worldproof **leadership**

CCBS Press

Cross Cultural Business Skills Minor

Worldproof Leadership

Twenty-one leadership perspectives for the interconnected world

Amsterdam University
of Applied Sciences

CCBS-Press
First edition 2018, ISBN: 978-90-79646-44-9, NUR: 812
Editorial managers: Aynur Doğan, Sander Schroevers
Assistant lecturers: Natalia Kempny, Poland, and Kalin Tsanov, Barcelona
Academic English and citations editor: Isabella Venter, University of Pretoria, South Africa
CCBS is an elective course at the Amsterdam University of Applied Sciences (HvA)
Inner and cover design: Sander Schroevers, Jaguar Print, Netherlands
Logo design: Erica Frank, Designer Gráfico, Vitória, Espirito Santo, Brazil
Cover graphic: Sergey Nivens, Russia

A catalogue record for this book is available from the Netherlands Deposit Collection of the royal library in The Hague.
Books from this series can be ordered via **GooglePlay** as an e-book.

Table of Contents

Preface

Welcome to an intercultural benchmark on local leadership practices in no less than twenty-one countries. Our world is internationalising at a fast pace, and more and more of us choose to find work elsewhere. As a result, we find ourselves confronted with culturally diverse management expectations. After working on this series, we now understand how knowledge of such local leadership conventions, can represent an important competitive advantage.
This book is the result of the collaborative research of seventy-six participants to the 'Cross-Cultural Business Skills' elective (minor) course. They have explored what leadership entails by doing a one semester - desk and field research. Together they have asked thousands of business professionals in selected countries on their preferred managing practices. The result of their efforts constitutes a relevant reference. We are grateful that this wonderful group can now share its gathered knowledge with people from around our world.

We first and foremost would like to thank all individual co-authors for their thoughtful research and constructive writing for this first edition of 'Worldproof Leadership'. Additionally, we would like to express our deep appreciation to all survey correspondents and interviewees who helped, despite their busy schedules, to make this innovative and applied way of education possible. We also acknowledge that this book would not have been here, without the engagement of Part-time Academy Director Hans Seubring-Vierveyzer. Then we owe a debt of gratitude to Isabella Venter for her hard work in authenticating all our academic sources.
Furthermore, we would like to thank Kalin Tsanov, and Natalia Kempny for their much-appreciated and professional assistance. Lastly, we take responsibility for any errors that may have inadvertently found their way into this book. May we close here, by wishing you all a remarkable read?

Aynur Doğan & Sander Schroevers

About CCBS

Since 2010, Cross Cultural Business Skills (CCBS) aims to educate bachelor students in the fundamentals of cross-cultural business skills and selected methodologies. CCBS is an elective course ('minor') initiated by prof. Sander Schroevers, and taught together with Aynur Doğan [MA], at the Amsterdam University of Applied Sciences (Netherlands).

Educational approach
At CCBS we believe that effective learning takes place through engaging in first-hand experiences. We challenge our students to produce new knowledge from a localised perspective. They often research in an unknown language, alphabet or cultural legacy which facilitates our students in developing meaningful skills for today's interconnected world. Our main objective is to co-create country-specific bodies of knowledge. We do so through expert-interviews (video and audio) with natives, and through in-depth analyses of local academic and trade literature.
In order to create a truly international classroom experience, we try to host students from across the globe. We attempt to connect our students with representatives of the business, media and diplomatic communities, during home-staged professional symposia. All CCBS-learning materials (print, digital and video) are 100% custom-tailored. We care about having the university's highest evaluation scores and have done so for many semesters now.
We therefore try to frame our lessons to be 'eye-popping', our work-shops to be clarifying and hands-on, and our social events to be warm and inclusive.
In short, let's do everything possible to make school a cool experience!

About CCBS global-fact-tank
CCBS global fact tank is our ongoing academic research project for the Amsterdam University of Applied Sciences that informs on cross-cultural business topics. Every six months, CCBS researchers survey C-level executives around the world. Our key focuses cover the following five areas of activity: management, meetings, leadership, recruitment and business presentations. Since its first international poll in 2012, the CCBS global-fact-tank has conducted interviews in 79 trade nations, with thousands of professionals. Thank you!

Consultation methodology

For the information in this book, results from three main data collection methods were applied. Firstly, insights around cultural aspects of leadership were gathered by conducting country-specific literature research, in both scholarly articles in journals, and preferably in-country books, and thus creating an extensive foundation for the validity of this book and its contents. Secondly this quantitative research was strengthened by a global online survey about leadership (CCBS Survey, 2018). To select qualified respondents for the survey, expert sampling was used. Furthermore, snowballing techniques were introduced as often the target population is difficult to get in touch with.
In total over 2,700 respondents participated after visiting our survey link, but almost two-thirds were not used because of stopping the survey too early, or their background or sometimes IP-addresses did not match our target group. The survey was created in English and translated by competent bilinguals who were either research collaborators or were supervised by them. The present study made use of translations into Arabic, French, Indonesian, Italian, Korean, Portuguese, Russian, and Spanish. Checks on translation accuracy were completed by back-translation or parallel translations, where possible.
The English version was used in eleven countries. The questionnaire comprised of 27 items, with multiple-choice and open questions, providing descriptive information on the national views on leadership). The multiple-choice responses were made on six-point Likert scales, anchored by terms ranging from 'not at all' to 'a lot'. All qualitative data provided comprehensive knowledge on the subject of local leadership cultures. The current multinational survey and interviewing was conducted between 04 October and 18 November 2018. Results using the outcome have not been reported prior to the present study.
Thirdly, in addition to the survey respondents, a selection of 58 leadership experts has been interviewed. These interviews lasted 20-40 minutes on average and were video and audio recorded and transcribed (a selection of these will be published on the YouTube and SoundCloud channels of CCBS minor).

Baas

Генеральный Директор

Geschäftsführerin

Bölüm Başkanı

Executive Vice President

Patrão

Økonomidirektør

Direttore Generale

CEO

회장님

Dyrektor

Président Directeur Géneral

Consejero Delegado

Τομεαρχης

MAIN DUDE

Country profiles

Sander Schroevers

For this paragraph I checked Amazon.com for the number of books using the word 'leader' in their titles, and saw an astounding 60,000 results. A quick search on ProQuest (a database we recommend for scholarly journals), resulted in almost a million hits on the subject of 'leadership'. But as the Global Leadership and Organizational Behavior Effectiveness (GLOBE) Research Program noted, "to date 90% of leadership literature reflects US based research and theory". Estimates like this keep us in the dark of how effective all this leadership knowledge is across national frontiers. Seeing that the number of countries expands, so do the differences... I have always liked that Peter Drucker quote: "Management is doing things right; leadership is doing the right things.". The point being that leadership partly focuses on the people-side of business, while management is often about systems and processes. Research has proven us that leaders' communication styles are influenced by the geographical region in which they operate. Regrettably some business leaders overlook local managerial and cultural practices, acquiescing in management-styles that have been grounded in Western concepts, that may undermine performance of an organisation. And as ineffective managers risk organisations costing large sums of direct and indirect costs, we nowadays see human resource professionals as well as senior executives pursuing more localised leadership strategies.

Chapter makeup

This book consists of 21 country chapters, each describing the local leadership perspective. All country profiles have been written in a standard format as to create a clear overview of the cultural features, while painting a contrast when comparing these leadership profiles to each other. Most of the twenty-one country profiles in this book contain the following sections:

- *Country introduction,*
- *How the indigene characterise leaders,*
- *Survey results and what local respondents say,*

- *An in-country literature review,*
- *A transcribed telephone interview with a local leadership scholar,*
- *A summarised video interview with a local cross-cultural trainer,*
- *A description of an in-country best-selling book on leadership,*
- *Understanding hierarchy in the chapter's country,*
- *How to achieve leadership empathy in that particular culture.*

Allow me to shortly introduce some of these sections to you here;

Local leadership analysis

The more I work abroad, the more I realise that it takes something else than just a survey to categorise national cultures by. There seem to be so many local variations and nuances, that simply do not fit into such constructs. But these nevertheless may have a substantial influence on how effective one can operate in a particular country. There are a great many books that have western authors explaining countries, but the local perspective often seems missing. This localised focus became pivotal to our approach of investigating country-specific leadership characteristics. Which we try to accomplish by introducing such sections as: (i) survey-results and what local respondents say, (ii) an in-country literature review, (iii) a local leadership scholar, (iv) a local cross-cultural trainer, (v) an in-country best-selling book on leadership, that all specifically draw on indigenous leadership research. For some teams researching in other languages or even scripts, has been challenging but allowed for rich ethnographic descriptions with the aim of discovering how leadership is enacted in eighteen selected markets.

Understanding hierarchy in a country

Much of the western leadership trends in the twentieth century has been about abandoning hierarchical command-and-control processes. Management literature and business school education started introducing a more egalitarian and facilitative style of leadership. We started to see open-plan office architecture, and 360-degree feedback. There is a striking disconnect between cultures on attitude toward authority. In India the teaching staff is addressed with Madam or Sir, and I occasionally saw students stand up when their 'senior-lecturer' entered the classroom. In my own Dutch course (CCBS - authoring this book) local students address me by my first name, and at times feel free to contradict me in front of the class. Perhaps inspired by this, we asked about a thousand qualified respondents in our global survey if they expected to be addressed by first name rather than by title. For the selected twenty-one national cultures, the following average scores were obtained;

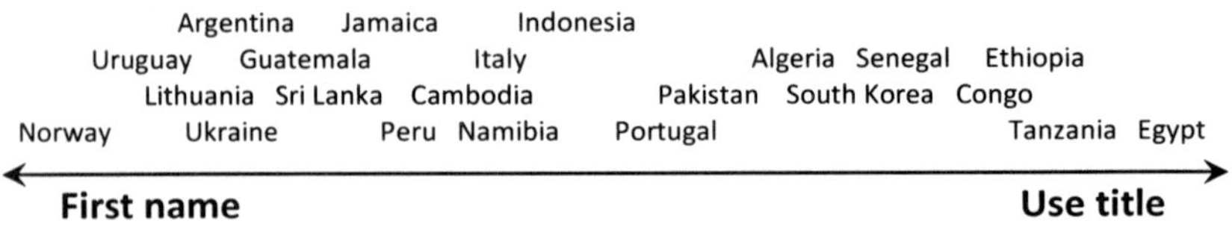

Figure: Employees can address their leader in this country by the first name.

Relational hierarchy

Eight out of ten Swiss survey participants admit that employees greet their leaders by the first name (CCBS Survey, 2017). This low level of hierarchy results in equal harmonious relationships between superior and employee, based on trust. To have a clear notion of someone's relative level of authority, is of critical importance in for instance a country like Korea. This as it determines how colleagues interact with each other, including choosing amongst the many different linguistic levels of politeness. Organisations tend to have a great many more levels of management, and corresponding forms of address. The informal way of doing business in for instance Australia might confuse the average Korean. Especially those who have risen to high positions in their organisations, who often are accustomed to a V.I.P. treatment.

Power Distance

The words *Hierarchy* and *Power Distance* are often used as equivalent expressions. The latter being defined as "the degree to which members of an organization or society expect and agree that power should be stratified and concentrated at higher levels of an organization or government" (House & Javidan, 2004, p. 12). Countries that have scored high Power Distance values in for instance the Hofstede or Trompenaars research, believe that power dispenses agreement, social order, and role stability, and therefore power should be concentrated at higher levels. In high power-distance cultures, paternalism characterizes leader-subordinate relationships, where a leader will assume the role of a parent and feel obligated to provide support and protection to subordinates under his or her care (Yan & Hunt, 2005).

Many of the twenty-one country profiles in this book make mention of a country's Power Distance Index score (PDI) by Dutch cultural scientist Geert Hofstede. However, just a value score number will not yet explain how hierarchy is understood in a particular culture. For example, even though Greece and South Korea both have equally high PDI values (of 60), leadership is enacted in a fundamentally different way in both countries. In this book we therefore try to remedy such cultural contingencies through culture-specific qualitative research, like interviewing local cultural intelligence experts.

How to achieve leadership empathy

Under this header each country profile will focus on a people-oriented leadership requirement: empathy. We here define empathy as a leader's capacity to relate to the feelings and experiences of others. Empathy as such, is broader than sympathy, and several researchers believe empathy to be a key part of emotional intelligence, and a critical element to being an effective leader (Bar-On & Parker, 2000). The successfully building and maintaining relationships, is a fundamental managerial skill. The point however is that according to the Center for Creative Leadership in some cultures empathy is more important to job performance than others (Gentry, Weber, & Sadri, 2016). Additionally, the way empathic emotion is expressed is subject to considerable local variations and nuances from country to country. It touches upon a leader's understanding of *role requirement*. Several questions of our online survey (CCBS Survey, 2018*)* refer to what particular expectations respondents have on this matter. Furthermore, each country team has tried to interview local experts, scholars and cross-cultural trainers on country-specific ways of demonstrating empathy in order to be effective. To give an example: in Nordic countries empathy is partly established by a low-key and modest behaviour, where for instance Latin countries much prefer a warm, personal and 'simpatico' approach, Koreans on the other hand value a courteous leader that protects face (Kibun). How to connect with people seems to depend on cultural background, and an ability to be empathetic is especially important for leaders working across cultural boundaries (Alon & Higgins, 2005). The results of our CCBS survey (2018) reflect this as all cultures discussed in this book, a large majority agreed to the statement that a manager should actively spend time on the personal well-being of team members. When comparing the actual country scores (Dell, Eriks, 2018), South Korea and Ukraine realise significantly lower on empathy compared to countries like for instance Uruguay and Portugal. As generally Ukrainian and South Korean leaders prefer to keep more personal distance from their employees. But note that having empathy, is not the same as demonstrating empathy; as staff expectations may vary considerably per national culture in areas like: (i) the amount of verbal attention employees require, (ii) the expected praise and encouragement by staff, or for instance (iii) the daily routine of managers. When managers increase their awareness of this empathic cultural context, it often has a direct impact on performance, the organisational climate and more productive working relations between leaders and employees.

Concluding

It was Darwin who has shown us the supreme value of diversity. The growing cultural diversity of today's workforce, and the global locations of organisations, transforms the way we lead teams. This calls for leaders with an ability to decode cultural differences and to adjust their leadership-style to fit the relevant context. In sum, I hope that our findings may lead to a richer leadership literature and allow professional leaders to recalibrate their skills and mindsets and use them as an advantage.

Algeria

Chakib Boulachioukh, Mats Grobben, Tarik Ceylan & Mo Soran

Algeria is the largest country in Africa and the tenth largest country in the world. Also known as the People's Democratic Republic of Algeria, Algeria is bordered by Morocco, Tunisia, Libya and the Mediterranean Sea. Their motto, شالوب ع بعشّالٍ essentially means by the people and for the people, which is reflected in their government system, the semi-presidential system. The country gained complete independence in 1962 when it broke out from French colonial rule. This has had a considerable influence on Algerian culture. For example, although French has no official status in Algeria, it is the second largest French-speaking country in terms of speakers (Esterhuysen, 2013). Nowadays, Algeria is still trying to distance itself from the centuries of conquest and domination by outsiders. The official religion is Islam, and it is forbidden to advocate or promote another religion in the country (Sawe, 2017). Algeria has possibilities to develop the country's economy because of its abundance of natural resources, such as arable land in the north and hydrocarbons (crude oil and natural gas) in the south. Other significant resources include iron, uranium and mercury. This makes Algeria potentially one of the richest countries in North Africa, according to Budhwar and Mellahi (2006).

How the Algerians characterise leaders

The management style in Algeria is based on a powerful hierarchy. Thus, authority should be respected. If someone with a higher position gives an order or assigns a task, there is no room to challenge his or her orders. Algerians operate in large groups, but they still tend to look for a strong PDG (*Président Directeur Général*) to take control and guide them through the process (CCBS Survey, 2018). Algerians tend to look for a leader who is charismatic, has the right (family) network and is resourceful and intellectual (CCBS Survey, 2018). In general, Algerians tend to value friends and family, and this is also the case on the work floor. Nepotism is considered positive among Algerians as this shows that a person cares about his or her friends and family. Seniority is also respected as Moran, Harris and Moran (2006) suggest. Algerians put a lot of value on authority. An Algerian leader can and will limit the freedom of his employees for the own good, mostly for a better performance. Moran, Harris and Moran (2011) make clear that the French background of Algeria still has its effects on the leadership values present in the country today. Family, education and qualifications are all characteristics of a (good) French and Algerian leader. As stated above, leaders can and will limit the freedom of employees for their own good. Those lower down the hierarchy expect leaders to make decisions based on what will benefit their employees (Moran et al., 2006). Algeria lies in the MENA (Middle East and North Africa) region. In broad terms, MENA countries are attributed to have a lot in common, including leader characteristics. Maghreb leaders, including Algerian leaders, are known to be: team players, a father figure, visionary, performance-oriented, diplomatic, collaborators and decisive (Kabasakal, Dastmalchian, Karacaya & Bayraktara, 2012).

Survey results and what local respondents say

The outcomes below are the ones that stood out most in the CCBS survey (2018) that was completed by local Algerian professionals. Each of the participants has a connection with management and leadership. To start off, an interviewee known as PDG notes that Algerian residents are *"generous, friendly, direct etc. the strong point of the Algerians is their generosity and hospitality, impulsive, they are also [direct] but very diplomatic."* (PDG, 19 October 2018). More than half of the respondents agree with the fact that the manager should actively spend time on the personal well-being of his or her subordinates. The results further indicate that respondents feel that a manager should encourage some competition within a team in order to achieve better results.

When asked about the specifics in leadership in Algeria the answers were mostly negative. One respondent notes: *"The leadership in my country [is] biased and not well defined. Managers mix between authority and leadership and think that [...] fear is the key"* (CCBS Survey, 2018). From the survey, we can conclude that a professional business card and e-mail signature should contain the leader's academic title. In Algeria, the position of CEO and chairman are combined and called *président directeur général* or PDG for short (CCBS Survey, 2018). It is important for subordinates to address superiors by their titles or positions when talking or writing to them. However, more than half of the respondents agree on being able to address their leader by the first name. Salary is still a big motivation for employees: *"Most of the employees are motivated just by the salary"* (CCBS Survey, 2018). Respondents have also experienced that superiors may bend the rules without asking, in order to improve their performance or achieve better results. In general, employees are expected to follow the established procedures. However, they may bend the rules without asking, in order to improve their performance or to achieve better results (CCBS Survey, 2018). Some respondents claimed that they looked for the following in a leader: a strong charismatic leader, a leader with the right (family) network, a leader who is resourceful and intellectual (CCBS Survey, 2018).

Local leadership analysis

In-country literature review

Today, knowledge has become an essential component of power and wealth, in an economy based primarily on knowledge. As a result of this most organisations work on developing and exploiting their knowledge-pool, in order to gain competitive advantages. Therefore, knowledge management has emerged as a necessity in the field of organisation management. Applying knowledge management has become one of the major challenges since it requires the availability of different means, mechanisms and changes in the culture of organisations. The study by Nouiri Madji (2011) examines this area by focusing on 'knowledge transfer' as an essential part of knowledge management in an organisation. More specifically, this literature examines what type of leadership style contributes to the transfer of knowledge within the organisation.

The study concludes that sharing knowledge in an organisation requires an environment of open communication, caring and understanding (Madjdi, 2011). However, the essential requirement for knowledge transfer is leadership. Leadership is the foundation of the institutions' success or failure. The leader should adopt a method that is consistent with logic, and the organisation should take into account the needs of his leadership. This is one of the most important factors in his success in managing any company, which is what applies to the process of transferring knowledge that requires a particular method without the other (Madjdi, 2011).

A recent study by Abderrahmane (2017) identified the level of Algerian worker's attitude towards women's leadership, according to the functional variable grade. The study contains data of a lot of employed workers of different companies. The data is divided into five basic areas such as: physical and mental competence of women as a leader, the organisation and internal communication of women leaders, the influences of values and social culture on the acceptance of women in leadership positions, the legal framework for women's leadership in Algeria, and the impact of women's leadership positions on Algerian society. The results show that the overall level of female leadership among the Algerian workers in local communities is low. Neither are there significant differences in the trend according to the functional rank variable. There is no existence of statistically significant differences by gender of the variable.

Omar Aktouf: an Algerian leadership scholar

Dr Omar Aktouf, born 22 October 1944, has a wide range of expertise and work experience. He has a bachelor's in general psychology as well as a PhD in management from the University HEC Montreal in Canada. Aktouf claims that the culture of an organisation can be influenced by the way a leader presents him or herself. In *Management and organization* (2009), he states that a well-cultured leader should pay attention to subordinates and act accordingly to different problems. Furthermore, he mentions that it is important that a leader is specific about the criteria when it comes to rewarding and promoting employees but also in terms of punishing and sanctioning anyone in the organisation. People are likely to think that the actions of a leader are the reality. While the formal arrangements are being seen as the rhetoric difference between doing and saying. *"Leaders and in-group members tend to believe that competence is the major reason why they are members of that group, but out-group members argue that it is ingratiation, favouritism, and politics"* (Aktouf, 1996). According to Aktouf, it seems that interpersonal attraction has to be important for a leader and his in-group members. Research even shows that in-group members see problems and solutions in the same way as their leader. This concept is an indication that leaders prefer subordinates that are like them. This also has the danger of 'groupthink' and the 'yes-man' mentality where everybody easily agrees with each other without discussing or arguing about any subject.

In-country leadership best seller

'La stratégie de l'autruche. Post-mondialisation, management et rationalité économique', which translates to *The strategy of the ostrich. Post-globalisation, management and economic rationality*, is written by Omar Aktouf who is currently a professor at HEC Montréal, a business university in Canada.
In his book, he focuses the fact that half of the world is living with less than $3 a day, while 225 billionaires in the world collectively own the same amount of money as 2 billion people. He claims that at the beginning of the twenty-first century more voices are against the mistakes that are being made by central banks of the world, and that we are not just talking about mere errors in

calculations and forecasting. He proclaims that there are serious mistakes being made in areas of management and economics. Mistakes so big that they influence the very conception and functioning of the world. The first step to repair these mistakes is to acknowledge and observe the 'three revolutions of modernity' (industrial revolution, automation and computerization-information). The main question in the book is if the people who are in charge of these modernities are willing to admit that everything in Algeria that is dominated by management and economy seems to crumble inevitably. He also claims that economic and management gurus continue to act like their heads are in the sand, while explaining why it is justified to keep their heads in the sand. Hence the title of his book.

Local leadership book	
Title	La stratégie de l'autruche
Author	Omar Aktouf
Publisher	Ecosociété
Year	2005
ISBN	978-2921561679

Algerian leadership YouTube review

Another way to find out more about Algerian leadership and what is expected of them is by looking at YouTube material of people talking about Algerian leaders. Over the past decade, the number of Algerian women who are entrepreneurs or leaders has risen substantially. "*Being a female entrepreneur in Algeria has the same advantages and disadvantages for both men and women*" (Khodja,Fekkan & Sofiane, 2018). Here Lamia Khodja simply states that nowadays women have the same opportunities as men in terms of entrepreneurship and leadership. In her experience, it is not any harder for women. "*Personally, I'm not against the idea because everybody brings something, women think in a different way*" (Khodja et al., 2018).

Karim Oumnia, CEO of Glagla Shoes International, states that companies need to be flexible, competitive and they must have a winner mentality to compete in the international market. "*Employees are part of the company, they must be hand in hand with the boss"* (Oumnia, 2013). Oumnia adds that leaders should be able to take their responsibility in good and in bad times.

Understanding hierarchy in Algeria

The Power Distance in Algeria scores higher than the world average. This indicates that it is considered socially acceptable to experience differences in hierarchy. It furthermore indicates that employees have a certain expectation that leaders will separate themselves from their subordinates. As A. Yahia-Berrouiguet (2016) explains, this means that Algerian organisation structure has more gaps in between levels; for instance, the businesses have a high proportion of supervisors to give commands or give orders to others who operates in a lower scale. Subordinates expect to be consulted because the ideal boss is a resourceful democrat who has a clear view of how the right things should be done. From an organisational perspective, it is clear that men in Algeria are scoring a higher masculinity score than the world average, which means that women are limited in their rights (Yahia-Berrouiguet, 2016). Education is also an important standard in Algeria, and highly educated employees do have more respect than lower or uneducated employees. According to Largosen (2002), age is also a factor that affects the respect shown to a person because Algerians attach a lot of value to the elderly. In Algeria, meetings are not held to make a decision but to discuss the issue. A meeting is planned far in advance, while the confirmation is made just one or two days before the meeting date. *"The decision-making process is hierarchical and anticipating may be seen as a defiance of authority"* (Santander, 2018).

In an interview PDG, (19 October 2018) claims that the strong point of the Algerians is their generosity and hospitality. He notes that they tend to be impulsive and that they are direct but very diplomatic. The interviewee also claims that the hierarchy is respected regardless of whether the person in the position of power is a man or a woman. In the interviewee's view, it is not difficult for a woman to gain access to a leading position because the most important things are the skills, competence and strength of a character with a spirit of leadership (19 October 2018). This means that titles, seniority and, above all, personal relationships are critical for a leader in Algeria. This results in Algerian leaders needing to have integrity, honesty, and transparency to obtain respect, trust and empathy (Kabasakala et al., 2012). According to a survey (CCBS Survey, 2018), it is important for subordinates to address leaders according to their titles or position when talking or writing to them.

How the Algerians achieve leadership empathy

Achieving leadership empathy in Algeria is built on some essential values, most of which are based on Islam. Inside the Islamic religion, there is a collectivistic culture with an emphasis on strong family and kinship relationships (Kabasakala et al., 2012). Other factors would be the possessed titles and seniority.
Because of this, Algerian professional life is mostly relationship-oriented, it values being polite to each other and, for example, not giving negative feedback to either superiors or employees. Algerian employees gain motivation through incentives and receiving rewards (Mezrig & Bouguesri, 2017).
In addition, a PDG can gain empathy from employees by looking out for their well-being (CCBS Survey, 2018)
Obtaining empathy can be a big challenge for a foreign manager, who will need to be sensitive, respectful and understanding of the cultural differences by adapting his or her leadership styles to the local expectations. Most of the time, it is the context, including religion, history, language, rules and laws, political systems and ethnic subcultures, that determines the effective way of leading (Fiedler, 1967).
Employee compensation plays a big role in the employment relationship because it has a critical importance to both employees and employers. For employees, compensation decisions affect their loyalty and job satisfaction, but for the employers, compensation decisions affect their cost of doing business (Mezrig & Bouguesri, 2017). However, personal relations are in some situations placed above the earning money for Algerian companies. And this concludes the leadership perspectives for the People's Democratic Republic of Algeria.

Argentina

Rick Springer, Ashley Scheenloop, Jordan Simpson, Daan Kossen & Doeun Park

Argentina is South America's second biggest country after Brazil. Due to its sheer size, it has a vast range of differing terrain, from the massive Andes mountain range to the Pampas grassland, which is the grazing land for the famous beef cattle. The country is, in fact, the largest Spanish-speaking nation, with over forty million Spanish speakers (Pariona, 2018). Argentina ranks second after the USA, in having received the most immigrants from the old world. Ethnically, an estimated 99 per cent of Argentines are of European descent, primarily from Italy and Spain. The largest Christian denomination in the country is Roman Catholicism. Many claim that *Argentinos* both culturally and emotionally, relate and act more similarly to European values than to those of surrounding nations. At the beginning of the twentieth century, Argentina was one of the richest countries in the world, as portrayed by Díaz Alejandro (1970). Defiantly Argentina's economic performance of the last hundred years has seen many severe recessions. Recently, the Argentine Peso was at a record low level, and the nation's old enemy, *inflation,* has appeared again (Gallas, 2018). This chapter presents a synthesis of Argentine culture, and leadership to help develop an understanding of the idiosyncratic nature of management roles in Argentine business (López, 2008).

How the Argentines characterise leaders

For Ruiz, Hamlin and Carioni (2016), the Argentine leadership styles tend to be authoritarian rather than democratic. Due to this fact, Argentines have a propensity for decisive leadership. A *'gerente'* is likely to be most effective when being a strong decision maker, a good listener as well as an eloquent speaker, as was mentioned by an Argentine manager in the CCBS survey (2018). In a recent interview, Santiago Sena (19 October 2018) emphasises that a leader also has a mission to improve his or her workforce. In order to do so, a leader needs to be supportive, motivating, caring and above all, a role model. Furthermore, Sena states that successful managers are often seen helping their employees further with their careers.

A commercial manager voiced in our CCBS survey (2018) that *"Leadership could have cultural specifications, but experience, education, and social commitment build a leader"*. According to Altschul et al. (2007), solid leaders in Argentina are known as *'Figuras Señeras'*, this term refers to a solitary and unique individual. Research by Aimar and Stough (2007) suggests that in Argentina decisions are made at the top level of the company. This is due to Argentines placing a great deal of respect on executive leadership, which also explains why managers and non-managerial employees avoid contradicting their superiors. But, although effective leadership in Argentina often calls for such an authoritarian approach, the average Argentinian *gerentes exitosos* are seldom 'know-it-alls' as indeed leaders in Argentina will consult employees. However, once a decision has been made, there will hardly be any discussion about it. As Lasky (2001) explains, appearance is an important point for an Argentine leader. Being negligent with clothing choices can affect a person's reputation. Answers in the CCBS survey validate this need of grace in one's appearances. A substantial amount of the survey responses even indicate that elegant appearance may have some influence on a successful career in Argentina.

Survey results and what local respondents say

Over fifty Argentinian managers have shared their opinions on local leadership with CCBS (2018). By looking into the results of the survey, we can distinguish certain traits which are present in most Argentinian front-leaders. For example, over 60 per cent of Argentinian managers agree with the statement that a leader should encourage competition within a team, to achieve better results (CCBS Survey, 2018). In terms of support at the workplace, the majority of the managers believe that a relationship with their subordinates is key to creating a solid working environment. This result indicates that leadership in Argentina is driven by networking and relationships. A leader who promotes strong relationships with the workforce increases not just revenue but also employee satisfaction. This point is backed up by PhD graduate Santiago Sena (19 October 2018) in an interview which reveals that employees are trusted to complete tasks and can always reach out to their manager for support. Pablo Sojo, an HR manager in the IT industry, adds to that: *"We are used to focusing on teams and team relationship, so as to get a performance hand on team"* (CCBS Survey, 2018). The CCBS survey (2018) defines the biggest difference between Argentinian business culture and other countries - flexibility and unpunctuality. Around half of the Argentinian managers in the survey disagree with the statement that a management decision *cannot be changed easily* after it has been made. This is significantly different, compared to surrounding countries, where instability and potential confrontation are much more avoided. A number of respondents note the economic and political influences in Argentina and how introducing flexible processes helps them to adapt to them. For instance, country manager, Gabriel Duarte clarifies: *"Economy and politics in Argentina change so dynamically, management has to be able to tackle and adapt to those changes"* (CCBS Survey, 2018). This reactivity to instability is possibly further reflected in the fact that only half of the respondents strongly consider that missing a deadline is the same as failure. When looking at gender equality in Argentina, more than sixty per cent of managers think that gender discrimination is present at the workplace. Women do not have the same opportunities as men to become senior managers. Nahuel Francica, a director in the Argentinian government, mentions *"Men have greater opportunities than women"* (CCBS Survey, 2018).

Local leadership analysis

In-country literature review

Lawyer and publisher César Daniel González wrote a paper in 2017, titled *Management en Argentina: Cultura y una perspecitva innovadora*. In this article, González (2017) established that leadership is influenced by culture. Employees often expect their leaders to have the same values and beliefs as they have. In addition, he states that for a leader to have a close relationship with his or her employees is the most suitable leadership style for many. González (2017) came to this conclusion while considering the guidelines and the values of the country. The effect that culture has on leadership has diminished slightly for the future generation, the so-called Millennials and Generation Z (González, 2017). White, Arcienaga and Gonzales (2010) give a more in-depth view on how relationships work and state that the *"Close bonds between manager and subordinate will often run deep, but can be more easily compared to the parent-child relationship than the best-friend relationship. Managers expect to be shown respect at all times. In return they offer help, protection, and future prospects"* (p.25). Professor Oller, of the Business University of Argentina, gives more details about leaders in the country. Through his survey among executive managers in Argentina, Oller (2012) was able to identify the most valued leader characteristics, which are decision-making, operating during times of uncertainty, a realistic look at the company and maintaining good relationships with employees.

While these are skills that can be acquired through experience and knowledge, this is not the case with gender. The Universia Argentina (2016) found that "*Eight* out *of ten women and seven out of ten men believe that men are favoured over women to access management positions*".

Santiago Sena: An Argentinian leadership scholar

Adviser to the chief of cabinet of ministers, Santiago Sena is an accomplished academic. Having finished his PhD in business management at IAE Business School, he now seeks to work in an environment where the commitment is to promote the economic, social and environmental development of Argentina.
An interesting point made by Santiago was the value of time in Argentina. "*We are not very attached to time. Of course, there is a social understanding if you are some minutes late which is okay in general. One can be 5 till 10 minutes late and nobody will feel uncomfortable with that*" (Sena, 19 October 2018).
One can see that there is a clear correlation between the relationship of Argentinian managers and their employees. One particular question in the CCBS survey states that managers have a distant relationship with employees to maintain respect. The reaction from Argentinian managerial respondents was resoundingly the opposite. In fact, approximately two-thirds of the respondents disagree or strongly disagree with this notion (CCBS Survey, 2018). Sena shares this view: "*In general people try to keep a good relationship. They share most of their feelings and opinions with each other*" (19 October 2018).

Federico Montelatici: an Argentinian cross-cultural trainer

Federico Montelatici is a business executive and consultant working in Argentina. Having graduated as an industrial engineer from the University of Buenos Aires, he completed an MBA specialised in marketing and finance at the Universidad Católica Argentina. Montelatici was interviewed based on his experience of leadership in Argentina as a consultant. Montelatici points out that there is not one specific management style in Argentina. This is mainly due to Argentina's mixed cultural background from European immigration. This seems to be supported by the results of the CCBS survey (2018) as there was not really one predominant answer choice.
Montelatici points out that the long economic crisis that the country faces influences leadership expectations amongst the Argentine workforce. "*The main strength is the ability to solve problems, to look for solutions and to make things happen and work to find a way to help the business*" (14 November 2018).

Lastly is discussed how Argentinian leadership seems to slowly be changing. He notes that the levels of hierarchy between managers and their employees are fading somewhat, and people are becoming more punctual. Towards the future Montelatici feels that: "*We do not have much experience going outside on enterprise in other countries, but we need leadership on that, to make the difference with the past*" (14 November 2018).

In-country leadership best seller

One of the best-selling books this year about leadership was written by Joaquín Sorondo and is called *Liderazgo para los número 1* (*Leadership for number 1*) which was published in 2018. The author, who is from Argentina, wrote the book as an MBA leadership professor and based on his 25 years' experience as a director in large companies, as well as a consultant in leadership and human resource management. He graduated from the University of Buenos Aires. In the book, Sorondo offers the reader guidance on leading groups or companies and on developing leadership empathy. The book is written not just for the Argentine context, but also for those who aspire to be *'número 1'* within global companies.

Local leadership book	
Title	*Liderazgo para los número 1*
Subtitle	-
Author	Joaquín Sorondo
Publisher	Paidós
Year	2018
ISBN	9789501296372

Argentina leadership YouTube review

Emanuel Richard (2018) is a managing director at Impex Telecommunications and previously a manager at Philips in Argentina. When asked what makes the Argentinian leadership style special? Richard answers: *"Everything. Argentina is not like any other Latin country, it has its own rules"* (Richard, 2018). According to Richard, the relationship between a manager and the subordinates should not be taken lightly, and that it is the basis for any working environment. For a leader to build the correct relationships, it starts with identifying who the key players among the employees are, as they are to be considered as the most valuable employees in the workforce. Through building close relationships, managers can, in fact, delegate staff through these key players. This in return allows managers to keep some distance from their employees. Most relationships are based on personal contact. Furthermore, Richard emphasises how managers acquire their status since in Argentina this is not just gained by education or work experience, but just as much by age and the way managers speak (Richard, 2018). In another video, Argentinian leadership speaker and author Eduardo Braun provides more in-depth information on the ideal leader. Eduardo Braun (2016) states that the purpose of a great leader is to light the spark in people. Therefore, a *'gerente'* needs to give employees a sense of purpose. Most people lack clear dreams and goals. Leaders should give them the right direction and goals in life. Once this is done to effect, businesses may see their performance multiply (Braun, 2016).

Understanding hierarchy in Argentina

Hierarchy in the Argentinian workplace is strongly manifested. Chhokar, Brodbeck and House (2007) state that the power distance score in Argentina is above average. This means that in Argentinian businesses, managers and leaders are seen as experts; they are aware of the power that they have and expect respect from their subordinates. Leaders also prefer a personal distance to be kept between them and employees, in order to maintain that level of respect (CCBS Survey, 2018). Therefore, it is likely for employees to only perform according to their manager's instructions. For an employee to correct the manager is considered rude and frowned upon, even if the employee is right. This is because managers are meant to be more knowledgeable and should not be questioned. People with a high-profile status often expect to only deal with individuals who belong to their own status group. Approximately two-thirds of the CCBS respondents expect extra services to match their position. Additionally, confrontations and orders ought to have a top-down structure (CCBS Survey, 2018). As Root (2016) states, not responding to this top-down structure could be seen as a disappointment and even a sign of weakness. The decisions that are made are impulsive, spontaneous, places the emphasis on a concept and cannot be changed easily. This is strongly in keeping with the CCBS survey (2018) results wherein approximately 80 per cent of respondents agree with this statement. Andres Hatum (2006) notes that Argentinian employees are predominantly collectivistic, which leads to efficient teamwork.

Argentinian managers see themselves as team-oriented, participative and charismatic leaders (Chhokar et al., 2007). The decision-making process tends to be centralized and hierarchical. Furthermore, Lewis (2006) states that the social aspects of an individual play an important role. For example, educational background or even the *barrio* where one lives can determine success. According to Sena (19 October 2018), people who come from a poor or disadvantaged background can still make it to the top. He mentions that individuals can educate themselves from primary school to a graduate level because all education is free and available. Even the poorest can get a scholarship if they wish to do so. However, in line with the CCBS survey (2018), the hierarchy in Argentina is changing. The top-down structure in a company is becoming less vertically-oriented. Employees are getting more responsibility and the gap between *gerente* and employees is gradually reducing. A person's title is becoming less important, as people are allowed to address their leader by his or her first name. This statement is backed-up by Montelatici (14 November 2018) as he mentions: "*My way of working is not to make a lot of distinction in dealing with people. I try to take the best of all of them*".

How the Argentines achieve leadership empathy

First and foremost, employees appreciate when a manager listens to them and shows that he or she is sincerely interested in what they have to say. This is due to the people-oriented culture in Argentina (González, 2017). Juan Serrano, a manager in Argentina and respondent of the CCBS survey, states that "*The social contact with friends, colleagues and family is important. The relation between one another is definitely stronger than it is in other countries*" (2018). Montelatici (14 November 2018) also confirms that the *gerente* should act like a paternal figure. To strengthen a relationship, Santiago Sena (19 October 2018) suggests that it is very common to share personal information while having dinner together. He also puts emphasis on listening skills, explaining that "*Mostly an empathic leader would understand what is going on with the people he is managing or leading*" (Sena, 19 October 2018). He adds that it is important that a *gerente* tries to keep the employees motivated and help them progress with their career. About 85 per cent of the respondents agree with these sentiments (CCBS Survey, 2018).

The vast majority of the respondents answers that they do not prefer having a distant relationship with their employees. They want more personal interactions instead, which can be explained as a diffuse culture. Aimar and Stough (2007) note that Argentines often find that their work and private life are closely connected. According to Chhokar et al. (2007), Argentines are likely to express their emotions and are emotionally sensitive in daily communication. They prefer to meet in person and converse, as opposed to phone calls or messages. They will also decrease the physical proximity with others, and touching between men and handshakes are common (Moran, Harris & Moran, 2011). When it comes to giving feedback, over 60 per cent of respondents indicate that they prefer when employees are direct with any feedback or criticism (CCBS Survey, 2018). Managers can also create empathy by being flexible and able to make quick decisions in the face of any rapid changes brought on by, for example, the economic crisis that Argentina finds itself in (CCBS Survey, 2018). Argentines find it very important to attain more responsibility within the day to day operation of a business. As Montelatici (14 November 2018) affirms, training people to innovate the business is highly appreciated. And on this note we now leave the Republic of Argentina, *¡Buen viaje!*

Cambodia

Julia van Winden, Agnes So, Tim Hofma, Sander de Vos, Quynh Nguyen Pham & Jan van den Berg

The Kingdom of Cambodia has been an independent country since 1953. The majority of the population identifies as Khmers, and the official language of the country is Khmer. Cambodia is one of the poorest countries in Southeast Asia and the greater majority of Khmers tend to have a very simplistic lifestyle. Most rely on owning their own land and working in agriculture (Sheehan & Cooke, 1996). In order to paint a picture of Cambodia's culture nowadays, Tully (2006) states: *"Modern Khmers are the inheritors of an ancient tradition"*. Khmers believe in the Theravada strain of Buddhism and are very devoted to their beliefs, traditions and culture. They believe life and religion are inseparable. This statement is further supported by Brown (2000), who confirms that the devotion of Khmers to the Theravada is unyielding. In the seventies, the capital Phnom Penh fell into the hands of a communist group named Khmer Rouge, led by Pol Pot. Punishment, torture and murder led to an eventual genocide, with over one-and-a-half million victims. Throughout history, Khmers have overcome hardships by believing and staying loyal to their own culture and beliefs. The transformation which Cambodia went through after the destructive Pol Pot regime is truly remarkable. Aside from the strong faith and colourful traditions of the modern Khmers, an increasing number of people migrated to the capital city of Phnom Penh and other urban areas. They moved, in order to find work in the corporate world (Sheehan & Cooke, 1996). Cambodia has overcome their economic and political crisis. Eventually, the agricultural lifestyle paid off. The growth in production of rice, garments, cashews and sugar resulted in large profitability. Other contributing factors, such as the oligarchy, international relationships and support of other countries, have caused a rise in provincial business in Cambodia (Hughes & Un, 2011).

How the Cambodians characterise leaders

According to research by Southiseng, Ty, Walsh and Anurit (2008), Cambodians agree that entrepreneurs should have a clear vision, specific goals and clear objectives when doing business. The results of the CCBS survey (2018) confirm this, indicating that employees in Cambodia expect their leaders to be visionary thinkers, powerful decision-makers and good listeners (CCBS Survey, 2018). It is also important that they possess the educational background and talent necessary for certain business activities in their field of work (Thon et al., 2009). The economic environment is unpredictable. Therefore, leaders should be innovators, instead of followers, who create added value in their product or service. Moreover, Cambodians see entrepreneurs as people who are decisive and risk-taking (Southiseng, et al., 2008). Cambodia has been heavily influenced by other countries in the areas of religion, culture, language, politics, ideas and education (McNamara, 2015). One of the main characteristics of Cambodian business is patronage. This factor is also the 'main thread' of Cambodian society (Ledgerwood & Un, 2002). Maintaining a good relationship between a leader and an employee is considered central. Moreover, it is believed that authority and loyalty work better among people than organisations (Mabbett & Chandler, 1995). According to the respondents of the CCBS survey (2018), a leader should have a strong charismatic personality and access to the right networks. Both are necessary skills to build lasting relationships within the business world.

The education of councillors, especially the chief, is a main factor for gaining professional legitimacy and trust. The majority of them are trained in pagodas, which, in addition to literacy, focus on ethics and are religion-based. Some of the elders have joined the monkhood, which usually equips them with even more religious education. There is more traditional authoritative legitimacy than administrative leaders (CDRI, 2009). A local software engineer Piseth Ben (11 November 2018) gives his opinion on the issue: *"I used to work in those big and small companies, so I think it depends on the size of the company. Large companies have a division, departments, managerial control, etc. but, we, Cambodians tend to be more flexible and lenient towards [one] another in smaller companies".*

Survey results and what local respondents say

The CCBS survey (2018) on leadership around the world has been filled in by Cambodian professionals, leaders and managers. The results indicate the relevance of respect between a leader and a subordinate, but also that a leader who possesses emotional intelligence and reason is preferred. Cambodian business culture seems to differ greatly depending on the work environment and company. This is illustrated by the fact that the CCBS survey respondents are split when it comes to whether it is disrespectful to address a leader by his or her first name or if a leader should always be addressed using his or her title. A regional acquisition leader in the private partnership sector, Rithy Kong, comments: *"It is informal and impolite to use first names in my country"*, but a founding director in the hospitality training sector, Michelle Morin, claims: *"We are very informal and call each other by our first names and nicknames, not the same in other offices"* (CCBS Survey, 2018). Furthermore, two-thirds of the survey respondents argue that managers should actively spend time on the well-being of their team members. This adds up to the certain expectations employees have towards their leaders. They expect them to be a visionary thinker, good listener and powerful decision-maker. Being a powerful decision-maker is important and seventy per cent of the survey respondents state that when a decision has been made, it will not change very easily (CCBS Survey, 2018).

Regarding gender equality, two-thirds of the respondents agree with the fact that men and women have equal access to senior leadership positions. However, some respondents responded differently. Founding director Michelle Morin believes that: *"[in] Cambodia, women are still greatly undervalued and the gender gap at the workplace, especially in public office and government, is massive"* (CCBS Survey, 2018). This means that within the business world in Cambodia women are suffering from gender inequality. She adds that development can still be observed, and that: *"[t]his is changing with the younger generation with more and more [women] attending university and making their mark at the workplace"* (CCBS Survey, 2018).

Local leadership analysis

In-country literature review

In an article by Ai (2006), Cambodia is identified as a high power distance country. What is worth mentioning is that people seem to accept the fact that power is distributed unequally in society. Those with positions of authority and power do not feel obligated to understand the needs and wants of those at the bottom of the hierarchical ladder (Ai, 2006). Cambodia has one of the lowest gender-equality indexes in Southeast Asia. This is because of the cultural practices, which traditionally grant women a lower status than men (Chhoeun, Sok & Byrne, 2008). As Dhatt et al. (2017) note there are male managers who choose to emphasise women's traditional role and to emphasise that their priorities should be in their homes. Many researchers have been exploring this phenomenon. Nowadays, the professional relationships between women and men seem to be shifting. Research shows positive trends in Cambodia in terms of gender and power distribution. Many national and provincial government organisational working groups are now providing training on gender and leadership skills to health workers. The aim thereof is to ensure a proper representation of women at all levels.

Irea Skocir: a Cambodian leadership scholar

A businesswoman who runs a resort and teaches hospitality in Cambodia has been interviewed on the topic of leadership in Cambodia. Working in the hospitality sector and having lived in the country for eight years, Irea Skocir (12 November 2018) says that Cambodia has been greatly affected by the regime of Pol Pot. After the genocide, there was no indication as to how a leader should behave since most Cambodians who had an education fell victims to the regime. However, the situation in Cambodia is constantly improving because more and more non-corrupt leaders are taking part in elections and the general population is fighting for a revolution in leadership style. Skocir expects it to take another ten years before the country is finally restored. She claims that the most important factor for Cambodian people is to eradicate corruption among leaders. Especially now, with foreign influence on the rise as Cambodia uses Chinese labour for building resorts and casinos. Skocir characterises Cambodians as very peaceful people. Nevertheless, in her experience, dealing with male colleagues has caused her a few conflicts. Women in Southeast Asia are not as free as in Europe. As someone who has done business in Western countries and in Cambodia, Skocir says that the biggest difference is the fact that Western leaders and entrepreneurs want to generate revenue and still give something to society in return, rather than Cambodian leaders who tend to only take. Skocir provides some final advice regarding doing business and being a leader in Cambodia: *"If you play according to their rules, you and your business will end up just fine. This would generate respect and acceptance"* (Skocir, 12 November 2018).

Piseth Ben: a Cambodian cross-cultural trainer

A native programmer and current software engineer at Acleda Bank gave his experienced input on corporate leadership in Cambodia in an interview. Piseth Ben (11 November 2018) has work experience in small and large organisations. In his opinion, a good leader treats his or her employees respectfully and guides them towards constant improvement. The traits which a prime leader should possess are: *"clear strategic management, communication, approachability and friendliness"* (Ben, 11 November 2018). He follows up with the negative traits for a leader: *"I think if a leader does not listen to their employees, he cannot ever be successful. Another bad trait is not giving an opportunity to the staff to speak and express their ideas. So is blaming the employees, should they make a mistake. Often times managers they do not care about the well-being of their employees"* (Ben, 11 November 2018). There is a difference between Cambodian and Western leadership. Ben points out: *"I think we do have differences, because of culture"*. Cambodian leadership is more about following orders, whereas in Western leadership effort tends to be collaborative. In terms of religion, based on his personal experience, Piseth Ben opines that faith does not play an incremental role in leadership. An example of this is an Indian company he worked with previously, where topics were strictly professional and religion did not play a part in their cooperation. On the other hand, he admits that in the Cambodian business world, *"... age does play a role, in terms of respect"* (7 November 2018). According to Ben, women in Cambodia do not often have access to higher education. Personally, he has not met any female leaders. *"Men get more opportunities than women, but I do believe that female leadership needs to be present at the workplace"* (Ben, 11 November 2018).

In-country leadership bestseller

Leadership in local politics of Cambodia: a study of leaders in three communes of three provinces is written by Thon Vimealea, Ou Sivhuoch, Eng Netra and Ly Tem. As the title suggests, it entails leadership research among three communes of three different provinces in Cambodia. It describes various aspects and characteristics, such as networking and employee motivation. Furthermore, the book discusses the activities and constraints of local leaders. The results are based on local valuable qualitative research and can be easily found in English.

Local leadership book	
Title	Leadership in Local Politics of Cambodia
Subtitle	A Study of Leaders in Three Communes of Three Provinces
Author	Thon Vimealea, Ou Sivhuoch, Eng Netra and Ly Tem
Publisher	CDRI
Year	2009
ISBN	978-99950-52-29-4

Cambodian leadership YouTube review

Sath Sodany, a successful Cambodian businesswoman, talks about women in leadership positions during her TEDx presentation in 2018. Sodany studied Marketing, Public Communication and Accounting and has work experience in different fields of business. In the video, she expresses how hard it is for a Cambodian woman to be successful and independent. The expectations of getting married and becoming a housewife are not uncommon. According to Sodany, there are a few things you should do as a Cambodian woman if you want to achieve independence. The most efficient road towards it is pursuing an education and focussing on personal development (Sodany, 2018). Another intriguing video on leadership in Cambodia is from the YouTube channel INSPIRED.Cambodia. It is a video by Toastmasters; a Leadership Community Club at Paññasastra University of Phnom Penh. One of the guest speakers in the video claims that being an excellent leader in Cambodia means taking care of others, and giving up one's own benefit for the gain of others (INSPIRED.Cambodia, 2017).

Understanding hierarchy in Cambodia

Power distance in Cambodia is extremely high, which is commonly seen throughout the whole of Southeast Asia (Karbaum, 2015). According to the Constitutional Council (2010): *"Khmer citizens are equal before the law, enjoying the same rights, liberties and duties regardless of race, color, sex, language, beliefs, religions, political tendencies, birth origin, social status, wealth or other situations"*. However, Theravada Buddhism states that wealth and similar factors which improve social status are granted to an individual for doing good deeds in their previous life. On the grounds of this belief, a person is able to reach a higher level up the social ladder. They will also receive more respect and be treated differently (Karbaum, 2015). The CCBS survey (2018) respondents confirm that hierarchy is of importance in Cambodia, with about seventy per cent agreeing that the leader of an organisation should have a respectable office space and transportation equivalent to their position. Also, three-quarters of the respondents think subordinates should address their leaders by their title or position (CCBS Survey, 2018).

How the Cambodians achieve leadership empathy

In terms of professional relationships in Cambodia, employees treat each other with respect. As previously mentioned, religion is a way of life, and this phenomenon also has an impact on their working field. The corporate world of Cambodia has a leadership dimension. It consists of two factors, individualism and respect. Both factors are affiliated with the philosophies of Theravada Buddhism (Selvarajah, Meyer & Davuth, 2012). A high number of Khmers are lay people and supporters of Theravada Buddhism. They assist and practice together with the Buddhist monks and nuns (Kent, 2003). Their opinion on 'the individual journey' of a person is a high priority, and this also contains the exploration of the 'self'. To establish the fundamental relationship between a leader and employee, the leader needs to be aware of every employee's personal life. This means their home, financial situation, friends, etc. The previous statement is verified by the CCBS survey (2018), where approximately two-thirds of the survey participants agree that a manager should actively spend time on the personal well-being of their team members. The relationship between leader and employee should preferably be like family. As Selvarajah et al. (2012) state, the manager must be able to understand that the happiness of his or her employees always comes first. Cambodian employees expect intelligence, honesty and persistence from their leaders. They disapprove of leaders who have traits such as egoism, corruption, selfishness and dictatorship (Zepp, 2012). As Piseth Ben explains, when a leader receives respect from his or her employees, it is an indication that he or she is a good leader. Therefore, one needs to take care of staff, correct them, be responsible and make sure they achieve their tasks (Ben, 11 November 2018).

Congo-Brazzaville

Thijs Keuchenius, Jevon Ribbens & Yorick Verhagen

Step out of the Congo's wilds and into Brazzaville or Pointe-Noire and discover what some call the heart of French Africa. Both urban centres exhibit a distinctive Francophone style that cannot be replicated elsewhere on the African continent. Pointe-Noire is a coastal metropolis with oil riches which account for over sixty per cent of the government's revenue in 2016 (ITA, 2017). There are also many expats located in Pointe-Noire. On the other hand, Brazzaville is a classic central African city with a sense of peace that is missing from its neighbour, Kinshasa, across the river in the DRC (Democratic Republic Congo). The two cities are expected to be the biggest metropolitan cities in Africa (Paul, 2014). The official spoken language is French but there are numerous other native languages. The most spoken one is Kikongo, which directly translated means hunter. Despite the troubles in the Great Lakes district and other locations, the country flourishes with its beautiful nature. Some of the most beautiful riches of Africa are found in the region around the path of the great Congo River and its forests, volcanoes, and mountains sprawling ever eastward. Today, the region contains roughly 4 million inhabitants in an area that is almost the same size as Germany (with over 80 million inhabitants). Congo-Brazzaville is emerging from the long stagnation of civil war into an open environment for business, with an upwelling of cross-cultural opportunities with Asia, Europe, and America.

How the Congolese characterise leaders

Accountable, responsible and transparent leadership is something the Congolese people and inhabitants of many other African countries are longing for, claims Professor Mwangi (2014). An employee working in the communication sector points out that leaders are needed to help develop the country and guide it in the right direction (CCBS Survey, 2018). Congo-Brazzaville is a country which has been plagued with prolonged wars and conflicts. Lots of images that are associated with leadership have their roots in these conflicts. This has a direct consequence on peoples' expectations of a leader, claims Mwangi, in his study about African leadership (Mwangi, 2014). He continues to argue that leadership is associated with the ability to govern advise and dictate on certain issues. Age is also an important factor. The older one is the better opportunities become available in leadership positions. A manager working in the oil and gas sector claims that *"respect is earned through age and not through competence"* (CCBS Survey, 2018). This last point isolates the younger people and causes them to potentially have different opinions on leadership than more experienced professionals. The latter group is very considered important in Congo-Brazzaville. As a result of it, individual competition is discouraged. In order to keep conflict to a bare minimum, internal promotions are common and leaders aim to create a familial harmony (Shonhiwa, 2008). Furthermore, consensus and cooperation are highly valued, and motivation comes from a sense of belonging (Matondo, 2012a).

Survey results and what local respondents say

The findings below are academic survey responses from professionals in Congo-Brazzaville. While investigating what the difference is in leadership between Congo-Brazzaville and other countries, it was discovered that a Congolese leader has more responsibilities than just his job - they should instead help develop the country by improving the sector they work in. The reason for this is because Congo-Brazzaville is economically behind a lot of other African countries. In addition, another comment on the same subject mentions that age is a big factor in the workspace (CCBS Survey, 2018). Respect is another key part in the workspace. At a company in Pointe-Noire, employees have to respect the schedule and their superiors. Olga Ombondo, a sales and marketing director, explains: *"Otherwise, the employees do what they want and no one works properly and they always arrive late; we are obliged to follow them all the time to be sure that the work is done correctly and well finished"* (CCBS Survey, 2018). Ruth Lago, a journalist and presenter for Africanews, mentioned in a recent interview with CCBS (22 October 2018) that young leaders are very open and willing to listen to their employees. She continues to press that the group is very central. Ideally, achievements are made in groups meaning that responsibilities are also shared. In her experience, a virtuous leader in Congo-Brazzaville is a good listener, concessive and competitive. Great leaders will also take into account the well-being of their employees. On the subject of motivation, she comments the following: *"If they continue to pay workers' salary, workers will stay motivated. In my company, we motivate each other with words. Sometimes I will say; good work! Always work with words!"* (22 October 2018).

Regarding the subject of women in leadership positions, the respondents had varying experiences. Some mention that there is no difference in leadership styles between a male or female leader. Others indicate that a female leader acts more motherly and is more demanding of other females in the company. Finally, a group of respondents note that, in their experience, people will not accept a female leader because of their cultural background (CCBS Survey, 2018).

Local leadership analysis

In-country literature review

In their article, titled *Le management Africain introuvable* (2014), Bakengela Shamba and Yves Livian explain management models in Africa from an external point of view. They explain that in Congo, when leadership fails to be effective, it is because management practices are influenced by a culture of institutional constraints that is external to the economic logic of the company. Exercising great leadership skills in a country like Congo is quite hard as cultural factors play a huge role in the workplace. In their view: *"Africans would place greater emphasis on the need for usability in organisations, rather than on relationships based on the logic of efficiency"* (p. 5).

In other literature, the most effective leadership technique is the one which is less known in management textbooks. A technique where a leader behaves as a so-called 'enlightened autocrat'. Bourgoin (1984) explains this technique in his book which has a quite evocative title: *L'Afrique malade du management (Africa, sick by management).* In the book, he claims that in the countries south of the Sahara where the distances are great, people give preference to theories which favours authoritarianism. These ways of approaching leadership tend to have one major thing in common - that power is not divided but in the hands of one person or a small group (Bourgoin, 1984).

When understanding the applicability of management theories in Africa, there are four major theoretical perspectives, according to Oghojafor, Idowu and George (2012): divergence, universalism, convergence and contingency. The last theoretical perspective refers to either the personality of the leader or the nature of the owner's enterprise and its hierarchy. Establishing a strong presence at the workplace is a key factor in the application of one's principles and translates into work efficiency.

Lastly, it is shown that when a superior exercises his or her power normally, which is explained as correcting the abuses of their subordinates using their power, it is seen as a sign of insecurity and lack of protection. Why would this, which is seen as a normal way of acting in certain parts of the world, for example, in The Netherlands, be a bad sign in Congo? D'Iribarne (2009) explains that the leader, in this case, risks that the subordinates address a dominant political figure who could overturn the decision against him. In conclusion, the superiors fear their subordinates at the same time that they are feared.

Jean Pierre Miahouakana Matondo: a Congolese leadership scholar

Who earned his PhD in business management at the Donghua University in Shanghai. He has gone on to write multiple scientific articles on the subject of cross-cultural management with a focus on Congo, Middle-Africa and China.
In 2014, he released his first book, entitled: *At the cultural crossroads: Chinese companies in middle Africa: cultural values and cross-cultural management.*
In his article, *Cross-cultural values comparison between Chinese and Sub-Saharan Africans*, he discusses the complex and sensitive issue of business identity.
In Congo, identity still primarily revolves around ethnic affiliation. Managers will need to tread carefully around personal questions when first introduced to their teams. Matondo bases individuality on ethnic, linguistic and geographic affiliation. This is different from many other areas in the world, where affiliation is based on race or nationality. Matondo gives the following example as clarification, *"ethnically speaking, an African may be in this order Lari (ethnic group), Congo (linguistic group), South or North (Regional appurtenance), Congo (nationality), Central African (regional affiliation), and African (ancestral origin) all at once"* (Matondo, 2012b, p. 39). He continues to mention that awareness of these distinctions is essential in order to effectively deal with the local populace. This can be quite a challenge for a manager. Considering that Congo-Brazzaville has a population of around 4 million, yet ethnologists recognise 62 spoken languages, 15 principal ethnic groups with over 70 subgroups. Being aware of all the distinctions can result in a competitive advantage for an organisation. The art of dialogue and conversation is a cherished part in human relationship management. Open dialogues and the free discussion of employee problems are key in leveraging a business. When people are unwilling to talk about private or public affairs, it can be interpreted as having bad manners and deter productivity. Should there be an open dialogue, one should respect individuals' sentiments; hence conversations that may cause misgivings should be avoided (Miahouakana, 2008). This perception of human relationships describes the climate of the African business environment (Matondo, 2012b). This is also observed in the well-known African management style, *Ubuntu*, which means 'humanity towards others' (Mbigi, 1995).

Erika Amoako-Agyei: a Congolese cross-cultural trainer

Erika Amoako-Agyei is an intercultural trainer, consultant, speaker and writer working with global companies operating in Africa. She has over 17 years of experience. Amoako-Agyei delivers cross-cultural training programmes for executives, multicultural teams, expatriate families and international students. In 2011, she founded Africa Intercultural Consulting, a management and cross-cultural training firm in the US that services global companies and organisations expanding to Africa. She is the author of the article, *Cross-cultural management and organisational behavior in Africa* (2009). She has also written a business person's guide to the social and professional cultures in sub-Saharan Africa. According to Amoako-Agyei (2018), having a workforce that is well-versed in the ways of the world is no longer a luxury, but a necessity in order to be a competitive business. However, for most Western executives, sub-Saharan Africa is still one of the most challenging destinations to do business in due to the various cultural differences. The business styles and ways of communicating can differ greatly from region to region. Amoako-Agyei takes, for example, the negotiating process. Most Westerners need to produce quick and tangible results and this can clash with Africans' slower pace and long-term outlook. When confronted with a slower pace, you should not press for an immediate response as it will look as if you want your employees to act prematurely. This is known to cause anxiety and distrust and can undermine the negotiating process. Ignoring the local culture and applying pressure to influence decision-making will not only risk breaking the lines of communication but could potentially cause irreparable damage and costly mistakes. When it comes to decision-making, there is a strong belief in tapping into the collective wisdom of the entire team, regardless of the high degree of hierarchy. Amoako-Agyei reckons that this approach does not mean that it is not possible for a quick decision to be made or to get things done individually if needed (Amoako-Agyei, 2018).

In-country leadership best seller

A popular book in Congo regarding leadership is written by the French YouTuber Olivier Roland, which was published in 2014, titled: *Tout Le Monde N'a Pas Eu La Chance De Rater Ses Études* (CCBS Survey 2018). Olivier Roland has been an entrepreneur since the age of 19, blogger, YouTuber, amateur archaeologist, diver, aeroplane pilot, globe-trotter and international motivational speaker.
In his book, Roland writes on how to break the routine and succeed outside the system, by following a step by step method, based on the experience of hundreds of entrepreneurs and supported by more than 400 scientific

references. Roland wants the readers to *"Understand the limits of the education system and why it is becoming obsolete, hack their education by boosting their IQ, learn how to really learn effectively, and become free in creating a business that serves your life, rather than your life at home"* (Roland, 2014).

Local best-seller	
Title	*Tout Le Monde N'a Pas Eu La Chance De Rater Ses Études*
Subtitle	-
Author	Olivier Roland
Publisher	Alisio
Year	2014
ISBN	9791092928228

Congolese leadership YouTube review

The video by Well Grounded (2018) is on the topic of leadership development programmes around the Congo Basin. The local conception of leadership is first and foremost related to the internal development of oneself. It is about increasing awareness of the impact of individual actions, inactions, attitude toward others and toward bringing change. The aim of the course is to improve employee participation so that they can be better individuals, colleagues and change-agents. Bringing transformation seems a reoccurring theme not only in this video but also in our survey answers and in research papers. Evariste Mbayelao believes that: *"Poor leadership is the root cause of the challenges that Africa is facing today"* (Well Grounded, 2018).

In an earlier video by Well Grounded, Mireille Kayijamahe mentions that technical skills are not enough to make a successful leader (Well Grounded, 2017). Organisations need people who are aware of the internal attitudes and must build constructive relationships with their team. She emphasises that there are three critical things for an organisation: people, purpose and projects. People are generally seen as the least important of the three by the management, while in reality, they are at the basis of every organisation.

It seems as though leadership is changing in Africa. More importantly, in Congo people are changing their expectations of a leader and what a leader should represent. Together with this change come more incentives to learn about leadership and ways to improve and bring change. Effective leadership is no longer just a position or particular role, but it is about knowing one's self and what you believe in, being clear on the changes you want to bring around you and taking action and inspiring others to do so too (Well Grounded, 2017).

Understanding hierarchy in Congo

According to professor Bakengela Shamba, Congo-Brazzaville is a country with a high hierarchical distance - meaning that there is a big gap between superiors and subordinates (CCBS Survey, 2018). Subordinates expect to be told what to do, and close supervision is seen as a positive attribute. A lot of prominence is given to leaders and business partners (Matondo, 2012a). Nevertheless, it is possible to come with personal matters to your superior and talk about your well-being (Lago, 22 October 2018).

According to William Conton (1966), there is a deep and ingrained respect for seniority. This is notable in business relationships, where the age of a person is a key factor. Old age is associated with authority, business wisdom, rank, title and experience. Regardless of rank, title or education, an older person holds a certain level of superiority. Nevertheless, a Congolese proverb says: *"Mpu buzitu ntu buzitu"*, which means *"in order to be respected, you should also respect others, no matter their age and status"*. As a result of the high power distance and the importance of status, there is a clear process of business communication. For example, during meetings, the seating arrangement will be in the order of hierarchy and one should not look an older participant in the eye - this is to show respect. Employees are expected to follow the instructions of their manager as they see themselves as benevolent decision-makers. According to Professor Muamba Mumbunda, at the Catholic University of Congo *"Everything is made in accordance with the statutes and internal regulation"* (CCBS Survey, 2018). Leadership is vital to job commitment and satisfaction with only workers' salaries being more important (Miembazi-Massamba, 2017).

How the Congolese achieve leadership empathy

Leaders in Congo-Brazzaville are expected to safeguard their employees' well-being and have a concern for social responsibility. It is highly valued for a leader to be understanding and nurturing. Employees rank low on uncertainty avoidance, so they value simplicity and clear messages. The leader should also keep a close eye on employees, by ensuring that everything goes as planned. Most people are not taught to be assertive decision-makers but to respect authority. As a leader, you will always need to make sure that there is a certain group harmony and avoid personal criticism. This is mainly because Congolese do not want to be singled out, which is owed once again to their collectivist values. Be that as it may, a manager will still confront their employees in order to obtain the targeted results (CCBS Survey, 2018). Wholesome leaders make sure that every team member is given a meaningful role. While still making sure that everything revolves around the team, personal achievement is underplayed in favour of group achievements (Booysen, 1999). Teams will work most effectively when achieving cohesiveness and solidarity. One way of reaching this state is by creating a common purpose (Mbigi, 1995).

Due to the current financial situation in Congo, the two most common reasons for job satisfaction and commitment, according to research done by Miembazi-Massamba, are salary and job security (Miembazi-Massamba, 2017). Still, the Congolese also want to be a part of something bigger, due to their collectivist values. As individuals, they want to know exactly what is expected of them in the workforce. Thus, assuring close supervision and setting realistic goals could be a better motivator than money. Therefore, a manager who is strong but also sympathetic can work wonders in the Congolese workspace.

Ethiopia

Loula van der Sande, Maurice Boukbrass, Jo-Mairro Burnet, Mairéad Carter & Ornela Johansson-Segunda

The Federal Republic of Ethiopia (*□□□□□*) is twice the size of its neighbouring countries: Somalia, Kenya and Eritrea. Ethiopia is positioned in the Horn of Africa and currently holds a population of 100 million residents, making it the 10th biggest country in Africa and 12th biggest country in the whole world in terms of population (World Population Review, 2018). Addis Ababa (*□□□ □□□*) is the capital city of Ethiopia and has a high diversity rate for different ethnicities such as Oromo, Amhara, Tigre, Somali, Sidama, Wolaytta and Afar (Background Note, 2004). Ethiopia's official language is Amharic which is used broadly across the country (Background Note, 2004). Birr (*□□*) is the national currency. The Ethiopian banknotes are printed with images of national heritage such as ploughing farmers, which indicates the integral part that agriculture has played in the history and economy (Background Note, 2004). Ethiopia's main unique selling point is the production of the finest coffee. The country is identified as *"the land of coffee"* ("*□□□ □□□*") by Sanath Bhaskar Baikadi (24 October 2018) which is one of their main exports. A common saying is *"Buna dabo naw"* which translates to *"coffee is our bread"*, this demonstrates the role coffee plays in the diet and as a source of sustenance (Background Note, 2004). A part of the steady increase in GDP is due to Europe investing in Ethiopia (Bayiley & Teklu, 2016). With the growth of exportation to European countries of products such as coffee, sugar, fruit, oilseeds, marble and gold. These products for the European market make up almost half of the country's GDP, employment and the mass majority of export earnings (Berhanu & Poulton, 2014).

How the Ethiopians characterise leaders

The attitudes of Ethiopian leaders differ based on age, according to research conducted by Yemer (2009). For this study, Yemer examined the opinions of 56 Ethiopian leaders on national leadership that were gathered through interviews. The participants were divided into three different age groups: 20 to 29, 30 to 39 and 40 to 49. Furthermore, leadership was split into two categories: participative versus directive and contingent versus consistent leadership. More than 90 per cent of the respondents in the age group 20 to 29 argue that both participative and directive leadership is important. More than half of the respondents of the remaining age groups preferred participative leadership. This result is remarkable as it appears that the younger age group prefers a combination of participative and directive leadership over just participative leadership, which is preferred by the older age groups. To conclude this research, all of the respondents in the 20 to 29 age group prefer the contingent approach over the consistent approach. The 40 to 49 age bracket, however, felt that the consistent approach is the best approach (Yemer, 2009).

An interesting aspect of leadership in Ethiopia is the role of females in business. In an interview with a cross-cultural consultant, Abigael Teklu (24 October 2018), she shared her opinion on higher management opportunities for women. Teklu claims that women, in general, have many social responsibilities besides work which can make it more difficult for women to rise up the hierarchical ladder compared to men. Women are judged on their status as a wife or mother. Nowadays, men and women are equal in the law, but in daily life, it can be different (Teklu, 24 October 2018). Historically, Ethiopian women have suffered from economic, as well as sociocultural discrimination. A USAID report states that the primary school enrolment rate of girls has doubled in the past two decades (USAID, n.d.). However, of all students enrolled in university, only 30 per cent are female. Besides that, the number of female teachers at a university is as low as 10 per cent. To conclude, seniority is highly respected in Ethiopian leadership. It is unusual for younger men to manage a senior aged team (USAID, n.d.). If the manager is younger in age than his or her subordinates, he or she may find difficulties in gaining respect from the team. This is because in Ethiopia seniority is considered a sign of wisdom. Furthermore, the academic opportunities for women are growing, but are not yet equal to the opportunities for men.

Survey results and what local respondents say

Ethiopians identify themselves as unique and different from all other African countries. This is due to their diverse variety of religions, cultures and traditions which makes them more patriotic (Teklu, 24 October 2018). Results of the CCBS survey (2018) confirms this as it shows that the majority of respondents feel that there is something unique and specific about leadership in Ethiopia that differs from other countries. Even the word 'leadership' in Ethiopia is looked upon differently when compared to a Western country. The difference is entailed into the act of leading, Ethiopian leaders tend to give orders as opposed to leading and showing how things are done. Tekola states: *"A leader in my country is often seen as 'the boss'"* (CCBS Survey, 2018). This supports their autocratic behaviour, which is directly linked to the high score of 70 of Hofstede's power distance (Hofstede Insights, 2018). Pascale Sztum, a cross-cultural management expert, explains that leaders in Ethiopia do not positively influence their subordinates, *"they just command"* (CCBS Survey, 2018). When asked if an employee may bend the rules without asking in order to improve their professional performance, the results of the CCBS survey reveal that more than half of the participants disagree. It is not possible to bend the rules without permission. Another interesting result illustrates that the majority of the respondents agree that employees are expected to follow the established procedures. This supports Hofstede's power distance theory: authority is important and the decision-making process is conducted at a top management level.

Ethiopians have a different concept of time compared to Westerners. With Ethiopia being close to the equator, there are two ways of reading the time: European and Ethiopian time. Ethiopian time runs on a twelve-hour day with the sun rising at one. When asked what time would be best to schedule a staff meeting, the CCBS survey respondents displayed a variety of time preferences with a third preferring to have a meeting after 11 am and another third between 9 and 10 am. In addition to following procedures, Ethiopian leaders are expected to meet deadlines. Half of the respondents agree that missing a deadline is more or less the same thing as a failure (CCBS Survey, 2018).

According to the survey respondents, Ethiopian men and women do not differ in leadership style. One of the survey participants argues: *"The style of leadership depends on individual characteristics [rather than] gender. There are good leaders from both categories as well as bad leaders"* (CCBS Survey, 2018). The participant points out that it is harder for women to reach the top positions as they need to prove themselves more than men (CCBS Survey, 2018). One of the respondents states the following: *"Women who made [it] up the ladder usually are powerful decision makers. While men I came across are soft and possess good political connections"* (CCBS Survey, 2018). A CCBS survey respondent adds that *"In large organizations, very few women reach the top, but many entrepreneurs are female. There is no big difference in leadership style"* (2018).

Local leadership analysis

In-country literature review

Mitiku, Hondeghem and Troupin (2017) conducted a study on leadership roles of Ethiopian civil service managers. In this research, they conclude that Ethiopian leaders have three characterisations of leadership roles, labelled as the 'change agents', 'affective leaders' and 'result-orientated realists'. The 'change agents' characterise themselves by emphasising change as a leader. The 'affective leaders' distinguish themselves from other leaders by focusing on people and relationship management. Finally, the 'result-orientated realists' highlight goal achievement and consider tasks of more value than the relational aspects of the firm. The majority of the leaders who were interviewed in this study preferred the 'change agent' leadership style. In contrast, Baikadi (24 October 2018) states that Ethiopian leaders are far from change agents. This is accounted for by Mitiku et al. (2017) who notes that the current civil service reforms could have affected the leadership role preference of 'change agents' as in such a political climate 'change' could easily be a politically correct mantra.

Sanath Bhaskar Baikadi: an Ethiopian leadership scholar

A personal interview with an Ethiopian scholar was conducted to gain more insight into Ethiopian leadership. Sanath Bhaskar Baikadi is a business management graduate from Angla University. Baikadi has 10 years of experience in the Ethiopian culture, and in 2014, he was chosen to be a curriculum designer, teacher-instructor and trainer to the University of Gondar. According to Baikadi, there is a huge difference in leadership styles between urban and rural areas. The rural areas show a lack of economic and social freedom, and these areas seldom encourage expats to come and grow their businesses in the country. As for the urban areas, it is the opposite. Leaders of rural areas are very autocratic, whereas leaders from the urban areas are a mixture of autocratic and democratic (Baikadi, 24 October 2018). A consistent characteristic of Ethiopian leaders is that they are highly policed, stubborn and very rigid in their delegation of authority (Baikadi, 24 October 2018). This strict and stern behaviour is a result of the militant governments of the past. Baikadi expresses that *"children will mostly grow up under domination and control of the parents. Consequently, they inherited this leadership style because of their family values"* (24 October 2018). Ethiopians and Westerners have a different view of leadership. According to Baikadi, the key difference between Western and Ethiopian leadership is the communication between the top and bottom of an organisation. Ethiopian leaders command their subordinates whereas in the Western leadership styles, a conversation is more common. In Ethiopia, subordinates sometimes are afraid to ask questions or communicate problems to their superior. One of the respondents of the CCBS survey (2018) adds that: *"The Ethiopian workplace can definitely be seen as an individualistic one."* People focus more on their own success and their own goals rather than team achievements. Furthermore, Baikadi believes that Western leaders are very adaptable and innovative, whereas the Ethiopian leaders do not feel such encouragement to adapt or to innovate new production methodologies or techniques. Lastly, he notes that, in comparison with Western leaders, the Ethiopian leadership style lacks delegation of authority (Baikadi, 24 October 2018).

Abigael Teklu: an Ethiopian cross-cultural trainer

Abigael Teklu was born in Addis Ababa and has spent most of her life in Ethiopia. Graduating from Addis Ababa University with a BA in management and public relations, she has over 10 years' experience in leadership development, with some years in different parts of the world, such as the United Kingdom. Based in Addis Ababa, Teklu is now working as an independent cross-cultural trainer, preparing expatriates who move to Ethiopia. Having worked with many different cultures moving to Ethiopia for business, she reveals that the main challenge for foreigners is the need to: *"understand that Ethiopians see themselves as unique and different from other African countries"* (Teklu, 24 October 2018).

Teklu (24 October 2018) expresses that the Ethiopian leadership style is based on the cultural and religious history of the country, which has led Ethiopians to be more tuned to an authoritarian style of leadership. This can be a challenge for expatriates from European countries, such as Switzerland, Ireland and the UK, who may be more accustomed to a *laissez-faire* leadership style. Although, she states that Ethiopian leaders can connect with individuals on a personal level, increasing the 'human element', meaning it is not only about the business. Teklu suggests that this relates to how Ethiopia is a collective society with a Hofstede individual score of 20, and therefore it is incorporated into a high level of trust in doing business and leadership deliverance (Hofstede Insights, n.d.).

In-country leadership bestsellers

One of the best-selling Ethiopian leadership books is written by Agitu Wodaja in 2014: *The secret to finishing well.* The book highlights the differences in leadership between Ethiopia and the United States of America. Agitu Wodaja gives insight into leadership styles that shape the decision-making process. *The secret to finishing well* is a mix of different types of stories on spiritual tenets, the logic of human rights, the inspiration of serving others, global events and the current state of our society. Wodaja includes the history of humans in the book as it relates to our behaviour and applies to our current situation. The author describes the main points of leadership and gives a starting point for new changemakers.

Local leadership book	
Title	*The secret to finishing well*
Subtitle	Quest for authentic leadership
Author	Agitu Wodaja
Publisher	Xulon Press
Year	2014
ISBN	978-162-871-620-7

Ethiopia leadership YouTube review

This paragraph will discuss a seminar held by Ethiopian business people from different industries talking about the state of leadership and the dearth of female leadership in Ethiopia. Ethiopia is one of the fastest growing economies in the world. In addition, Ethiopia has grown socio-economically. This all has a positive effect on the society, especially for women in the country. The fast-growing economy has opened up job opportunities for women who were traditionally limited to domestic labour and economically dependent on men. Furthermore, enforced policies against early marriages and female genital mutilation opened doors to equality in leadership for women and girls (Earuyan Solutions, 2018). According to Haddis D. Tadesse, Bill and Melinda Gates Foundation Deputy Director, Africa and representative to Ethiopia and the African Union, *"Social construction is based on their family lineage, wealth, level of education and other privileges"* (Earuyan Solutions, 2017). She notes that men have the tendency to react negatively towards women in a high position. Tadesse adds: *"Men feel threatened by women at the top."* A female participant suggests that *"As a woman you need to show more effort and hard work than a man to get to the same position"* (Earuyan Solutions, 2017). A businesswoman in the seminar illustrates that in a situation where three women are at the top of a company, there still will be a man above them. This shows the high rate of gender inequality in Ethiopia. Companies always see the weakness of women and not the strong points they bring to the company. In contrast to men, in which companies see mostly only the strong points and not the weak points. However, companies in Ethiopia, especially big corporations, offer support to employees to study more. For example, a female in the discussion added that *"they pay for the master's of their employees"*. Of course, this depends on the company and the leadership structure. *"Study is very important for women in Ethiopia to become successful."* According to a former employee of Ethiopian Airlines, salaries of men and women are equal and the salary depends on the position you have and not on your gender (Earuyan Solutions, 2017).

Understanding hierarchy in Ethiopia

In the work environment of Ethiopia, hierarchy has a strong presence and is widely accepted. The power distance in Ethiopia is fairly high. An explanation for the high score is that people in Ethiopia accept hierarchy without expecting any justification (CCBS Survey, 2018). When further analysing the CCBS survey, roughly three-quarters of the participants indicate that leaders should keep a personal distance from their employees to maintain the right level of respect. These results confirm that the power distance in Ethiopia is has a strong presence, again referring to Hofstede's power distance score of 70 (Hofstede Insights, n.d.). Touching again on the issues Baikadi (24 October 2018) raised with the military base governments which have had a strong influence on hierarchy within businesses and governments alike. The military that was once active in Ethiopia had a traditional hierarchical structure, with many different levels of command. In traditional Ethiopian companies, a strong hierarchy is more visible in comparison to Ethiopian international companies where there is a more open relationship between subordinates and their leaders. This style is becoming more common in Ethiopia due to globalisation. However, Teklu (24 October 2018) mentions that there is room for personal relationships in traditional companies. It depends on the leadership style, which is influenced by the origins of the leader. Baikadi (24 October 2018) states that there is a difference between rural areas and urban areas, with leaders in urban areas having an international approach to hierarchy due to the influx of students gaining education outside of Ethiopia in places such as Germany and Ireland. However, in rural areas, the traditional approach is more common due to the religious and policed areas.

How the Ethiopians achieve leadership empathy

Achieving empathy is an important aspect that Ethiopians consider essential towards increasing employee morale and productivity. According to Baker and Campbell (2013), the vital components of forming empathy among employees involve cultural and social aspects, such as the value of religion and tradition, and incorporating this within the workplace, as well as adapting to cultural diversity. Ethiopia is home to many European expatriates that emigrate for work. Empathy should also enable foreigners to progress and grow within the workplace. All these factors play a part in the successful achievement of effective leadership empathy in the workplace. These components comply with the Maslow's Hierarchy of Needs, in which specific stages must be met for fulfilment in the workplace (Oleson, 2004).

Ethiopians achieve empathy through communication and specifically in having the ability to communicate between different hierarchical levels within the workplace. This allows employee involvement and opinions within decision-making in the workplace, which results in a relationship forming between the employees and employer. Subsequently, listening to employees is another way through which to achieve empathy. In order to build relationships between employee and employers in the early stages, the employers will need to listen to the demands and needs of employees. This is in agreement with the opinion raised by a cross-cultural trainer, Abigael Teklu (24 October 2018), who believes that leaders need to listen more as they miss out on opportunities and great ideas from their own employees within their department.
Additionally, the sense of recognition for employees is a way of achieving empathy. The success of the company is based on employee's productivity and efforts in implementing the business' beliefs and instructions. Recognition of their hard work is a factor in motivating employees and boosting their morale within the workplace, which is a common incentive for the needs and wants of employees (Oleson, 2004).

As Transparency International (2018) illustrates, the corruption level in Ethiopia is high due to current political status and government. This poses a risk to Ethiopian leaders in their effort to achieve leadership empathy as trust is a key element that helps boost effectiveness and productivity at the workplace. This issue is being tackled with the incorporation of legal documents, such as contracts for employees which protect their roles and positions at the workplace.

Although this is a negative element that Ethiopia is working on, it is also an advantage for achieving leadership empathy as these legal aspects will build trust in the workplace. Employees will feel secure within their role and valued as they have documents to rely on. Furthermore, legal protection enforces some of the key factors of achieving leadership empathy such as organisational experience. This could also be observed in the CCBS survey, where more than half of the local respondents agree that this is essential in achieving leadership empathy, but also in making a good quality leader (CCBS Survey, 2018).

Guatemala

Alexandra Rossman, Bryan van de Groep, Floor Buikema, Rik Visser & Savannah van der Ploeg

Bordering Mexico, Belize, Honduras and El Salvador, Guatemala is a country known for its Mayan roots (Nelson, 1999). The landscape still embraces the heritage of the natives with ancient ruins, volcanoes and farmlands. Agriculture has historically been important to their civilization and remains the main export sector in their economy (Bossen, 1982). A large part of the population resides in the countryside due to their farming abilities but also as a factor of high income inequality. The rural regions are home to many of the remaining minorities, while the Ladino population (of Spanish-European descent) make up the urban majority. Since the conquest by Spanish conquistadors, the official language is Spanish with approximately half of the population additionally knowing one of 23 regional Indian languages (Becker, 2009). This blend of cultural decent has added a sense of distrust, mostly due, in part, to their rough history of violence and political greed. Therefore, in Guatemala, communication revolves around trust and loyalty, with relationship building at the highest level of importance.

How the Guatemalans characterise leaders

In the article, "El liderazgo es para presidir y no para ocuparse", Samuel Berberián (2018) writes about leadership from the Guatemalan perspective. In the article, he highlights that a person's capacity and profile are much more of a determinant for one to be a leader than, for example, charisma. A leader needs to be able to guide a group and create a team atmosphere where goals are set and achieved above expectations. A Guatemalan scholar, R. Yesid Barrera Santos (18 October 2018), further extends the role of a manager by adding that they should be the paradigm of the perfect employee. This weight of performance in serving the community originates from the ideals held by the indigenous groups of the country (Santos, 18 October 2018).

Along with being of service to employees, Berberián (2018) continues by stating that many leaders today do not concern themselves with explaining nor justifying what they are doing. They simply make it happen. He warns that this can create a barrier between the varying positions, and while Guatemalans often see disparity as normal in the workplace, this is not without discontentment. The authoritarian leader thrives off of a family-based culture that Ernesto Solares explains is an outdated tactic (CCBS Survey, 2018). When it comes to critical traits of a leader, being future-oriented as well as performance-oriented is not as important to the labour force (House, 2014). Rather, encouragement and support for staff members are traits that stand out to employees.

Survey results and what local respondents say

In order to gather greater data about leadership in Guatemala, an online survey has been distributed to various Guatemalan experts who have had noteworthy managerial positions. The Guatemalans who participated in the CCBS survey (2018) communicated a range of opinions on desired leadership traits. There is a strong agreement on expecting a leader to be a visionary thinker who listens well to employees. Our local scholar, Barrera Santos, enunciated the value of being a visionary by explaining that leaders who are focussed on the present will only lead their team to the present (18 October 2018). A capable leader should also be strong, effective and most of all, a powerful decision maker with a strong charismatic personality (CCBS Survey, 2018). Additionally, leaders in Guatemala have more success in becoming favourable managers by having organisational experience and technical competence.

When it comes to communication, a Guatemalan leader tends to give feedback with a direct approach. Evaluations are normal in the workplace in order to attain the preferred outcome. Progress with a project can take precedence over the well-being of the employees. Mr Cuevas, a sales manager in the banking industry states: "*the most successful managers are well known to be authoritarians*" (CCBS Survey, 2018). Nevertheless, when looking at the CCBS survey (2018) there is surprisingly no distance between leaders and subordinates. In most instances, employees and managers share the same kind of offices or equipment. The procedures are not always followed by the employees as imposed and the leaders are mostly called by their first names instead of the titles belonging to the positions. Also, despite being focussed on project progress, it is still seen as of high importance that leaders pay specific time and attention to the personal well-being of their employees (CCBS Survey, 2018). Balancing these may be a challenge, and as stated by a business professional, the quality of a leader can be diluted when having to service a larger task force.

When it comes to gender roles in today's society, the biases are still present in Guatemala. Alejandro Pisquiy (CCBS Survey, 2018), a regional buyer for Central America and the Caribbean, confirms the disjunction between the genders in managerial positions. Nevertheless, there is a still a representation of women in Guatemalan high-end managerial positions. They have generated their own style of motivating in a country where gender inequality still exists. A director in the food and beverage industry states, *"Yes, women are more [positive]. They give the extra mile. They enjoy the hard work and are extremely competitive"* (CCBS Survey, 2018).

Local leadership analysis

In-country literature review

In *El liderazgo laboral*, Tecoloco (2012) writes about leadership within Guatemalan business culture. According to Tecoloco (2012), leadership in the work environment is important for harmony and performance. A good leader at work is someone who sets an example, is honest and has principles (Tecoloco, 2012). A leader is someone who has gained the trust of the employees and works hard to maintain that trust. Montejo (2005) expresses the value of being a reliant leader from the context of survival by Mayan tribe figureheads. A more recent take has been explored by Jose Toasa (2016). The younger leaders that he describes, also called grassroots leaders, are more inclined to try innovative approaches to problem-solving, questioning older leaders and collaborating with differing groups. According to Toasa (2016), the Guatemalan inhabitants feel that the grassroots leaders represent them better as they listen to every group. Rafael Sologaistoa (2018) defines a leader as one who facilitates both professional and personal growth for the people surrounding them.

R. Yesid Barrera Santos: a Guatemalan leadership scholar

Santos (18 October 2018) is a skilled business administrator with a PhD in political science and sociology. His specialisations include conflict resolutions, negotiation themes and coaching. His firm is dedicated to supporting the universities and local corporate leaders in Central America. During an interview, Santos explains five fundamental traits for being an effective leader. These include serving, possessing excellent communication skills, being visionary, having character and, most importantly, having discipline.

In his experience, leaders in Guatemala tend to appreciate formality and hierarchy. The end of Guatemala's 36-year war has left a feeling of agitation which can explain why the leadership styles are often direct, hard and intimidating. Guatemala is considered to be a '*Machista*' society where mostly men are given high positions in the workplace, but a higher number of female students could create a big change for women in Guatemala.

Gabriela Contreras Aguilera: a Guatemalan cross-cultural trainer

Having over ten years of experience, Gabriela Contreras Aguilera (12 November 2018) is well positioned to shed light on distinct leadership traits in Guatemala. From her experience, the attribute of ingenuity is the main characteristic of what makes a leader valuable. The performance of a team should not be dependent on the authority inflicted by the manager but by the recognition given for positive performances (Aguilera, 12 November 2018). The cross-cultural trainer explains that the support of a nourishing work environment can generate a highly skilled task force. The role of a leader among employees should be to maintain a balance of control and leniency. An example would be to give recognition in public but provide feedback in private (Aguilera, 12 November 2018). When asked whether a manager adjusts the way they manage for the benefit of their employees, she points out that many will, but that there are still cases of managers who limit their employees in fear of the subordinate's advancement.

In-country leadership best seller

Created by Mariano Codoñer C. and José Antonio García Mayorga (2008), *La paradoja del liderazgo autocrático* (*The paradox of autocratic leadership*) describes the leader/worker, or *jefe/trabajadores,* relationship that currently exists in Latin America. Having years of experience with managerial work, the authors describe the current work environment. They place the emphasis on the despotic leadership trends that are widely used in the Guatemalan workplace to showcase ineffective leadership skills. Their research exhibits a number of traits that are seen as quintessential to the leaders and employees alike. As the reading continues, Mayorga and Codoñer (2008) develop methods through which current leaders could increase their workforce output by becoming a more desirable boss. Utilising empathy and patience, the authors have found that many firms have had success when creating a comfortable work environment for the hired staff.

Local leadership book	
Title	*La Paradoja del Liderazgo Autocratico*
Subtitle	-
Author	Mariano Codoñer C. y José Antonio García Mayorga
Publisher	Self-published
Year	2008
ISBN	-

Guatemalan leadership YouTube review

In the video *Experiencias de liderazgo empresarial por Daniel Panedas*, Daniel Panedas (2014) gives a lecture on his experiences in leadership after living in Guatemala for ten years. In another video titled *Formación de líderes*, Miguel Moreno and Pedro Moreno (2012) present their view on leadership. Notable in both videos is the importance of interconnection. According to Daniel Panedas (2014), trust-based relationships are the foundation of a successful career. Therefore, it is extremely important that leaders develop and utilise empathy with their team. In addition, Miguel Moreno (2012) is convinced that values and principles are fundamental for being a good leader. The reason for that, according to Miguel Moreno (2012), is that a leader's actions will one day affect his or her family, the community and even the nation.

The value of understanding the community expands past country borders. Panedas (2014) asks the MBA students in the lecture to develop their general knowledge since it will be extremely important when interacting with other professionals and leaders. Miguel Moreno (2012) implies that understanding the era we live in is paramount to leading effectively. Understanding new politics, shifting of thinking processes and behaviour transformations allow us to make the right decisions. According to Panedas (2014), being grateful and never fearing risks are qualities that create a great leader. He declares that projects will not succeed if there are no risks taken. In addition, he insists that we all need a little bit of luck, a push in the right direction and someone who can help (Panedas, 2014). According to Miguel Moreno (2012), not only your own experience is important, but also the knowledge you gain from people with other experiences.

All in all, according to Pedro Moreno (2012), leadership begins with the life of the individual. *"If an individual's life is a disaster, he cannot be a good leader"*.

Understanding hierarchy in Guatemala

In Guatemala, emulating those in higher positions is existent among the workforce. According to Ernesto Solares (15 November 2018), a Guatemalan general manager, people often seek to be on good terms with their superiors regardless of collaborative ties. Solares also discusses the significance of hierarchy by stating that it is necessary to have control over individual tasks and as a result reach the desired organisational goals (Solares, 15 November 2018). Measurements of the hierarchical separation have been made available by the Dutch psychologist, Geert Hofstede (Hofstede, 1983). According to his power distance measurement, Guatemalans rank high indicating a general acceptance of the separation between different levels of work hierarchy. Acceptance of this ranking does not imitate the feelings and mindsets of all those within country borders. Carlos F. Rodriguez, a political advisor, agrees that transparency is vital for constructive leaders. He states, *"..lamentablemente en la mayoría de empresas o entidades públicas, entre más alto sea tu puesto más inaccesible te vuelves,"* which expresses the inaccessibility of higher-ranking members within a firm (CCBS Survey, 2018). This system of unreachable management has been tied with the traditional *machismo* gender hierarchy that exists in Latin America. Men with these privileges hold formal leadership positions and are enabled to make decisions for the firm (Musalo, 2013). Surprisingly, there has been a noticeable change among the strict social scale. Many respondents, including a local country director, affirm that using the first name of a manager has become a trend (CCBS Survey, 2018).

How the Guatemalans achieve leadership empathy

When discussing the Guatemalan business realm, it is important to highlight the way in which the indigenous Mayan community approaches empathy. In many of the aboriginal towns, the citizens gather frequently for town meetings (Ekern, 2011). This is in regard to the significance associated with respect for the community. A leader who lacks regard for the fellow townspeople and their well-being lacks the ability to be a successful leader. The deep-rooted traditions of the Mayan culture have settled into the evolving metropolitan areas as well. When asked what employees expect from their leader, Rodriguez responds with,

"Considerado al colocarse en los zapatos del empleado," or in other words empathy (CCBS Survey, 2018). Santos explains that being congenial is one of the main distinctions of a good leader (18 October 2018).

The importance of working together as a collective is similarly important in the Guatemalan workplace. As Jose Velez, a commercial director in Guatemala describes, treating employees like a family has strengthened the engagement and overall quality of work life (CCBS Survey, 2018). Showing care and appreciation for employees can also be witnessed through *la hora chapina*, or the Guatemalan hour (Republicanew, 2016). On one hand, it means that workers arrive late to functions. The other view is that time is given for relationship building, which inevitably establishes trust. Treating employees with the same esteem as a family member is an easy way to show compassion.

Indonesia

Yasmin Ehrhardt, Aikò Dreesen, Ruben Siekman, Joey Agterberg & Ivan Tsjarachtsants

After a long history of occupation by different foreign rulers, at first by the '*Vereenigde Oostindische Compagnie*' (Dutch East India Company), by 1949 Indonesia embarked on a new journey and is thriving. The Republic of Indonesia is one of the world's most densely populated nations. According to the 2010 census, its population exceeds 260 million inhabitants. These residents are divided amongst more than seventeen thousand small islands which, when combined into a massive land mass, would be four times as large as Thailand. The biggest portion of the population can be found in Jakarta.

The Indonesian linguistic landscape is extremely diverse, with over three hundred languages spoken. The Indonesian congress deems the Malay language (or Bahasa Indonesia) as official.

Indonesia is a democracy that has been heavily influenced by Islam, with the majority of its population being Muslim. The three following religious groups, which are significantly smaller in proportion, are Protestants, Catholics and Hindus. The Indonesian constitution guarantees all citizens the freedom of worship, each according to their own religion and beliefs. Across the thousands of islands of Indonesia, one single currency is utilised for all trade which takes place - the Rupiah (abbreviated as Rp).

How the Indonesians characterise leaders

It is important to emphasise the link between Indonesian culture and the most prominent leadership style (Dubrin, 2001). Culture is the framework of norms that shapes a leader's attitude, which is clearly seen in Indonesia (Carroll & Gannon, 1997). The link between the cultural visualisation of little assertiveness and a highly humane-oriented society represents the most efficient type of leadership. This cultural profile fits the globe's average rating of humaneness and charisma of the Indonesian leaders (Globe Project, 2016). Being charismatic refers to the capabilities of the person in charge to inspire and motivate individuals (Moore, 1995). It also involves being able to have certain expectations of individuals which they should live up to according to the society's core values.

This is relevant to the highly valued in-group collectivism in Indonesia and adds to the prominent values of loyalty, pride and group cohesion. All of these values aid managers in building strategically strong teams (Globe Project, 2016).
Since power distance is relatively high in Indonesia, there is very little conflict and prominent synergy, which is reflected in a high-performance orientation score. It relates to the extent of group compliments and mutual motivation towards excellence. However, this relationship between leadership and culture results in the individual in charge having to take on a lot of responsibilities. This reliance results in the leader having to make most of the decisions alone, which is directly reflected in the country's relatively low participative value (Globe Project, 2016).

Indonesians expect their leaders to not only be a manager but also a protector, a mentor and most importantly a father figure (*bapak* in Bahasa) (CCBS Survey, 2018). This *bapak* style of leadership can be characterised as attentive and paternalistic. According to Gani (2004), the leader of an organisation indeed assumes the role of a *bapak* and, as such, is expected to behave wisely and virtuously. Furthermore, in an interview with Chris Hainsch (17 October 2018), a consultant in Indonesia, this paternalistic style (or in some cases maternalistic) is said to strengthen the relationship between employees and managers. This creates a more personal bond which leads to loyalty. This is in accordance with the results of the CCBS survey (2018): *"Indonesian company is communal. Employees within the company feel like one big family and leaders [are] usually seen as the parent".* One respondent, a hotel manager, summed up Indonesian corporate culture simply as *"family feeling"* (CCBS Survey, 2018). A leader who is paternal/maternal is, in theory, expected to be approachable, relatable and accepting of their employees (Irwanto, 2011). However, as Antlov and Cederroth (1994) point out, leaders use their governmental connections as an asset to gain legitimacy. This might indicate a distant relationship with their employees as some did not gain this legitimacy fairly. Nevertheless, there are many leaders in Indonesia who do not exploit their connection to the government.

For Antlov and Cederroth (1994) there is another leadership style prevalent in Indonesia which is based upon the ethical and moral qualities of the individual. This refers back to the paternalistic leadership style described by Irwanto (2011) and shows that Indonesian leaders maintain responsibility in terms of tasks and people. As such, leaders in Indonesia find maintaining relationships with their people important, and they also take responsibility for their own achievements. The CCBS survey results support this with over half of the respondents stating that leaders prefer to have a more personal relationship between them and the

employees, instead of maintaining distance (CCBS Survey, 2018).
Moreover, Antlov and Cederroth's research indicates that Indonesians are tolerant towards organisations with an authoritarian environment, characterised by the willingness to work with the superior in a patron-client relationship system. This is reflected in traditional Indonesian culture and is called *'tepa selira'* which means mutual respect. Thus, leaders and employees try to ensure that respect is reciprocated and well-maintained in order to achieve the company's goals together (Irwanto, 2011).

Survey results and what local respondents say

The Cross-Cultural Business Skills (CCBS) survey extends globally. A number of Indonesian professionals participated, revealing detailed insight on local leadership. From the results, it can be concluded that two-thirds of the respondents are convinced that when a management decision is made, it is not likely to be amended. This is in line with a manager's view on this matter: *"Leadership in Indonesia, I think it could be a little dictatorship-like in a sense that once a decision is made, it cannot be changed"* (CCBS Survey, 2018). The investor relations manager continues: *"Although, a lot more leaders are now more open to discussion and not just a decision maker"*. This way of thinking also applies to deadlines. When asked if missing a deadline is considered a failure, almost all respondents found this to be true (CCBS Survey, 2018).
Several noteworthy results were seen when asked whether bending the rules at the workplace in order to achieve better results is acceptable. From all the respondents of the CCBS Survey, Indonesian respondents voted 'yes' the least. The Indonesian results almost unanimously indicate that bending the rules is not acceptable no matter the outcome (CCBS Survey, 2018).

Chris Hainsch (17 October 2018) states that the majority of the population grows up with the fact that they must listen to a person with more power. *"When children are growing up, they have to listen to their parents when they are going to school they have to listen to their teachers"*. This indicates that the Indonesian population follows a certain mindset which citizens have been indoctrinated by across multiple generations. Hainsch elaborates further: *"It continues like this and of course then also the companies have to adopt this leadership style"* (17 October 2018). Sunu Widianto (8 November 2018) confirms this statement in terms of giving employees orders. When they comply with them, the employees in turn ensure organisational harmony. Knowing that the rules are very strict,

one might think immediately of a very tense work environment, where managers are not likely to take criticism in a direct manner or consider the well-being of their employees. However, almost half of the respondents of the survey would prefer direct criticism, by which they mean that the criticism is within the staff meeting (CCBS Survey, 2018). Besides receiving criticism in a direct manner, around the same number of respondents state that having a strict work environment does not correlate to being distant towards their employees.
On the contrary, it shows that checking up on the well-being of employees is a significant task, on which time should be actively spent. Edhie Sarwono further explains this sentiment by stating: *"Balancing religious and professional behaviour. More balance, means more respect from subordinate or others"* (CCBS Survey, 2018). Thus, achieving a better relationship with your employees can be done by aiming towards balance in religion and work-related behaviour. This, in turn, will grant the leading figure more respect. These are all part of the characteristics of a strong employer, or as Chris Hainsch states: *"If you are running a business in Indonesia locally then you are running quite fine if you have a strong employer character"* (17 October 2018).

Local leadership analysis

Sunu Widianto and Budi Harsanto (2017) researched the impact of transformational leadership and organisational culture on firm performances in Indonesia's small to medium- enterprises (SMEs). The aim of this research was to apply resource-based theories to achieve a high level of performance within the firm through entrepreneurial orientation. In their paper, Widianto and Harsanto use a mix of several studies on these topics, where studies are used as the basis of their hypothesis and key variables (2017). The first variable, transformational leadership, is based on multiple sources that have shown the positive effect that transformational leadership has on firm sales growth. Peterson, Walumbwa, Byron and Myrowitz (2009) carried out a study among 49 start-ups and 56 established firms. The results reveal that transformational leadership has a stronger influence on start-ups compared to larger organisations. Their second variable, which is culture, indicates that competitive and innovative cultures have a positive influence on organisational performance. Not only does culture impact on how members of an organisation solve issues and view their business ecosystem, but it also means that people tend towards entrepreneurship when they are supported by an entrepreneurial environment and culture.
For the third and final variable, the researchers use entrepreneurial orientation

(EO). This variable is used as a mediating variable, looking at the link between transformational leadership and organisational culture on organisational performance. Based on these three variables, they developed two hypotheses: 'EO mediates the relationship between transformational leadership and firm performance.' and 'EO mediates the relationship between organisational culture and firm performance.' Moreover, to assure that the research could create generalised results, Widianto and Harsanto performed 100 surveys in Bandung, Indonesia. For the research, they conducted both offline and online questionnaires. The reason Bandung was chosen is because the city is considered to have significant SME development with a lot of young entrepreneurs and several SMEs in production and trade areas with specific products. The study concludes that a transformational leadership style relates to the rate of survival in dynamic environments, especially in emerging markets in Indonesia. As such, a transformational leader has a considerable influence on how entrepreneurial orientation flourishes in SMEs through inspiring, motivating and acting as a role model for employees to perform better. SMEs in emerging markets need more agility to cope with limitations in the near future, and for this reason, a transformational leadership might be the best way to overcome these challenges. Moreover, transformational leadership might be an intangible resource associated with strategy-making to support firm performances. Therefore, there is indeed a link between transformational leadership and EO which leads to strategic decision-making and achieving superior firm performance (Widianto & Harsanto, 2017).

Sunu Widianto (8 November 2018) is an assistant professor at the Department of Management and Business of the University of Padjadjaran in Bandung, Indonesia. After obtaining his PhD at the University of Twente, Widianto focussed on researching leadership, team performance and organisational behaviour. By conducting research, such as the one published in the article: "The impact of transformational leadership and organizational culture on firm performance in Indonesia SMEs" (2017), Widianto expanded his knowledge in order to create a more in-depth understanding regarding leadership.
Widianto (8 November 2018) explains that, contrary to common belief, Indonesia does not adopt a paternalistic leadership style equally over all industries. Current leadership styles vary among different industries. He highlights the relationship between the increasing amount of young entrepreneurs and new technology and innovation. Emphasis is put on the ways in which the current generation is more open-minded and strives for a more direct way of communicating. It is important to note that Indonesia is a collective society with a hierarchical structure,

creating a foundation of values which are reflected in a leader's behaviour. Another relation is contrasted between the behaviour of leaders and their characteristics. For the Indonesian public, it is important for a supervisor to have certain traits, especially because Indonesians dislike conflict and value harmony. The different characteristics of an individual in a managing position decide how effective they are in managing an indirect, high-context group of employees. The most important characteristics are charisma, intelligence, empathy, appreciation and decisiveness, which translate directly into respect. This earned respect makes it easier for the individual in charge to motivate and delegate to their employees. Being able to gain this respect is crucial in order to maintain the top-down hierarchical structure. Widianto states that *"[w]hen a leader says something we have to comply with his decisions"*, emphasizing the harmony in the working environment the leader has created which satisfies the needs of the employees. He goes on to explain that *"[t]he leader is like a role-model making them want to comply with whatever he does"* (Widianto, 8 November 2018).

Christian Hainsch (17 October 2018) is a managing partner of Indoconsult. Indoconsult supports foreign companies entering the Indonesian market. There is a variety of areas where they provide support, but the emphasis at Indoconsult lies on cross-cultural management, cross-cultural training as well as legal and tax issues. Hainsch is mainly responsible for the cross-cultural and legal aspects. With regard to the cross-cultural business management in Indonesia, it seems that the paternal leadership style is not the only aspect of the Indonesian culture that takes this shape. As Hainsch (17 October 2018) formulates: *"The whole society is based upon this paternal leadership"*. Emphasis is put on the way that managers care about their employees. Moreover, the importance of having a good personal relationship with your employees is highlighted as this translates into loyalty. Thus, the cultural aspect reflects the type of factors that are important for a successful leader. In relation to these cultural factors, Hainsch (17 October 2018) explains that these change over time. The current leadership style may be paternalistic. However, this is mostly due to the way individuals are raised and what type of education they grew up with.
The concept of feedback in Indonesia is considered a one-way street where the top gives feedback to the bottom, without giving any feedback back up the ladder. This is in stark contrast to the Western style of giving feedback, where it goes both ways. This process is prevalent throughout the entire education system, resulting in companies having to adapt their management style to the type of graduates they have. This management style is top down, and the feedback that does take place is usually a 'yes' or 'no' answer to whether or not

something has been taken care of. Furthermore, there are reports and meetings explaining the situation in a formal matter. Nevertheless, the decisions are mostly made by top management which has analysed the situation.
Running a large company in Indonesia is considered to be prestigious due to having a strong character and the courage to start something and having the connections necessary to run operations. These abilities come with a certain type of charisma which is key for a leader to exude credibility that will allow him or her to delegate effectively.

Theodore Permadi Rachmat began his journey as a businessman right after graduation. He was hired as a sales employee at Astra International. Throughout the years, he held senior executive positions within several companies in Indonesia, including United Tractors, Mahanusa Capital, Unilever Indonesia and Protocol One. Rachmat eventually grew to become the president of Astra International. Throughout his life, Rachmat tried to absorb as much knowledge as he could from various sources, such as his professional experience as an employee and CEO, but also through a high number of reading material.

Local leadership book	
Title	*Pembelajaran T.P. Rachmat*
Subtitle	-
Author	Theodore Permadi Rachmat
Publisher	Gramedia Pustaka Utama
Year	2014
ISBN	978-979-228-764-6

His book, *Pembelajaran T.P. Rachmat*, is a dialogue between management concepts and practices of Rachmat: how to start, manage, grow and maintain the sustainability of a business. These values are of key importance in order to show leadership within a firm, so that it, in turn, can provide a real contribution to the nation and the country. This book is also equipped with stories concerning Rachmat's personal growth that have never appeared, including the recognition of bitterness and failure experienced, and the responses to it. *"If one falls ten times, stand up eleven times"*; that is the invitation.

Indonesian leadership YouTube review

The Leadership (Kepemimpinan) video published by Victorious Networkers (Soemarsono, 2017), represents the network marketing and trainer Agus Soemarsono. He is the founder of Victorious Networkers - a company focussing on giving guidance to the Indonesian society and offering them an opportunity to get health support, personal growth and achieve financial freedom. In this video, Soemarsono gives a lecture about Kepemimpinan (leadership). The focus of the video is on 10 lessons about leadership. Soemarsono starts the video off with a quote: *"It often occurs in departments that the managers say: 'follow my orders or leave the business'. In my opinion, this expression is wrong"* (Soemarsono, 2017). A leader needs to have certain characteristics to become a good front-runner. First and foremost, before someone wants to be a leader, they must observe. What this means is that everybody first starts at the bottom and works their way up by watching and learning from other people. A leader is not born but formed. It is not possible to suddenly become one as it takes a lot of time. Another very important characteristic of a leader is, *"Pemimpin itu harus melakukan dengan perbuatan dan tidak hanya berbicara"* (Soemarsono, 2017). The meaning of this quote is that leaders need to do their tasks and achieve results. Instead of only speaking about their objectives, they will need to do everything in order to achieve their goals. Leaders never stop learning. They acknowledge their strengths and weaknesses and learn new things from everyone in the company. When Indonesians look at what they expect of leadership, the majority of the population seeks honesty in their leaders. Another quote to remember is: *"Jujur mengakui kesalahan dan serta memberi dan tidak suka menerima"* (Soemarsono, 2017). This means that leaders need to speak the truth about their mistakes and should give instead of take. This is crucial because for Indonesian people integrity is central. Another important aspect of a leader is that he or she needs to have a broad view, understand the company and the direction in which it is heading.

The leader of a company will need to have the ability to solve problems and understand the worker's needs. The most essential principle is that the leaders of a company must listen to their employees. *"Mendengarkan adalah cara yang paling hebat"* (*listening is the most powerful way*) (Soemarsono, 2017). Altogether, employees want a leader who understands and listens to them, someone who has a lot of knowledge and still accepts their mistakes. One who empowers them to do better and to learn new things.

Understanding hierarchy in Indonesia

To understand Indonesian culture, it is important to first understand what the Hofstede metrics for Indonesia actually mean in practical terms. The high power distance defines that to be seen as valued by their peers, the Indonesian worker should obtain a high rank within the organisation. Indonesia scores relatively high on power distance compared to European countries. This high score also indicates that the middle manager should provide lower co-workers with clear instructions and information, just as the co-workers expect (Hofstede Insights, n.d.). This data can be confirmed by Globe Project (2016). The 'Country Practice Score' scores relatively high in comparison to the average range of globe scores. From Hofstede one can also conclude that compared to European countries Indonesia is a relatively collective society, which means that they rather think in terms of 'we' instead of 'I' (Hofstede Insights, n.d.).
The power distance has a huge effect on the leadership style. Depending on hierarchy, results will lead to indirect communication, where negative feedback is most likely to be hidden. Communication is limited because of the great inequality between power holders and non-power holders. As a result, the superior officers of the company are hardly approachable by non-power holders. The centralised power within the management creates a direct communication flow from top to bottom, but this remains a one-way communication flow (Hofstede Insights, n.d.). Legislation and other external market factors are slowly forcing Indonesian companies to decrease the power distance. However, as literature tells us, the external forces as well as the average organisational culture are not challenging this leadership style sufficiently. For example, in the tobacco and textile industries, it can be seen that there is a relatively higher preference for female employees when conducting comparative analyses with regard to the employee diversity compositions across these respective industries as opposed to other industries.

This is due to the fact that female employees are found to be more patient than their male counterparts, but more importantly, because they are seen as generally unassertive. At the same time, legislation does not forbid gender discrimination. This leads to little incentive for companies to change.
To worsen the situation, most of these women do not even have a contract and their pay is lower than the Indonesian minimum wage. However, leaving is not an option considering the high unemployment rate within this demographic (Bennington & Habirb, 2003).

How the Indonesians achieve leadership empathy

Indonesians have a clear view about their management and leaders. They expect the leader to be paternalistic, meaning a strong hierarchical way of leading. Whenever an employee requires assistance, the leader is expected to have advice and personal help ready (Lewis, 2006). The paternalistic way of leading will result in being a good leader. However, certain key features are required. When looking at a leader, Widianto (8 November 2018) asks himself whether they have charisma, a charming personality and high intelligence. It will be easier for leaders to motivate their subordinates if they have most of these features. Irwanto (2011) points out that there is a big difference between the Asian and Western patterns of leadership. An effective leader in Indonesia should emphasise the collective well-being and show a strong humane orientation within society. Indonesian leaders have to show appreciation towards their subordinates in order to gain respect, which in turn will make their subordinates more responsive to their demands (Widianto, 8 November 2018). According to Gani (2004), leadership managing can only be achieved by team-trust, ego identification, action, skills and methods.

Laksamana (8 November 2018) mentions that the most imperative part of achieving empathy lies within one's region. *"In my view, in Indonesia leadership styles are highly influenced by a leader's local culture and background. For instance, Javanese has its own style, so is someone from North Sumatra"*. This means that wherever you are, it is important to adjust to the local inhabitants. Changing your behaviour to the leader to whom you are speaking, based on his or her regional culture, will result in more empathy. *Semoga sukses!*

Italy

Elisabetta Ghermandi, Eva McLaughlin, Giulia Nasti & Mirre van Wesemael

Often referred to as *Lo Stivale* (the Boot), due to its peculiar shape, Italy is located in the heart of the Mediterranean Sea. A country of arcane bureaucracy, Italy itself has only existed since 1860. Analysing *il Bel Paese* (the beautiful country) by focusing on the North/South divide, would be a major over-simplification – dismissing the different cultural backgrounds of more than 250 regions within the country (ISA, 2018). These cultural differences can be seen in the language, as half of the population speak their regional dialect along with Italian (De Renzo, 2005).

The label *Made in Italy* is known globally for its excellence in clothing, design and motoring (D'Achille & Patota, 2016). Due to the rise of Italian emigration through the 20th Century, Italian food and drinks have reached all four corners of the globe (Motta, 2016). Tourism plays a key role in the Italian economy as Italy is one of the world's most visited countries (ANSA, 2017; Statista, n.d.). The Italian business environment is highly influenced by the predominance of small to medium-sized enterprises (SMEs) which produce the majority of Italy's GDP (Derr, Roussillon & Bournois, 2002) and are typified as family businesses (Ghislieri & Gatti, 2012). The economy is also heavily reliant on their trade surplus with neighbouring countries, Germany and France being the main trading partners (Statista, n.d.).

Leadership is not a modern concept, one of the first leadership books was first written in about 1513 by an Italian, Niccolò Machiavelli, describing a candid perspective on how business operated back then. As Massimo d'Azeglio, a political figure during the creation of Italy, wrote: *"Fatta l'Italia, bisogna fare gli Italiani"* (we have made Italy; now we must make Italians).

How the Italians characterise leaders

As globalisation has impacted nearly every country in the world, Italy has seen a change clearly visible in its leadership style. However, charisma has always been an integral trait of Italian leadership. Prior to the nineties, even though Italian leaders were characterised as authoritarian and hierarchical

(Windtrebusinessfactor, 2011), charisma was a key element to guide people towards leaders' vision (Dormagen, 2008). This was already seen in its oppressive past, and can still be seen in today's business culture whereby professionals still hold respect for their leaders, due to charisma being an imperative attribute for leaders. Status, understood as a set of benefits attached to a role, is considered an acquired set of rights and symbols of power. This is supported by Bobbio, Van Dierendonck and Manganelli (2012) who affirm that Italians, in general, operate in an individualistic and charismatic manner as the leader gains higher rewards from such traits. The consistency of charisma could be attributed to the deeply rooted subculture of the Roman Catholic Church which, over several centuries, significantly influenced Italy, both politically and socially (Grigoreva, 2017). Findings from the CCBS Italia survey (2018) concur, with more than 80 per cent of Italian respondents holding charisma as one of the most important characteristics of leadership in modern day Italy.

As a male-dominated country, Italy has little improved its gender balance in the 21st Century. Modern businesses expect a level of dedication and sacrifice from their high-potential employees to the extent that their work should have primacy over family and personal interests (Derr et al., 2002). Due to this mentality, the majority of women suffer from "*segregazione verticale*" (*vertical segregation*), which in turn causes a limited number of women in the workforce (Marri & Mallen, 2013). Linked to the male dominance, one interesting point to raise is the importance of phonetics in Italy, as seen in the case of a right-wing politician Umberto Bossi. A stroke in 2004 left Bossi with weakened muscles, affecting his vocal tone which impacted his follower's perception of him, making him appear not to be the same dominant leader he had previously sounded, prior to the stroke (Acoustical Society of America, 2014). Our CCBS Italia survey further emphasises some additional key characteristics, with 70 per cent of participants stating that Italian leaders are expected to possess an entrepreneurial mindset. Furthermore, an Italian respondent, the head of Group Leadership Training, points out that peculiarities like formalism and egocentrism are greatly accentuated. Several other survey participants highlight that short-term vision is a growing concern in today's business environment. Alekos Scognamiglio, CEO of several businesses in the digital industry, observes: "*[i leader] siano portati a scelte più conservative che hanno lo scopo di ottenere un immediato benessere economico, senza però creare un piano a lungo termine di crescita sostenibile*" ([Italian leaders] are inclined towards more conservative choices with the aim of obtaining economic prosperity, without creating a sustainable long-term growth plan) (CCBS Italia Survey, 2018).

Survey results and what local respondents say

The CCBS Italia 2018 survey, received over 125 native responses from both academics and professionals living and working in Italy, who shared their experience and views on leadership. After closely analysing the quantitative and qualitative data, the following observations were made.

Firstly, more than half of our respondents have experienced gender inequality within the professional environment. Men and women do not share equal opportunities when it comes to promotions to senior executive positions. Giorgio Bonfiglioli, an Italian business owner in the electric motors industry, has observed that even when Italian women reach higher positions, it has not always been easy for them to get recognition from their male subordinates. *"Generally, they are therefore more capable, tenacious and stubborn than their male colleagues of the same level"* (CCBS Italia Survey, 2018). Although, Francesca Gammicchia, owner and founder of Talento Umano Formazione Esperienziale, points out that: *"It is difficult for a woman to be a leader without giving up her feminine side"*. In addition, a general manager in telecommunications observes that women are paid less and have fewer benefits in comparison to their male counterparts. Subsequently, the CCBS Italia survey shows that more than 50 per cent of the Italian participants expect their employees to follow the established procedures and 40 per cent believes subordinates do not have any decisional power (2018). These findings reinforce Hofstede Insight's (n.d.) assertion concerning the power distance within Italy, where half of society expect and accept that there is equality of power and decision-making and the other half accepts a more centralised approach. Similarly, Trevisani, a business consultant, observes that in Italian businesses decision-making is a slow process since approval from a superior is required first.

More than half of the Italian survey contributors prefer to receive criticism directly, outside or even during staff meetings, and missing a deadline is seen as a failure by more than 80 per cent of the respondents. Furthermore, even though agendas are usually provided, they are often simply seen as a starting point for further discussion. A technical director in the research field asserts that there is a lack of respect for any agenda and difficulty to reach any clear decisions (CCBS Italia Survey, 2018).

Local leadership analysis

In-country literature review

Ghislieri and Gatti (2012) focus on the ability to transform followers into new leaders which is an important skill as it guarantees organisational continuity and generativity. This is a particularly growing concern in Italy, due to the growing age gap found within the executive levels, which is being slowly dealt with in intergenerational leadership transfer. This theme is especially important in Italy, as cultural values encourage the maintenance of firms within the family, which is significant when almost half of Italy's GDP is accounted for by these Italian family businesses which see the boundaries of family and business blend together and influence the management style (Ruggieri, Pozzi & Ripamonti, 2014). These blurred lines can cause major communication issues due to unconscious rivalries which are unrelated to the business, which in turn can hinder the organisation (Giovannini, 13 October 2018). All things considered, Isolabella and Kaneklin state that there is a need for greater trust and readiness to listen (1997) which is visible due to the general lack of external trust, a lack of civic commitment, and lower levels of participation in the world of work by women and young adults (Bertani, 2015).

Daniele Trevisani: an Italian leadership scholar

Daniele Trevisani is an academic researcher, writer, professional coach and trainer who received a Fulbright Scholarship in intercultural and effective communication. In an interview with in regard to the characteristics of Italian leaders, Trevisani (15 October 2018) identifies three main layers that, in his experience, occur in Italian leadership currently. The first layer contains the *super seniors*, those who founded the company and continue to be key stakeholders. This is characterised by a patriarchal leadership style where face to face communication is the standard. The second layer incorporates mature leaders who apply a more managerial leadership style who focus more on projects, objectives and the international environment whose communication is based mainly on email. The last layer is characterised by a more participative leadership style where project management is more common with a significant use of technology and social networks. He argues that a lack of linguistic clarity and precision within the professional context can cause project delay and confusion in communication, and sees this as a result of Italy being a high-context culture.

Trevisani also states that Italy is still in *"un mondo pre-culturale" (pre-cultural world),* where physicality counts more than ideas. He supports his opinion with a reference to neuroscience research, stating that human brains are divided into the reptile and mammalian brain and a neocortex. Trevisani asserts that, in Italian leadership, the part of the mammal brain still is predominant and influences social interactions within people in different positions within the organisation. Trevisani concluded the interview with his belief of what it means to be a great leader: *"Ecco, questa è la mia visione, cioè di un leader che sa prendersi dei rischi e sa uscire dalla zona di comfort, sa arrivare anche nella zona della ricerca vera e propria"* (This is my vision, a leader who knows how to take risks and knows how to get out of the comfort zone, who knows how to get in the real research area) (Trevisani, 15 October 2018).

Lucia Giovannini: an Italian cross-cultural trainer

Lucia Giovannini has a doctorate in psychology and counselling and a bachelor's degree in psycho-anthropology. Her main field of expertise is communication, with a focus on leadership, stress management, resource and talent development and, ultimately, change.

In Giovannini's (13 October 2018) opinion, leaders are not born but made. She believes in servant-leadership, the leader-sherpa and the leader-coach. A leader is a person who has developed the ability to listen, to support and to empathise and who possesses resilience. Successful leaders should have a futuristic and motivating vision that guides people toward a goal that is beyond personal gain and more toward the common good. Moreover, a good leader should be flexible enough to maintain a macro vision and, simultaneously, be able to dive into detailed procedures. Flexibility is also required to deal with cross-cultural teams. This is seen by Giovannini as a challenge for Italian leaders, considering the limited international mindset of Italian leaders.

Since leaders work with people, empathy is an essential trait to exhibit, and it is closely tied to communication. Empathic leadership can create cohesive teams, even when people are not sharing the same physical space, as in the case of remote and virtual teams. Such teams, as well as cross-cultural teams, can be the basis of communication challenges for the modern leader.

In the more traditional companies, there is still a high-power distance, it is *"as if they were at the top of a mountain alone [...] but nobody can do it alone, no matter how good their skills"* (Giovannini, 13 October 2018). Such distance only disappears during company dinners, often held before Christmas and the summer holidays. Here the leader *"scende dal suo 'piedistallo' e si mette fra le sue persone"* (comes down from his 'pedestal' and stands among his people). Giovannini ends with a reflection on what an honour and responsibility it is to be a leader and to guide people: *"Thus, always keep in mind to think about how what I say, what I do, can contribute, not just to my business, but to the whole world".*

Nicola Riva: an Italian cross-cultural coach

Nicola Riva has a law degree and a doctorate in psychology and counselling. He is a personal and professional coach for managers and executives in corporate and law firms. Riva (13 October 2018) believes that leadership is a global concept connected to the human being and not to geography or ethnicity, hence to be a successful leader in Italy requires the same characteristics as in the rest of the world. He points out five characteristics that are fundamental for the modern leader. The first is the ability to listen. This entails listening with the aim of *"creating a fascinating and attractive vision that can motivate and inspire people"*. The second is the ability to support. Leaders should *"know how to use the right, heartfelt, genuine words to support their people, especially in difficult moments of great challenge"* (Riva, 13 October 2018). The third is the ability to ask questions that stimulate the inner potential and resources of the individual. People tend to be more motivated if they are allowed to find their own answers. Lastly, giving and receiving feedback. Feedback is seen by Riva as feed-back, that is, give nourishment back. When giving feedback, we act as a mirror that reflects the other person's behaviour, which allows them to see themselves from a different perspective, thus enabling them to grow. It is important for leaders to receive feedback or they may find themselves *"surrounded by 'yes men' and 'yes women' that give them all but good, genuine feedback"*. According to Riva, these characteristics are inherently the basic skills of a good coach, *"un leader che è in buon coach è un leader eccellente"* (A leader who is also a good coach is an exceptional leader). Riva's final note was on female leadership and how giving space to female leaders would be a turning point for the entire world, not just the business world. For him, women, by nature, embody the characteristics of the modern exceptional leader. *"The notion that Italy is above the EU average in terms of [the] number of women in an executive position, makes me hopeful"* (Riva, 13 October 2018).

In-country leadership best seller

One of the best-selling books about leadership was written by the Luisa Macciocca Massimo and Raffaele Massimo in 2011 and is called *Leadership e Team building di successo. Come si diventa leader di una squadra vincente* (*Successful leadership and team building. How to become the leader of a winning team*). In this book, the authors describe the fundamental skills to be a successful leader. Modern leaders are defined as those who, thanks to their professional and personal experience, are able to motivate the creativity and consensus of their collaborators, produce a continuous flow of problem-solving and have a decisional and organisational flexibility deriving from a positive attitude. The team building is indeed described as the creation by a leader of a motivated and winning team which shares his or her vision. A good leader is, according to the authors, the one who manages to create a united team, which supports him or her with determination and contributes, with involvement and participation, to the decision-making process. Furthermore, the emphasis is on the ability of the leader to embrace and transmit business values. The book also touches upon the topic of emotional intelligence by analysing the interpersonal dynamics and the trust aspect that underlies the success of a leader. Indeed, an entire chapter is dedicated to the ability of the leader to develop a sense of belonging within the team. In the conclusive part of the book, the authors also analyse aspects such as communication and language, emphasising how every single characteristic of a leader is fundamental to his success.

Local leadership book	
Title	*Leadership e team building di successo*
Subtitle	Come si diventa leder di una squadra vincente
Author	Luisa Macciocca Massimo, Raffaele Massimo
Publisher	Maggiori editore
Year	2011
ISBN	8838757941

In-country leadership YouTube review

Carlo Messina (SDA, 5 February 2018), CEO of Intesa Sanpaolo, stresses the importance of taking care of people and being acknowledged by subordinates as the leader. Becoming a leader involves constant progress in gaining knowledge and competencies. Furthermore, leaders should be humble above all. Overall, organisational culture is very tightly linked to organisational value. Companies should be a synthesis of shared values (SDA, 5 February 2018). Whereas, Claudio Belotti (Windtrebusinessfactor, 2011), coach and trainer, has a more team-oriented view on leadership. In the speaker's view, leaders must create relationships and help team members to appreciate themselves, but above all to appreciate each other. This can be accomplished by getting to know each other and to see and appreciate the differences between team members. Above all, leaders must know how to listen (Windtrebusinessfactor, 2011).

Finally, a YouTube search has provided two other speakers that seem to have a more modern view on leadership; they focus more on the need to stimulate creativity and innovation for today's business environment. Luciano Boccucci (2014), facilitator of creative change, innovation coach and trainer, argues that before leadership has always been recognised by people of particular charm, charisma and sometimes genius. However, today the leader must be a creative innovator and know how to go further with courage and imagination. *"Se vuoi creare una cultura del cambiamento hai bisogno di leader del cambiamento"* (*If you want to create a culture of change you need change leaders*) (Boccucci, 2014). Subsequently, Stefano Sassi (SDA, 19 July 2017), the CEO of Valentino, states that leaders need to have mental agility and resilience. To be able to be successful in this quickly changing environment, creativity and excellent management skills are needed to support a unique vision. The formula for success is putting together the creative soul to the operational machine (SDA, 19 July 2017).

Understanding hierarchy in Italy

Italy has a typical top-down decision-making culture, as seen through Hofstede's framework (Hofstede Insights, n.d.), along with individualistic, long-term oriented and risk-avoidant. In addition to these, the leadership style in Italy is highly influenced by a hierarchical system. Trevisani (15 October 2018) asserts, *"è un sistema di leadership tribale, dove veramente contano i maschi alfa o femmine alfa, conta la seniority"* (Italy has a tribal leadership system where alpha males or alpha females are dominant and seniority matters). Within the Italian leadership, social functions are connected to the position that the person fills within the organisation. Inside Italian offices, there is a major communication distance where no-one or only a few will enter the office of a superior, according to an unwritten hierarchical law. Carlo Duronio, an Italian HR manager, highlights that there is a tendency to control from the top with a non-inclusive decision-making process due to a cultural imprint from the past (CCBS Italia Survey, 2018). Stemming from an authoritarian organisational structure, *"Italians accept and somehow expect that some groups in society are more powerful than others. They act accordingly in their exercise of leadership"* (Tavanti, 2012, p. 290).

Family-operated businesses play a vital role in understanding the hierarchy (Derr et al., 2002). A quick review of some of the largest companies shows they are still controlled by single families (Fiat, Benetton, Mediaset etc.). It is imperative to understand that the *"family cell fulfils a special function in firms"* (Marturano, Oriani & Quaglino, 2009, p. 96), and the Italian cultural values encourage the maintenance of firms within the family (Cucculelli & Micucci, 2008). In such situations, there can be *"no room for information coming from a person who does not frequent the family and business regularly"* (Ruggieri et al., 2014, p. 94). Many decisions may take place outside of the boardroom, due to the predominance of the leaders' interest in protecting their own benefit as well as the group (Luiss, 2008). That said, many enterprises are moving from a vertical to a horizontal and polycentric approach recognising the individuals themselves as part of the organisation (Reggiani, 2004). Akin to family businesses, high hierarchy also relates to the tremendous respect for those with age, seniority and power. Additionally, Grigoreva emphasises that building business relationships takes time as Italians' main drivers are based on intuition and emotions and they prefer not to have time restraints (2017).

A qualitative analysis of our survey's outcome (CCBS Italia Survey, 2018) shows that employees look up to a leader on the basis of same-industry experience, technical competence or experience in the business organisation. Interestingly, mentioning an academic title is not deemed relevant. Focusing on traits related to hierarchical leadership styles, our survey shows that over 50 per cent of our Italian respondents prefers not to have a professional distance from employees whilst maintaining the right level of respect. It also shows that 60 per cent disagrees with the statement that subordinates should address leaders according to their title or position when talking or writing to them.

How the Italians achieve leadership empathy

During the Italian Renaissance, Cosimo de' Medici became a successful leader by identifying sentiments and mindsets of diverse teams of competitors in the field of banking, commerce and trade. With that insight *"he built new bridges of common purpose, resulting in a 'team' that produced greater, more sustained economic, social, and cultural value for all parties"* (Uzzi, 2015, para. 1). More than six hundred years later, Carlo Messina, a CEO from the Italian banking sector, addresses that the common objectives within a team still leads to greater synergy for the end result (SDA, 5 February 2018). Claudio Belotti, coach and trainer, follows suit by stressing the importance of *"Valori allineati fra leader e team"* (values aligned between leader and team) (Windtrebusinessfactor, 2011). In this modern business world, it is imperative to be able to lead teams and coordinate internal and external multicultural stakeholders. Boyatzis and Ratti's (2009) research into competencies distinguishing effective Italian managers and leaders, states that a set of emotional, social and cognitive intelligence traits are required. Empathy is needed to foster such competencies which in turn enable the leader to ask questions and listen to the answers with the goal of understanding the other person and not to simply appear to listen only in order to ingratiate him or herself (Boyatzis & Ratti, 2009). Above all, a leader needs to *"put oneself into another's shoes"*. Trevisani affirms *"C'è una sorta di empatia sul piano emotivo del leader rispetto ai collaboratori"* (There is a sort of empathy on the emotional level of the leader towards collaborators) (Trevisani, 15 October 2018). Furthermore, in his experience, the level of empathy in the professional environment is not sufficient in Italy, even though it is higher than in some other countries, e.g. Germany. Paradoxically, he noticed more empathy in the US and the UK.

In the CCBS Italia survey, when asked whether managers should actively spend time on the personal well-being of their team members, roughly 85 per cent of the Italian respondents gave a positive answer, of which 70 per cent were in strong agreement (CCBS Italia Survey, 2018). Riccardo Quattrini, a general manager in the food industry, believes that empathy is a distinctive trait of Italian leadership along with *"una certa dose di umanità"* (a certain dose of humanity). Concepts shared among several of our sources as well as participants of our survey include that women are more empathic than men, who possess more emotional intelligence, and pay more attention to interpersonal relations. It would be amiss to forget the use of space in the Italian culture, one where body distance is closer than the average culture, being present at 80 centimetres

compared to other nationalities at more than one meter (Lewis, 2006).
The use of gesticulation, where Italians are able to add emphasis to certain words, or even a simple gesture can be an entire conversation.
Joyce Scognamiglio, a business owner in the digital industry, states that in Italy leadership culture is non-existent. In his opinion, *"la vera leadership è sublimata esclusivamente dall'intelligenza emotiva"* (true leadership is sublimated exclusively by emotional intelligence) (CCBS Italia Survey, 2018).

Jamaica

Lars Eijman, Tugba Güler, Adi Hendriks, Brian Torres Rojas & Jeroen van de Weerd

Jamaica is one of the more diverse and colourful countries in the Caribbean. The island is known for its strong sense of self-identity, expressed through its music, food and a rich cultural mix that remains identifiable far beyond its shores. The country's national motto is 'Out of Many, One People', referring to its strong diversity, due to many different ethnic groups which immigrated to Jamaica. As a result, Jamaican people do not have a typical physical characteristic that they can be recognised by. The main spoken languages are Jamaican Standard English and Jamaican Patois. Jamaican Standard English is the official language of the island, while Jamaican Patois is the de-facto national language. Jamaican Patois mostly exists as a spoken language, although it is also sung a lot (Jordan, 2016). Since its independence, in 1962, the country has developed markedly but unevenly. Jamaica's economy is increasingly based on services, notably tourism and finance. The agriculture continues to be one of the bases of the island's economy (Buisseret, Black, Ferguson & Bryan, 2018).

Jamaica has a reputation for having the greatest number of churches per capita in the world. There is freedom and equality of religion in Jamaica. For instance, the Abrahamic religion Rastafarianism developed in Jamaica during the 1930s. Protestant churches nevertheless are dominant, with various denominations comprising over about 60 per cent of the total population.

How the Jamaicans characterise leaders

In Jamaica, leaders are known for their aspiring motivations (CCBS Survey, 2018). Jamaicans are often thought of as being motivated by the goals that they want to achieve and by their religion. It is up to a leader to choose how to inspire people or employees. Jamaica is a somewhat diverse country with various cultural influences. As a result, there is a range of management styles.

For Jamaicans, an important characteristic of a supervisor is to pro-actively help team members. This can be achieved by, for instance, showing an interest and also a willingness to give back to employees. An analysis of the CCBS survey results (2018) supports these statements: *"In Jamaica not only the leader creates expectations, but the team as well"* (CCBS Survey, 2018). What is more, leaders in Jamaica are expected to demonstrate respect for the fact that Jamaicans value a work-life balance and the ability to have fun while fulfilling their workplace duties. Notably, the answers from the CCBS survey (2018) demonstrate that older managers in Jamaica are known to have a more autocratic management style. The younger generation, however, which often has been exposed to North-American leadership styles, tends to be more hands-off and inclusive.

Survey results and what local respondents say

The CCBS survey (2018) has been completed by many Jamaican managers, former Jamaican managers and those who work in a professional business atmosphere in Jamaica. All polled professionals state that missing a deadline is more or less the same as a failure in the Jamaican business environment.
In addition, on missing a deadline, Jamaican management decisions most likely will not be changed very easily. As an anonymous respondent puts it: *"The rules are paramount and must be followed. If there is a need to bend a rule to improve the performance or achieve better results it must first be discussed with the manager"* (CCBS Survey, 2018). In addition, three-quarters of the participants might confront the team members or subordinates during a staff meeting if necessary, to obtain the targeted results (CCBS Survey, 2018). All the Jamaican respondents agree that a leader gets respectable office space and transportation, to match their position in the organisation. An interesting quote from an anonymous manager at a telecommunication organisation sheds some light on the issue of status and reputation: *"We have a high level of classism in Jamaica and it is recognized that leaders of foreign nationality within our organisation are more highly respected"* (CCBS Survey, 2018). Despite the importance of the organisation leaders, all our survey respondents do not consider their academic title on the business card or email signature to be important (CCBS Survey, 2018). However, it is desired from employees that they address their leaders and senior colleagues with their surname. According to one of our respondents: *"It is a sign of disrespect if leaders are addressed by their first names"* (CCBS Survey, 2018). In this sense, the Jamaican business culture can be classified as rather hierarchical.

Local leadership analysis

In-country literature review

According to the book, *Reflections on leadership and governance in Jamaica: towards a better society*, Jamaican society still has strong traces of the colonial era in its educational and legal systems. The truth is that the society can learn several aspects from the colonial history, but the author Canute S. Thompson states that "*We cannot blindly and slavishly adopt leadership and governance models from foreign contexts and try to impose them on our society and expect that we will see great results*" (Thompson, 2018, p. 144). Lloyd Smith (2012), a member of parliament in 2012 and deputy speaker of the House of Representatives, has written an article wherein he describes how the leadership should be, but also what the current situation is in Jamaica. "*It should be emboldened by two major principles: character and caring. Emanating from these two distinct characteristics are some necessary attributes such as trust, accountability, transparency and integrity*" (Smith, 2012, par. 8). The current problem in Jamaica is that a great many leaders are being appointed in a transactional way. "*What Jamaica needs is transformational leaders, leadership that is therefore proactive, not reactive*" (Smith, 2012, par. 8).

Phillipa Dianne Lawrence: a Jamaican leadership trainer

Phillipa Dianne Lawrence is a Jamaican specialist in leadership. With more than 30 years of working experience in Jamaica and abroad, she has knowledge of the way leadership works in different countries. Lawrence is currently working as international affairs professional in her home country Jamaica. She is the founder of Diplomacy and Protocol Solutions International, where she provides advisory services in the field of international affairs and cross-cultural communication. According to Lawrence (8 November 2018), Jamaica is one of the countries where women take the greater part of leadership positions. Lawrence says this is because in Jamaica women are seen truly equal to men. She furthermore states that even though Jamaican culture is a very laid-back one when it comes to leadership, Jamaicans tend to be most hierarchical and structured. Top level management decides what the lower level employees will have to do, making it a typical top-down approach. During meetings in Jamaica, the junior staff are not in a position of prominence since these positions are left for the people who are in more senior leadership positions. The junior staff members speak only when they are called upon and generally they perform the role of note takers in the meeting. Lawrence describes how a Jamaican leader combines this hierarchical leadership style with such a laid-back culture as follows: *"Although the leaders maintain an executive distance from their employees, they also incorporate the Jamaican culture, so that it's not too intimidating depending on who they are dealing with. They might not be as structured as if they are dealing with, say the man on the street, supposed they are interacting in their personal lives. They will bring in some local culture and local flavour and not be so rigid and structural in terms of expecting the same types of behaviour from the man on the street"* (8 November 2018).

In-country leadership bestseller

The bestselling book in Jamaica regarding the topic of leadership is *Edward Seaga: My Life and Leadership (Volume II: Hard Road to Travel 1980-2008)*, written in 2010 by Edward Phillip George Seaga. Harvard Graduate, Edward Seaga is the youngest member ever to have participated in the Jamaican Council. Seaga is one of the most outstanding Jamaican politicians in history having been the fifth Prime Minister of Jamaica from 1980-1998 as chairman of Jamaica's Labour Party (JLP), one of the two main political parties in Jamaica. Edward Seaga, as leader of the opposition for more than 20 years, always had a reputation for controversy, bravery and inventiveness (Martin, 2013). His book is an autobiography which offers an insight into the rise of present-day Jamaica. A voyage described with interest and optimism, triumph and struggle.

Local leadership book	
Title	*Edward Seaga: My Life and Leadership*
Subtitle	Volume II: Hard Road to Travel 1980-2008
Author	Edward Phillip George Seaga
Publisher	Macmillan Education
Year	2010
ISBN	978-0230021631

As a young politician, he made himself stand out with a speech on the 'haves and have-nots', announcing a mission *"to pull up the poor without pulling down the rich - in a country with little wealth both capital and labour are mutually dependent for success"* (Rogers, 2017). Furthermore, Seaga describes in his book his detailed strategy for financial and social recovery together with his investigation of the continuing problems (Seaga, 2010).

Jamaican leadership YouTube review

In the Jamaican business environment, women happen to be represented fairly well as the speaker in the *Women & Leadership in Jamaica* video states. Claiming that Jamaica is one of the few countries in the world that has reached or surpassed gender equality, as about sixty per cent of the Jamaican managers are in fact women, he further affirms that sixty-three per cent of female Jamaican professionals have a degree or diploma (Duncan-Price & Hamilton, 2015). In the Jamaican government, however, it is quite the opposite from the business culture of the country. Former Jamaican senator Duncan-Price (2015) asserts that just eight per cent of Jamaican parliament seats have been assigned to women over the past 40 years.In this light, we see that professor Hamilton (2015) notes that the Jamaican women are underrepresented in academies and absent in the highest level of economic decision-making.

Understanding hierarchy in Jamaica

The culture of Jamaica is a diverse one. Due to the island's immigration and its colonial history, there are many different cultures and cultural influences. This results in a variety of leadership styles, as can be seen in the divided answers on the CCBS Survey and various outcomes in research studies. Managers usually expect to be addressed with 'Sir' or 'Madam' and their surname, and there is the expectation for leaders to make powerful decisions (CCBS Survey, 2018).
On the one hand, research shows us that the power distance in Jamaica is low, which indicates that the leadership style is more people-orientated (Gooden & Preziosi, 2011). For example, respondents to the CCBS Survey agree that managers should actively spend time on the personal well-being of team members. The low power distance also shows that employees wish to collaborate on the decisions to be made (Gooden & Preziosi, 2011). *"Going directly to one's immediate supervisor for answers or feedback is expected. This is understood as respecting the chain of authority"* (CCBS Survey, 2018).

At the same time Jamaica's colonial history sometimes still shows in its management style which is top-down, authoritarian, hierarchical and control-and-punishment-oriented (Punnett, Dick-Ford & Robinson, 2005). As stated by one of the respondents to the CCBS Survey *"[..] We are developing local leadership in a post-colonial environment, in which the colonial leadership prevailed before. There is the struggle between the national culture and the organizational culture"* (2018).

How the Jamaicans achieve leadership empathy

In Jamaican businesses, relationships are likely to be prioritised since they are essential to getting business done, and as the power distance in Jamaica is fairly low. This indicates that the preferred leadership style is more people-orientated and superiors are more participative and consultative towards their employees (Gooden & Preziosi, 2011). Almost every Jamaican business professional actively spends time on the personal well-being of the team members (CCBS Survey, 2018). However, to achieve leadership empathy in Jamaica, it is also necessary to take into account the differences between top-level management and employees. Thus, there is clearly a difference between the relationship between managers and employees, which is much more formal, and the relationship between employees themselves, which tends to be informal (Mujuru, 2012). Jamaican business professionals tend to keep a personal distance from their employees, to maintain a right level of respect (CCBS Survey, 2018).
It is important to address someone by their correct title and surname. As one of the informants to the CCBS research, Phillipa Lawrence, puts it: *"It is a sign of disrespect if leaders are addressed by their first names"*. This stems from the fact that respect towards each other in the Jamaican business culture is crucial. *"If you breach the issue of respect then the whole relationship will break down. In fact, you may not get an opportunity again [...]"* (Lawrence, 8 November 2018).

Lithuania

Kasane Bos, Jamii de Heer, Michelle Heitmann, Chihhsin Lu (鲁直欣) &
Yelyzaveta Zakharova (Захарова Елизавета)

Located in north-eastern Europe, Lithuania (*Lietuva*) is the most populous and the southernmost of the three Baltic States (World Bank Group, n.d.). Together with Latvia and Estonia, two other former USSR Republics, they are often called the Baltic Tigers for their massive implementation of economic reforms after their proclamation of independence from the Soviet Union. Lithuania is a very diverse country. Old towns full of legends coexist here with modern museums, white sandy beaches and amber treasures of the country that attract tourists and businesses no less than the green parks and mineral waters of balneal resorts. Hundreds of years ago the territory of the Grand Duchy of Lithuania stretched from Baltic to the Black Sea and the rulers of the duchy were respected all over Europe. During the Soviet era the country was a prestigious resort destination for the government officials, and now Lithuania is a full-fledged member of the European Union.

As a country with a long and glorious history, it is quite surprising that the population remained rather homogeneous with Lithuanians making up the vast majority of the population. The official language is Lithuanian, although due to historical features, around eight per cent of the population uses Russian on a daily basis. As a former USSR republic, Lithuania inherited some features of the Soviet social system. For instance, women are not limited to a specific field of work, which is especially noticeable in an older generation which was brought up in the USSR. Dalia Grybaskaite, the first female president of Lithuania, is a vivid example. Although Lithuania was one of the last countries to join the EU, it has one of the highest literacy rates in the European Union and the world in general (UNESCO Institute of Statistics, n.d.). Lithuania is also in the top 20 best performance economies, outperforming two other Baltic Tigers (World Bank Group, n.d.).

How the Lithuanians characterise leaders

In Lithuania, leadership needs to be set on modernisation and openness founded on democratic principles to preserve Lithuanian identity. Leaders within Lithuania, as with other eastern European countries, do not really adopt a parental role towards those that they lead or manage and expect a more formal approach (Minelgaite & Littrell, 2018). On the other hand, research shows that Lithuanian leaders do not necessarily prefer to keep a personal distance between them and their subordinates (CCBS Survey, 2018). To properly inspire and motivate staff and to succeed in any form of intercultural management, leaders are expected to have knowledge and understanding of Lithuanian history. Besides that, leaders that possess organisational experience and market expertise in their field of work are valued by their subordinates. Additionally, soft skills are significant for a leader to obtain. Great listening skills, being able to compromise as well as encouraging others is from great importance (CCBS Survey, 2018). Lithuanian business and leadership consultant, Stankūnas, opines that as a leader: *"it is even more important to help people around you to become better"* (Stankūnas, 9 October 2018).

While older generations of leaders will have more of an authoritative approach to leading and seem very detached in order to achieve goals and objectives set by the company (Minelgaite & Littrell, 2018), the CCBS survey findings (2018) indicate a preference among respondents towards a less bureaucratic approach. Even though addressing a senior manager by the first name is accepted, it should be taken into account whether the company is Lithuanian capital or Western capital. Furthermore, criticism towards a leader can be given in a direct manner yet rules and regulations should still be followed. Survey respondent Inokaitis, a senior advisor in a Lithuanian company, suggests that: *"if you want to do something to improve the performance but it is conflicting with agreed norms in the organi[s]ation, it is better to consult with the management before bending them"* (CCBS Survey, 2018).

The values which leaders in Lithuania consider to be the most important revolve around success – not just in their own professional career but also to ensure that those same characteristics are valid for those they lead (Pacesa, Zakarevicius & Zukauskas, 2011). As stated by Stankūnas: *"A new generation of leaders which are focusing on good relations, organisational empathy and teaching new modern types of motivation [are developing]"* (9 October 2018). Ultimately, it can be concluded that a charismatic and a rather team-orientated leadership style is therefore preferred (Minelgaite & Littrell, 2018).

Survey results and what local respondents say

The CCBS survey results indicate a mixed view on how Lithuanian professionals perceive the local leadership style as compared to other countries. General Manager Jurgita Baksiene proposes that: " *[...] there are big differences among old, and new generation[s] of leaders. In the public sector, state-owned enterprises [and] old-generation leaders still prevail*" (CCBS Survey, 2018). Moreover, IT recruiter Jurga Kazarauskaite feels: "*that in Lithuania there is a lack of listening. Still there are organisations, where there [are] no 1-on-1's*" (CCBS Survey, 2018). Comparatively, a CEO in the public relations sector, Rytis Sabas, believes that: "*[...] it depends on the culture of the organisation more than country*" (CCBS Survey, 2018). Respondents of the survey have divided opinions on whether or not rules can be bent without consulting higher management beforehand. PhD Associate Professor and Business Consultant, Rasa Pauliene, suggests that: "*Observing practical situations, representatives of the Y generation are more likely to receive clear guidance from their managers rather than to take initiatives themselves. Paradoxically, research by Y's representatives show that they are thinking about themselves the opposite: they do not want guidance or rules, they want to be able to make decisions themselves*" (CCBS Survey, 2018).

Furthermore, the majority of respondents agree that men and women have the same access to senior leadership positions in Lithuania. However, leadership styles between men and women seem to differ. According to Pauliene, "*Men [...] tend to autocratic leadership (or transactional leadership); women [...] tend to a shared leadership (or transformational leadership)*" (CCBS Survey, 2018). Lithuanian Research and Development CTO concedes that: "*Women usually are better listeners to the needs of the employees, while men are more strategy focused and more result oriented*" (CCBS Survey, 2018). Although this may be true, Kęstas Breskus, Cross Functional Team Manager, disagrees: "*There is a difference between each person more than gender*" (CCBS Survey, 2018). A Lithuanian member of the board in the banking sector concludes that after all: "*Leadership [...] isn't about gender*" (CCBS Survey, 2018). When asked to provide the three most used leadership titles in Lithuanian businesses, divergent views were expressed by contributors. Among the most popular are *Direktorius* (director), *Vadovas* (leader) and *Prezidentas* (president). Moreover, other common titles also include *Generalinis direktorius*, CEO and director.

Even though data collected within the survey shows that it is more common for employees to address their leader by the first name, Aivaras Janusauskas, a director of a department in the banking sector, points out that it "*might be different among public institutions*" (CCBS Survey, 2018).

Local leadership analysis

In-country literature review

Taking into account the conservative national character of Lithuanians, one can say that they are less likely to take risks and are relatively suspicious of change. However, it has been noted that there is an increase in making risky decisions and innovation intake among the younger generation. Moreover, among the older generation of managers, it is common to strive for the best results even in the times of great uncertainty often ignoring how challenging the task may seem. On the other hand, younger managers attach great importance to work-styles oriented towards business-like objectivity and seek independence and autonomy, agonizing over the restrictions they face in these areas (Diskienė, Marčinskas & Stankevičienė, 2010).

Katilienė and Bakanauskienė (2012) explain that compared to younger executive managers, the interpersonal spiritual aspect is more common for senior managers, which suggests that senior managers have a more independent spirit compared to younger colleagues. Furthermore, Lithuanian people are regarded to be direct, formal and rather reserved. Strong traditions, respecting rules as well as procedures are typical for both society and the corporate environment of Lithuania (Diskienė et al., 2010). A recent study by Raisienė, Pulokienė and Valickas (2018) shows that local leaders are considered to be more balanced and practical as opposed to professionals from neighbouring countries. However, according to Diskienė et al (2010), there is a more one-sided situation in terms of staff- or task-orientation, where Lithuanians seem to be more task-focused.

Rasa Katilienė: a Lithuanian leadership scholar

Dr Rasa Katilienė is a lecturer of Managerial Decision Making at the Vytauto Didžiojo Universitetas as well as a self-employed consultant. Besides that, Katilienė holds a PhD in Social Science, specialising in Organizational Leadership. Having twelve years of practical experience in the areas of leadership and project management, Katilienė has been conducting leadership training at various organisations in recent years. In addition to coaching sessions and consultations, helping to develop leadership and spiritual intelligence skills for those who seek profound transformations both at the organisational and personal levels. According to Katilienė (9 November 2018), various leaders have different characteristics. Therefore, it is difficult to determine which the best characteristic for a leader is. However, she prefers leaders to be visionary and focused on development, but on the other hand also look at the life conditions of the employees. Moreover, a leader should have a skill of problem-solving and make sure that every department of the company works coherently together. When discussing what challenges leaders face, Katilienė states that Lithuania is a small but extremely proud nation with a very rich history and unique traditions which causes considerable differences and challenges in the country regarding leadership. Furthermore, Lithuania is a fast-developing nation and changes come quickly as, for instance, in 2015 Lithuania adopted the Euro which was a significant step forward. When talking about empathy, the expert notes that: *"In Lithuania, there are a lot of possibilities to improve [leadership] skills. However, the leader has to be aware that empathy is a skill that is very important. It has to have some meaning for him and for the organisation. If this is not the case, he will not be interested in the emotional part of being a leader"* (9 November 2018). Proceeding on this subject, Katilienė suggests that the level of empathy is connected with generations since younger age groups tend to be more empathetic than the older ones.

Almantas Stankūnas: a Lithuanian cross-cultural trainer

Almantas Stankūnas is a Lithuanian business development director and consultant at TEC Infrastructure which is one of the leading consulting companies in the Baltic states. Besides holding a Master's degree in Engineering, he has more than 20 years of experience within the consultancy branch of international companies such as AECOM in Lithuania. Furthermore, the main focus of his consultant service is to advise organisations with regard to leadership, communication among investors and improving overall performance. Stankūnas (9 October 2018) believes that having a managerial degree does not necessarily result in being able to lead others. A good leader needs to be passionate about what he is doing and needs to find that particular area of expertise he wishes to succeed in. Another highlighted key point is that it is important to follow business integrity and maintain humility as many former leaders have failed by not doing so. Moreover, Stankūnas illustrates that there is a high: *"focus on professional excellence and productivity and [Lithuanians] also tend to quite often use a more administrative approach to check if everything is in order and done"*. On the other hand, Lithuanians are striving towards learning new things and are thus becoming more open-minded. However, even though Lithuania is considered to be culturally flexible due to its location and historic past, it is important to know that: *"in Lithuania you can find organi[s]ations of various cultures [where] some of the leaders still [use a] formal, more or less, older [style] of leadership"* (Stankūnas, 9 October 2018).

In-country leadership best seller

One of the best-selling books about leadership in Lithuania is written by Nerius Jasinavičius, which is published in 2017, entitled: *Nuo amato prie verslo (From workplace to business).* Jasinavičius has been working as a process improvement (TOC, LEAN, SixSigma) expert and trainer in different European countries since early 2000. In 2004, he founded TOC Sprendimai, a consulting company which helps clients to become the leaders in their field.

Local leadership book	
Title	*Nuo amato prie verslo*
Subtitle	Pradžia
Author	Nerius Jasinavičius
Publisher	Kopa
Year	2017
ISBN	9789955772880

In this book, the author demonstrates his findings and methods, which have been trialled with owners of small and medium companies (with up to 100 employees) during ten years of work. In addition, this book is adapted to the standards of Lithuanian business and reflects the problems which they are facing currently in the country – creating and developing businesses. Jasinavičius (2017) emphasises that it will not be enough if you simply read the book; the theory only holds value if you put it into practice: *"The main purpose of this book is to help business creators and developers to achieve their business objectives much faster than they would have without the knowledge and insights I offer"* (Jasinavičius, 2017).

Lithuanian leadership YouTube review

In the constantly changing world, there is no company that has eschewed change, and Lithuanian companies are no exception. Nowadays, they are torn between the need to change and the wish to remain stable. It is the leader who should be able to solve this dilemma in a way that a company can benefit from. In an address at ISM University, Valdas Adamkus, the former president of Lithuania, points out that a leader is the one who sees opportunities and chances for the company to benefit even during the times of unexpected change and motivates others to contribute to the success. He also emphasises the features that characterise a good leader: *"freedom, responsibility, courage, honesty and compassion are crucial for us to be able to deal with change"* (ISM University, 2013). One of the most outstanding peculiarities of Lithuanian leadership culture is that it can be split up into two groups. An older generation of workers who were brought up in the Soviet Union and support traditional corporate values belong to the first one with the younger generation that represents a global way of thinking forming the second group. Bjornar Lund, CEO at DnB NORD, accentuates that the second group is becoming more numerous nowadays, but it is still a long way to go: *[...] there is still too much hierarchical way of thinking [...] there is a much more power game: people enjoy being in power, being dominant to other people. So, I think there is real willingness to really break down that hierarchy* (ISM University, 2016).

Giedre Simanauskaite, Communications Manager at Rimi Baltic Group, also pays attention to the newer generation of leaders highlighting features that are important for them in the workplace. First of all is the meaning; it is necessary for them to know what impact their work will have. Secondly, Lithuanians want to have similar interests with their colleagues and, perhaps, even become friends with them. Thirdly, a leader should serve as an example, guiding employees. She clarifies: *"We do not like when the people are pointing at our mistakes [...] We want to see you behaving [in the] same way you want us to behave"* (Simanauskaite, 2016). Lastly, employers want the employees to be happy. How much fun they have while doing this project matters as well as how successful the project was. This flows from the belief that happiness increases productivity and inspires employees to become more creative (Simanauskaite, 2016).

Understanding hierarchy in Lithuania

Lithuanian history and being a part of USSR in particular had a big influence on contemporary hierarchy in Lithuania. Mixed with new ideas spread all over the world, Lithuanian hierarchical culture appears to become very divided. The older generations are holding on to the structure of the USSR days. Nonetheless, the new generation is adapting to the Western method of leadership. According to Baltrimiene (2005), this new generation has a different mentality and worldview. The customs within Lithuanian businesses are changing and have resulted in less hierarchy between people. Within the power distance scale of Hofstede, Lithuania scores a 42 out of 100, which implies that Lithuanians prefer equality and a decentralisation of power and decision-making (Hofstede Insights, n.d.). Moreover, there is a sense of loyalty and a different attitude towards authority and status among the older generation, which have experienced Soviet dominance. The enormous gap between generations affects the way companies in Lithuania carry out leadership. As a result, corporations founded in the USSR days have a strong sense of hierarchy and a clear top-down communication.

On the other hand, in later established corporations, hierarchy is less heard of. Therefore, a horizontal communication approach, which is likened to the system in Western countries, is used. Chief Technical Officer of R&D additionally indicates: *"In Vilnius, we have international companies and relatively young leaders with international experience. The [Western] culture is dominating in those companies. The rest of Lithuania is very different with culture more closely related to Soviet epoch and understanding"* (CCBS Survey, 2018). Stankūnas asserts that: *"New organisations are changing the importance of hierarchy. However, in many organisations [hierarchy is] still present. These companies have challenges with team cooperation and decisions on a more horizontal level. Managers have to be fully involved, and they decide"* (9 October 2018). Nevertheless, a chief operating officer of an IT company in Lithuania (CCBS Survey, 2018) states that there is not a high position difference. As a result, the leader in the company is a friend to his or her subordinates. Thus, the person in charge tries to guide during the work process instead of giving orders like a stubborn boss.

How the Lithuanians achieve leadership empathy

Every culture has a different way or level of showing empathy. According to Chopik, O'Brien and Konrath, the Baltic countries are the least empathetic (2016). Leaders depend greatly on their experience when making decisions rather than intuition. Furthermore, they lack self-management skills in addition to empathy although the CCBS survey indicates that these qualities are what Lithuanians look for in a leader (CCBS Survey, 2018). Katilienė suggests that: *"empathy needs to be reflected in the organizational culture and that culture and leadership are two sides of the same coin"* (9 November 2018). Stankūnas believes that: *Leaders in Lithuania are very aware of this lack of empathy, but for leaders that have worked abroad and had experience in international organi[s]ations, providing higher motivation is important. To get more empathy and reaching higher motivation is getting better day by day in Lithuania* (9 October 2018).

Diskienė et al. (2010) discuss that in Lithuania a leader is someone who holds responsibility and navigates multiple objectives of a group with the same goal. It is crucial for a leader to make their words count by their actions. Planning, organisational skills and decision-making in important situations are generally respected in Lithuania. Management specialists agree that leadership styles are a combination of personal traits and how their subordinates behave. Thus, it is dependent on the personality of the leader and experience in certain situations. Moreover, a change in the attitude of managers resulted in a more democratic work style, based on cooperation, mutual respect and the authority of the manager. Successful personnel motivation is closely related to the manager's leadership and how effective it is. Consequently, certain factors that encourage this successful motivation include respect, awards, career prospects, a creative atmosphere and confidence in the leadership (Diskienė et al., 2010).

Malta

Menno de Baas, Sabline Schaaf, Thom Sliej & Yildiz Cincil

The Republic of Malta is an archipelago between Italy and Libya. Only the three largest islands, Malta, Gozo (*Ghawdex*) and Comino (*Kemmuna*), are inhabited. The Maltese people have two official languages - Maltese and English. However, a large portion of the inhabitants also speaks Italian. Maltese stems from multiple languages - mostly Arabic but also English, Italian and French (Sabine, 2017). English is an official language due to the colonisation by the British Empire. The Republic of Malta, hereafter referred to as Malta, became independent at the beginning of the sixties, but it remained a member of the Commonwealth. At the beginning of the new millennium, Malta joined the European Union, and it adopted the use of the Euro as the official currency. Being a popular holiday destination, Malta's main source of income stems from tourism. Another reason to travel to Malta is for medical reasons, such as cosmetic surgery. Medical tourism is actively promoted by the government in order to create an attractive medical environment (IMTJ, 2010).
One of the country's major problems is that it has very few natural energy sources available. In order to meet the fuel requirements, Malta is entirely dependent on the importation of fuels (Euromonitor, n.d.). One of the most influential sectors in Malta is banking. While this area may be the most prominent, only one per cent of the population works in it. However, in the last decade, the World Economic Forum's Competitiveness Index has rated the Maltese banking system as one of the soundest in the world, which creates an incentive for banks to set base in the country (Maltaprofile, 2017).

How the Maltese characterise leaders

The Maltese experience with leadership has been quite limited, partly due to its colonial history. The only way to carry out leadership was in a family environment and clubs or trade unions. In his research, Darmanin (2007) characterises Maltese leadership after its independence as paternalistic, where leaders keep a high hierarchical distance between themselves and their employees, but on the other hand, tend to comfort their employees with a 'godfather' attitude. The Maltese needed yet to understand that their leaders were not restricted by their colonisers anymore and that they were able to determine their own course of action within their businesses. This attitude characterised Maltese leadership for decades.

However, this attitude has gradually been changing. Since the beginning of the new millennium, Malta is in a transition, where the traditional way of leadership is transforming into a more modern way. By using their own creativity, directors are now able to find the most suitable form of leadership for their firms. Darmanin (2007) points out that the enterprise understands the value of a leader who is proactively participating in an organisation, rather than just being the face of the business. This makes the distance between leader and member shorter and enables interaction between the employer and employee. In an interview, Vincent Cassar concurs with this statement and mentions the following regarding current leadership in Malta: *"It's changed a bit to become more democratic [and] more distributive"* (Cassar, 4 November 2018). A changing attitude comes partly from the need for leadership training. Darmanin (2007) further asserts that more and more companies, governmental institutes and private institutes take this seriously and offer training courses, workshops and seminars for their leaders to grow within their position. Micallef's (2015) study confirms the importance of education in management, as she states that small- and microbusinesses in Malta adopt education into more informal and indirect measures, whichever fits best with their businesses.

A change in attitude can also be noticed in the distribution of leadership positions by gender. Maltese women are assuming more and more leadership responsibilities compared to a few decades ago. There has been a prejudiced attitude towards female leadership, which came from the "godfather" attitude and the image of a leader, based on masculine traits such as assertiveness, competitiveness and tough-mindedness (Darmanin, 2007). However, this attitude is strongly decreasing and female leadership is heavily encouraged nowadays. The impact of media is essential in this process. It can help reduce gender stereotypes even more if women are more frequently shown in authoritative roles (Cassar, 2004).
Cassar also mentions that there is not a typical leadership in Malta, and leadership could best be seen as a hybrid between trying to be professional and leaving space for personalisation (Cassar, 4 November 2018).

Survey results and what local respondents say

In order to gather data on the difference of opinions, preferences and experiences with local leadership, CCBS (2018) approached various professionals. The following opinions and quotes have been given by experts who are working or have worked in Malta in a professional context. One of the professionals states that there is not a specific style of Maltese leadership. He further explains his assertion: *"I consider leadership to be synonymous with the person carrying out the role of a leader. It will depend very much on the type of character such person is and his/her leadership style will match this. In Malta I do not recognize anything specific about leadership"* (CCBS Survey,2018). However, another professional indicates that Malta is going through a phase, a factor, further supported by Hofstede (n.d.), namely that long-term Maltese leadership is changing. Another professional explains this transition in leadership style in the context of the changing demographics. Currently, Malta is experiencing increased immigration, and employee demographics are shifting, due to foreign workers fulfilling local positions. These foreign workers incorporate their own unique culture, which affects work methods and, more poignantly, the leadership styles. This professional concludes that leadership approaches will vary according to different circumstances (CCBS Survey,2018).

Local leadership analysis

In-country literature review

In a lot of Western countries, including Malta, people want a more balanced man-to-woman ratio with regard to leadership positions. However, it is believed that men and women have different leadership styles (Pace & Pace, 2005). For example, women adopt a more inclusive and participative leadership style, while men tend to use a directive and controlling style. One of the professionals who filled in the CCBS survey states the following regarding female leadership: *"Most women leaders tend to adopt a task centred approach whilst the majority of men tend to apply a person-centred approach, also, most women expect subordinates to strictly abide with decisions taken and organisational policy"* (CCBS Survey, 2018). In general, according to Privitelli (2015), leadership styles are undergoing a considerable change, and there are different approaches to being an exceptional leader. One of them is for a leader to be very dominant. In such an authoritative leadership style, all decisions are made by him or her, and no discussion about these decisions is possible. The second approach to leadership involves experience and respect towards professionals who possess it. Another, less dominant, approach to leadership is found in the importance of building a relationship with employees, whilst trying to combine the remaining styles and approaches, previously mentioned (Privitelli, 2015). For Gatt (2016), this all comes down to whether a leader can be effective. He notes that effective leaders make sure that all employees are feeling comfortable in the company and see themselves as more like a professional coach (Gatt, 2016). For a small island such as Malta, it is important that employees have leaders with a combination of the qualities mentioned by Privitelli (2015) and Gatt (2016). When living on an island, resources are often limited (Bush, Purvis & Barallon, 2009), meaning that in terms of human resources, it is more difficult to find people with the right knowledge and education to fulfil leadership positions. According to Bush et al. (2009), being a small island is not a limitation to turning a company into a success, but the amount of people on this island is. Therefore, for a country such as Malta, it is important to motivate employees and enable them to get the best out of their careers. In order to understand what motivates employees, it is necessary to consider their local culture. In the study performed by Catania (2013), it is concluded that employees are motivated by numerous intrinsic factors. It also mentions that one should keep the Maltese cultural characteristics in mind as they act as the national moderators of intrinsic motivation (Catania, 2013). Being motivated by intrinsic factors means that employees act without an obvious external reward. One acts because the activity is considered enjoyable, or it is viewed by the individual as an opportunity to actualise potential, learn or explore (Cherry, 2018). In order for Maltese businesses to motivate their employees, they need to offer sufficient opportunities to their employees, encouraging them to stay and work on the island.

Vincent Cassar: a Maltese leadership scholar

Vincent Cassar is an associate professor and deputy dean of the Faculty of Economics, Management and Accountancy at the University of Malta. He also serves as a senior consultant at KPMG (Malta) People & Change Advisory and is Board Director at Resources Support Services Ltd.

In the interview with CCBS, Cassar mentions that there is no such thing as a typical Maltese leader. This is due to the approximately fifty thousand non-Maltese people living in Malta, who bring their own culture and business styles into the workforce. Cassar indicates that there once was a time where leadership in Malta was very directive and autocratic. However, since the increase in competition for human capital, leaders have to take a more cautious approach in order to retain employees. Cassar (4 November 2018) now considers Maltese leadership to be a hybrid between trying to be professional and leaving space for personalisation.

When comparing Maltese leadership with leadership around the world, Cassar sees an obvious difference. Due to Malta being an island, with a strong family-based culture, it may sometimes restrict the decision-making discretion of the person in charge. The leader always has proximity to other people, and with every decision, the personal reputation tends to be kept in regard because of the fear of being negatively perceived by the community. When looking at leadership in other countries, one often sees independent boards of directors or leaders who are not native to the country the business is in. This makes it easier to achieve task-oriented targets, where people could be fired if necessary. In Malta, firing people is not as easy because this might negatively impact the personal reputation of the leader.

Another important factor to remember is that Malta is a country with a Mediterranean culture, where, in Cassar's experience, men often dominate leadership positions. However, the women holding leadership positions are often highly competent and have a strong personality. Currently, there are numerous incentives to increase the number of women in leadership positions. If someone wants to start doing business with a Maltese company, it is important to bear in mind its Mediterranean culture. That means that relationships are a key factor. It also means that the Maltese people are open to doing business, but on the other hand, one needs to invest a lot of time in building a professional relationship. One of the things that can be done as a business partner is to share a meal together, in order to build on the relationship. Also, one has to invest a lot of time in finding out what kind of company they are doing business with, in order to effectively reap the benefits of its partnership (Cassar, 4 November 2018).

In-country leadership best seller

One of the best-selling books about leadership was written by Alfred Darmanin and is called *Developing leadership skills: a training manual for leaders*. Darmanin was a clinical psychologist from the University of Louvain, Belgium and obtained his PhD from Berkeley, California, with a specialisation in the psychology of leadership, he now lectures in applied psychology at the University of Malta. He has conducted several workshops for leaders and executives in various companies, both locally and abroad. Besides *Developing leadership skills:*

a training manual for leaders, Darmanin has written three other books and several articles on leadership (Times of Malta, 2004).

Local leadership book	
Title	*Developing leadership skills*
Subtitle	A training manual for leaders
Author	Alfred Darmanin S J
Publisher	Media Centre
Year	1992
ISBN	99909-2-000-1

In this 507-page book, Darmanin provides all those involved in leadership roles with about 200 activities and exercises, which can be used at meetings, seminars, workshops, training courses, or even on one's own. The 31 leadership skills covered are classified under four categories: organisational, group, interpersonal and intrapersonal, and these include basic skills such as communication, time management, interpersonal relations, team-work, delegation and conflict management. For each skill, the reader is provided with a set of practical exercises together with a systematic outline to serve as an input, and a list of suggested readings (Darmanin, 1992).

Maltese leadership YouTube review

To gather insight on Maltese leadership, important sources of information are the different business conferences held in Malta. During those conferences, multiple speakers from different companies give their views on theoretical or actual business cases. These talks are mostly focussed on strategy, growth and the focus of businesses. In general, the keynote speakers tend to emphasise long-term development. "We are all about people, we are all focusing on the customer and focusing on innovation. It's a much more long-term approach" is what the chairman and CEO of Toly Products, Gatesy states (Business Leaders Malta, 2014). Besides paying attention to the company strategy, growth and focus, leaders also need to be able to adapt to the changing circumstances, in order for their business to thrive. The COO of Melita, Rasterhoff states that managers need to be aware of what is happening around them and be able to adapt accordingly. A strategy could be applicable in the first moment, but in the next one, it may already be obsolete (Business Leaders Malta, 2013). During another interview, it becomes clear that there is a clear distinction between male and female leaders. On the question from an interviewer *"How did you manage as a woman in the telecom industry?"* Hernandez, the new manager of Vodafone Malta, replies *"Being myself, be the way I am. I never tried to copy a man in the leadership style"* (Hernandez, 6 August 2018).

Understanding hierarchy in Malta

In order to understand the professional hierarchy in Malta, it is important to understand its history as a colony. In this colonial past, the leadership positions were taken over by colonial rulers (Darmanin, 2007). It was often the case that employees had to comply with the orders that were given to them. This can still be seen in current business practices, as Malta is still a prominent hierarchical society (Hofstede Insights, n.d.). However, according to a senior manager from the transport sector, Malta is currently undergoing a transition, where the changing employee demographics cause work methods to shift. This, in turn, affects the leadership styles (CCBS Survey, 2018). A senior manager states that leadership approaches will thus vary in different circumstances. For instance, in some organisations leadership will be similar to what is stated in non-Maltese leadership literature, whereas in other organisations, particularly family-owned businesses, leadership styles have remained somewhat traditional (CCBS Survey, 2018). Cassar (4 November 2018) also states that most company structures have flattened over the past two decades. Younger companies are taking a different kind of leadership shape than the older, more traditional companies. This is also dependant on the size of the company and on the culture of its employees because there are around 50,000 non-Maltese inhabitants currently living in Malta. These people may have a different culture than the Maltese people, which affects leadership styles (Cassar, 4 November 2018).

How the Maltese achieve leadership empathy

In order to effectively do business in Malta, it is imperative to remember that the most efficient way to ensure a meeting is to have a personal or professional reference, who could introduce you to your business counterpart. However, if you have no connection available, it is also acceptable to send an email to a person in a higher position in the company hierarchy. Once a link has been

established, it is important to know that the Maltese will only enter into a business agreement if they feel that they know and trust you. Another key item is to always be on time for meetings as this is highly valued (Expatfocus, 2018). Cassar (4 November 2018) agrees that you need to have an established relationship, in order to effectively do business. *"[The] most important thing to become a good leader here are your contacts. It means that you have to be known and the people have to see you in action. People have to trust you"*.
He also stresses that leaders who are perceived as worthy are the ones who keep in mind their personal image when making business decisions. This is a result of the family-oriented culture, where many people in the community know each other, and actions influence the standing one has within the community (Cassar, 4 November 2018). Thus, in order for a leader to achieve empathy, they have to make decisions which profit the company and keep their personal image intact.

Namibia

Thomas de Vijlder, Maxime Woerdeman, Melanie Straatman, Shannon Sanches & Robin Smid

The Republic of Namibia has just over two-and-a-half-million inhabitants and is located in Southern Africa. Its population is relatively young, with over two-thirds of the inhabitants under the age of 30, and grows annually with approximately two per cent (Mckenna, 2017). Namibia's culture can be described as formal and diverse. An example of its diversity is the number of languages that are spoken in the country: these amount to about eleven (The Government of Namibia, 2018). Since so many languages are present in the country, people tend to speak two or three languages on average per person. The official language of Namibia is English, but about half of the population also speaks the native language, Oshiwambo (The Government of Namibia, 2018).

Another manifestation of cultural diversity in Namibia is found in religion. Belief is very important to many people's lives and every religion is accepted and respected. Christianity is the religion of a large majority of the inhabitants of Namibia (McKenna, 2017). The main driver of Namibia's economy is agriculture, with workers in this sector encompassing almost one-third of the entire workforce. Diamonds are one of the most important natural resources, with an export accounting for one-third of Namibia's foreign exchange earnings. Some of the other natural resources include gold, copper, lead and uranium; the country is famous for having the world's largest open-cast uranium mine at Rössing (Euromonitor, 2018). The export partners of Namibia are countries in Africa, the Middle East and Europe. These account for more than three-quarters of the entire country's export. Aside from these major export partners, the open economy of Namibia is intriguing to foreign investors, who are looking for new opportunities to expand their business to the African continent.

How Namibians characterise leaders

In Namibia, the leadership style tends to be straightforward and traditional, according to Dr Rowan van Dyk. He believes that the majority of leaders tends to fulfil a managing role rather than a leading role (Van Dyk, 11 October 2018). In Namibia, value-based leadership is about setting good examples to subordinates. In this way, supervisors will be able to maintain authority because subordinates are tempted to disobey orders from a leader who does not adhere to their principles. Namibian leaders are traditionally not focused on team orientation. In fact, participative leadership is very low. Subordinates have to obey their leader without any consultation or discussion. Thus, the supervisor does not involve his or her employees in any decision-making process (Van Dyk, 11 October 2018).

Correlated to low participation of employees, autonomous leadership is very individualistic among leaders in Namibia because of the top-down approach, wherein leaders see themselves as 'the boss' and others do what the boss obligates them to do. Frequently, leaders have a political agenda and act only in the way that benefits them. Additionally, all authority rests at the top, which makes subordinates afraid to take initiative. This is known as an autocratic task-oriented leadership approach (Van den Bosch, 11 October 2018).

However, contemporary managers show a progression towards a more humane-oriented leadership style. Millennials in Namibia are making a significant effort in doing business with people from other tribes (Van Dyk, 11 October 2018). This differs from the traditional practices since although Namibians are unlikely to discriminate against colleagues from other ethnic groups, the older generation tend to keep a certain distance due to colonial wounds stemming from the country's history. In Namibia, leaders are self-protective as it is essential to maintain a certain level of status and reputation. This also has to do with the hierarchy in Namibian business culture. People in top positions want to show their power; for example, when two businessmen engage in a venture for their company, each of them wants to be the greater person. *"When there is a cake, both parties want the biggest piece"*, quotes Dr Rowan van Dyk.

Survey results and what local respondents say

In the recent Cross-Cultural Business Skills Survey, native Namibian professionals have provided some insight into leadership and workplace practices in the country. Firstly, the CCBS survey (2018) results show that in Namibia, managers who actively spend time on the personal well-being of their teams are valued and appreciated. This statement is supported by one of the interviewees, Servaas van den Bosch, a media and communications professional: *"They are trying to create a culture where people want to work. This also has to do with the shortage of skills in the country. So, they really need to make an effort to retain the staff that they have"* (Van den Bosch, 11 October 2018). Further support for this utterance is provided by Hofstede as Namibia scores lower on the individualism indicator (Hofstede Insights, n.d.). This implies that its culture can be seen as collectivistic, placing greater value on the group rather than the individual. Secondly, even though Namibians prefer to have a manager who spends time on employee well-being, it is common that there exists a certain level of hierarchy within a team. The leader will keep a personal distance at certain times to maintain the right level of respect. In his interview with CCBS, Servaas van den Bosch states: *"Namibian leadership is rather top-down in my view and often a difference of opinion from that of a CEO or manager can be viewed as dissent as opposed to a possibly creative new approach."* (11 October 2018). This is also acknowledged by Hofstede's power distance indicator (Hofstede Insights, n.d.). Also, within this hierarchy, women do have to work harder and *"men are still seen as more reliable and likely to be more effective in roles of leadership"* (CCBS Survey, 2018). To show the right level of respect to leaders, subordinates also address leaders according to their titles or positions. More than half of all respondents agree with this statement (CCBS Survey, 2018).

Although one respondent, Tarah Shaanika, indicates that this can differ at times: *"It depends on what traditions allow. In some traditions, for instance, someone older than you should always be addressed differently from your agemates"* (CCBS Survey, 2018). Thirdly, more than three-quarters of the respondents agree that it is important to follow the established organisational procedures (CCBS Survey, 2018). However, these procedures do allow room for 'rule-bending' as more than half of all respondents agree that they can "bend the rules without asking, in order to improve their performance or achieve better results". Nevertheless, this practice is not excessive and overall applicable. According to Tarah Shaanika: *"There are some rules that cannot be bent such as having to bribe someone or receiving a bribe, [or being] dishonest in any manner to get better results and so forth"* (CCBS Survey, 2018). Lastly, Namibian business culture is a rather direct culture for people within an organisation. More than half of the respondents disagreed with the survey statement: "This leader prefers to hear criticism in an indirect manner, outside of the staff meeting", which suggests that leaders prefer to hear criticism directly from their team members and that giving criticism in a staff meeting is a possibility too. In a staff meeting, a manager might confront his or her employees if necessary, to obtain the targeted results in an efficient matter (CCBS Survey, 2018).

Local leadership analysis

In-country literature review

One of Namibia's most respected leaders is president Hage Geingob ("President's Birthday", 2018). His integrity and ability as a political orator and organiser, and his readiness to work with people from all walks of life set him apart from former presidents. Also, his openly displayed love and support for the Namibian sports, arts and entertainment sectors deepened his connection with the people of Namibia. The most important quality that any leader must have is the ability and willingness to reciprocate the loyalty and support of his followers. Bill Bradley in *The Namibian* notes: *"Leadership is unlocking people's potential to become better, an ability they might not know they had"* ("President's Birthday", 2018). It is important that a leader has a vision and gets people to believe in that vision. A leader cannot achieve the implementation of a vision all by him or herself, but only through a collective effort in which everyone moves in the same direction.

Servaas van den Bosch: a Namibian experience expert

In order to gain academic insight on the topic of Namibian leadership, scholar Servaas van den Bosch was interviewed. Van den Bosch has 20 years of experience as a media and communications professional in Europe and Africa. He has been contracted as a communications specialist for the United Nations, the European Union, the Deutsche Gesellschaft für Internationale Zusammenarbeit (GIZ), the United States Agency for International Development (USAID) and the Millennium Challenge Account, as well as numerous multinational corporations. In his spare time, he represents his country of origin, the Netherlands, as an honorary consul in Namibia. At this moment, Servaas also works as a CEO at Emergo (Emergo, n.d.).
According to Van den Bosch (11 October 2018), Namibians tend to be quite *"top-down"* in terms of leadership. They try to implement more Western ways of running a business. Furthermore, Namibians place a large emphasis on approaching challenges by drawing up long-term plans, but many of them are deemed unrealistic. Van den Bosch (11 October 2018) admits that authority rests at the top, with leaders trying to delegate power to their subordinates. Namibian people tend to be quite individualistic and are prominently looking out for their own interest. Van den Bosch concludes: *"I think that in larger companies that are kind of based on the South African 'white model', they tend to do teambuilding exercises, invest in employee-wellness and things like that. In government,*

I just do not see it happening. Some do, but a lot of them have a long way to go when it comes to teambuilding. I also think that it is part of the culture of the people [as they] are not accountable, because teambuilding is one side of the coin. But if people are not accountable, they also have no reason to be part of a team" (11 October 2018).
Another aspect, which Van den Bosch underlines is: *"When I speak to other Dutch entrepreneurs or business people, one thing that always comes up is that Namibians are quite difficult to work with [because] they understand the rights but not the responsibilities, [and they] tend to do the minimum. As a leader, first of all you [want] micromanaging, also because the skills are not here"* (11 October 2018). The people that grew up in Namibia, white or black, have more realistic expectations of their leaders, so as not to get frustrated easily. For foreigners, whether from Europe or the Middle-East, it can become very frustrating, since they may find it hard to understand the Namibian work ethic. Van den Bosch mentions: *"They [Namibians] will not answer emails, they will not read emails. Compared to other African countries the roads are good and the infrastructure is good, those are all things that are really good, but in terms of doing business, it is not easy"*. Last but not least, Van Den Bosch summarises Namibian business culture as: *"Very 'face-to-face' and what I always tell Dutch companies is that you need to com here and you need to understand the people if you want to talk to them"* (11 October 2018).

Dr Rowan van Dyk: a Namibian cross-cultural trainer

In order to fully understand Namibian leadership from a professional point of view, Dr Rowan van Dyk was interviewed. Van Dyk has worked in leadership and management training for the last 50 years. He has been actively running a company in Namibia for over 19 years, which provides leadership training to first-line managers and supervisors. Besides being a trainer, consultant and speaker, Van Dyk is also an author who has published three books on the topic of leadership.
According to Van Dyk (11 October 2018), Namibian leaders tend to be more managing than leading because: *"The problem with the people is that they are caught up in control and instruct environment [...] of the people I work with, 80 per cent of them makes a decision and informs this is the decision"*. Most of the time, leaders do not brainstorm but just inform their subordinates of their final decision. In their eyes, group effort is time-consuming. Traditionally, leaders in Namibia are more hierarchical, following the philosophy of:' *"I am in charge, I drive the fancy car, I live in the big house, so I have to keep up appearances"*

(Van Dyk, 11 October 2018). Leaders do not understand the essence and importance of developing lasting relationships, because currently *"there is no leadership in the sense that people are working to build relationships and develop trust, and actually get the people to want to be motivated to do what they want them to do"*, linking this to the fact that empathy and understanding drives employees to deliver superior work (Van Dyk, 11 October 2018).

However, Van Dyk emphasises that, currently, the Namibian government is going through a change: *"If you look at the president of Namibia, he is putting in a lot more effort to sort of build relationships [...] a while back when he had his birthday [...] he was supposed to speak at an event [...] instead what he did is he got a couple of hundred elderly people [...] and celebrated his birthday with them and provided cake [...] so that's for me more a leader that is trying to build relationships"* (Van Dyk, 11 October 2018).

In recent years, the effects of increased globalisation have resulted in more Namibian businesses realising that one does not have to enforce authority, instead they must focus on building relationships and trust. Dr van Dyk observes this in his workshops: *"people are eager to accept the new [...] you can see that there is a desire to change"* (Van Dyk, 11 October 2018).

In-country leadership best seller

Rowan van Dyk was born in the South African town of Stellenbosch in the Western Cape. Upon his high school graduation, he obtained a BCom degree, and then later also an MBA and a DBA. For the past 30 years, Van Dyk has been actively involved in leadership and management training and for the past 18 years has owned his training company that operates both in South Africa and Namibia as a training provider offering outcome-based training (Van Dyk, n.d.).

Penny du Toit is a business strategist and growth advisory expert with years of experience in the areas of risk, change and Catalyst Leadership. Together with Rowan van Dyk, he is the co-founder of the Wave-Crest Leadership Centre, where young and upcoming entrepreneurs are groomed into becoming Catalyst Leaders. Together, Du Toit and Van Dyk co-authored the book *Why great leaders are catalysts* and helped establish the principles of The Leadership Flag and Core of the Cabbage (Du Toit, n.d.). Today, one of the best-selling books about leadership is *Why great leaders are catalysts,* published by the two authors in 2017.

For more than a century, a debate has been raging on whether great leaders are born or made. The purpose of this book is not to enter into that debate and attempt to establish an answer; instead, it is aimed at creating an awareness that leaders need to act as catalysts. The highlight of this book is within the fact that all of us need to be leaders at certain stages of our lives, whether we want to or not. Whenever you are placed in a situation where you become responsible for someone else's actions, or you have someone that needs to report back to you, you are assuming a leadership role. A book born out of the frustration caused by the people who have climbed up the corporate or political ladder and project themselves as leaders, but will never truly fulfil their roles as they do not understand the concept of being a catalyst (Amazon, 2017).

Local leadership book	
Title	Why great leaders are catalysts
Subtitle	-
Author	Dr Rowan van Dyk & Penny du Toit
Publisher	Distributed through Amazon
Year	2017
ISBN	978-9994585304

Namibia leadership YouTube review

According to De Bruyn (2015), the moment of leadership is now. Leadership is not just a position, but rather a state of being in the world in an authentic way. We describe leaders as we describe ourselves - the art of leadership is about seeing matters in a new and different way. The ultimate goal is to make leadership an intrinsic part of oneself, to re-examine who we are and what is happening around us. For De Bruyn, this means that: *"As a leader, one must be able to see clearly, not only when the rain has gone but even in the midst of a storm"* (2015). The idea of metaphors is important to truly see the state of an organisation and one's own leadership. He goes on to explain that if we look at leaders, we often look at them, not through the prism of what they have done and the skills they have, but who they are as individuals. Therefore, the DNA of the organisation has to be synonymous with the DNA of the leader.

Understanding hierarchy in Namibia

According to Hofstede, Namibia is a hierarchical society. This means that in Namibia, people accept an organisational structure in which everybody is ranked according to levels of importance (Hofstede Insights, n.d). Additionally, Namibia scores low on egalitarianism. This is mirrored in its socioeconomic structure. Besides suffering from an extremely high level of income inequality, Namibia also displays high levels of gender inequality.

This general acceptance of hierarchy in Namibian society is reflected in its businesses where it is still a tradition that the higher levels of an organisation control the lower levels. *"Whatever the boss says, goes,"* says Dr Rowan van Dyk (11 October 2018). However, Namibia is currently experiencing a vast change. While Western countries started years ago with building relationships with the aim of achieving better results, Namibia is only now in the middle of implementing this new model of leadership. As Servaas van den Bosch sees it, the majority of leaders is still more autocratic and task-oriented, but they are willing to change their leadership style to a more Western way (Van den Bosch, 11 October 2018). There are more and more progressive leaders who are starting to look at developing relationships. It is a long process which takes practice and dedication, but the most important indication of its necessity is the desire for change in Namibia. This assertion has been supported by Dr van Dyk (Van Dyk, 11 October 2018). While the hierarchical structure remains a slowly changing reality, this does not mean that different levels in an organisation are not approachable. When it comes to negotiation in Namibia, it is customary to consult and hold meetings with various employees before making important decisions. Global Affairs Canada also mentions that it is common to ask for advice or directions from a supervisor. According to Dr Van Dyk, a lack of time is usually the excuse given during a brainstorm session about ideas or negotiation for an important decision does not take place. Furthermore, Namibians are proud of their independence. Given the history of South African occupation and Apartheid (inequality), they want to be sure that expats are not taking jobs or decision-making authority away from Namibian natives. This is mirrored in the hierarchical business society of Namibia.

To sum up, the majority of leaders remains task-oriented but is willing to change to a more humane-oriented leadership style. Businesses who do negotiate and put the effort in building relationships have come further in the process. As Van Dyk points out: *"It's like a soccer team. One player can't do everything, he needs the other ten players to help, otherwise he is not going to win the game"* (Van

Dyk, 11 October 2018). As this chapter has shown, Namibia is slowly starting to catch on to that idea.

How the Namibians achieve leadership empathy

As Namibia remains traditional regarding leadership, a majority of leaders does not put any significant effort in achieving empathy towards their employees. Nonetheless, there are more and more progressive leaders who are willing to make a change and work on improving this situation (Van Dyk, 11 October 2018). Furthermore, according to William Craig (2017), the success of a company is mostly tied to the loyalty of its customers. While this customer-first mentality is necessary for the continuation of a company, leaders forget another imperative element of success and growth: the employee-employer relationship. By building relationships with their employees, leaders can achieve empathy and therefore create a more positive work environment.

Nowadays, Namibians focus more and more on employee wellness. Namibian leaders are trying to create a business culture in which people want to work, so they really need to make an effort to retain the staff that they have (Van den Bosch, 11 October 2018). Big organisations in Namibia already focus on what is driving their employees and are taking this into account. Moreover, knowing their employees' interests and inspirations also helps towards building a strong and positive relationship. Having and showing such empathy and understanding of the drivers of employee efficiency will end up achieving much better work results (Van Dyk, 11 October 2018). Lastly, because - according to Hofstede (Hofstede Insights, n.d) - Namibia is a hierarchical society, it is still important as a leader to show who is in charge in an organisation. A leader should therefore show him or herself, in practice, to be educated, experienced, caring and hardworking. Besides that, it is essential for a leader to be amicable. This does not mean being everyone's best friend, but it does entail being approachable and having good listening skills. To summarise, being open, involving others in decisions and supporting the training and development of Namibian co-workers can be important for developing strong working relationships with employees.

Norway

Sarah-Lena Reindl, William Kallur, Kirsty Czaszewicz, Elias Karlström & Alessandro Asproso

Norway is a part of Scandinavia and is Europe's most northern country. The land is sparsely inhabited, with only four towns having a population larger than 100,000 residents. Norwegian living standards are one of the highest worldwide, and therefore, the country is ranked first on the United Nations human development index in 2018. This measurement puts emphasis on the individuals of the countries and their development in terms of key indicators, such as life expectation and education (United Nations Development Programme, 2018). In addition to this, Norway possesses two of the world's most sought-after natural resources: oil and gas. Tactically, they have opted to deposit their balance of payment surplus into a domestic oil fund - making the country the world's largest sovereign wealth fund (Visit Norway, 2018).
Since Norway did not gain independence from Swedish rule until 1905, the Norwegians have developed a certain proud and nationalistic mindset. The sense of nationalism can also be seen in the celebration of the "*Syttande mai*"- the Norwegian Independence Day, on the 17th of May. This nationalism together with Norway's assets contributed to the decision of not operating under the European Union's legislation. Norway's culture is heavily influenced by democracy. The nationalistic view and democratic practices have had a great effect on the way Norwegians look at leadership (Kirkhaug, 9 October 2018).

How the Norwegians characterise leaders

Egalitarianism is a concept which is heavily installed within Norwegian work culture. This is because managers who are in charge of organisations affirm that transparency and unity between all levels of the workforce are crucial for ensuring productive efficiency and reaching the company's optimal output (Meyer, 2014). A study in Norway analysed 162 Norwegian advertisements for leadership positions. The study reveals that the most demanded traits are personal and social abilities (Tollgerdt-Anderson, 1993). In his 1986 study, Eric G. Flamholtz stated that Norwegians use different kinds of leadership styles. However, a more recent study from Gibson (1995) has concluded, that

Norwegian executives tend to have a consensus leadership style. They work together with their employees as a team, in order to achieve the company's goals. A survey has been filled in by multiple executives in Norway, that have professional knowledge and experience in different areas of leadership. One of them states that: *"leaders are part of the whole organisation and interact with everyone as part of the group. That makes them stronger as leaders - not weaker, as many other countries seem to think"* (CCBS Survey, 2018). The fact that an individual in a superior position does not differentiate from their staff is also reflected in the CCBS survey. In it, 80 per cent of the respondents disagrees with the statement that leaders should get respectable office space and transportation, as to match their position.
Despite the fact that hierarchy is less prominent in Norway, almost half of the respondents believe that a leader should encourage some competition within the team in order to achieve better results in the end. Respondents found it best to describe a leader as an individual who is resourceful and intellectual, with a strong charismatic personality (CCBS Survey, 2018). Further, the CCBS survey (2018) has shown that characteristics such as organisational- and market expertise, as well as technical competence, are equally vital traits in a leader.
In addition to that, a leader should be a good listener, should act fair and possess visionary thinking. Nevertheless, the majority of the respondents also express the need for leaders to be target-oriented since employees seek a powerful decision-maker and an eloquent speaker (CCBS Survey, 2018).

Women as leaders

Regarding gender equality, Norway has been a role model in terms of policies and legislation. In 2004, Norway was the first country to have gender quotas on boards worldwide. Companies try to increase their transparency by hiring diverse people from both genders, with diverse skills (Danbolt, 2016). It appears that women tend to put more emphasis on supportive behaviour and personal development, compared to their male counterparts. The gender diversity of a company always reflects the fairness and innovation of an organisation. More than sixty per cent of Norwegian graduates in 2014 were female. This high rate provides women with bright opportunities to become future leaders (Danbolt, 2016). When comparing these results with the outcome of the CCBS survey (2018), more than half of the respondents agree that there is gender equality in leadership positions. Despite this, thirteen of the fifty-five disagree or have a neutral standpoint on the matter. One of the managers explains that from personal experience: *"Female leaders tend to be more efficient and thus [demand] greater clarity in leadership and organisational processes"* (CCBS Survey, 2018). These results can be linked back to Norway's strong egalitarian society, expressing that the country is ahead with its number of female leaders contributing to its economic success.

Survey results and what local respondents say

Over fifty Norwegian professionals ranging from *Instituttleders* to CEOs, have shared their views about leadership in their country in the CCBS Survey (2018). More than half of the respondents agree when asked if they prefer to keep a personal distance from employees, as to maintain respect from their subordinates (CCBS Survey, 2018). Regarding leadership styles, the CCBS survey illustrates that along with businesses endorsing a flat organisational structure, attributes such as *"openness"*, *"direct discussion"* and *"involvement"* are extremely sought after by the subordinates (CCBS Survey, 2018). They seek interpersonal relationships with their managers. One respondent believes that managers should: *"focus on empowering the staff – involvement in decision making..."* because the *"...staff need to truly understand the goals to perform at their best"* (CCBS Survey, 2018).

Contrary to Hofstede's findings of Norwegian's low power distance score between managers and subordinates, rather intriguing responses were revealed in the CCBS survey. Referring to whether employers would take the liberty to bend the rules without telling anyone in order to improve their personal performance or for group gain, half of the Norwegian managers agree, while the other half expresses disagreement. However, the reasons given the participants all had one similar theme; the issue is not the act but whether the task was carried out with integrity. Moreover, the respondents answered that the circumstances which make bending the rules permissible depends on factors such as company ethics and the extent to which they are violated. One male respondent explains that: *"Individual decision making is encouraged but within the boundaries of risk and law"*. Another Norwegian *Direktør* concludes that an *"Organisation is based on trust, as long as you perform well and reach your personal goals, you have the flexibility and trust to decide both when and where you perform your job"* (CCBS Survey, 2018).

Local leadership analysis

In-country literature review

A large amount of literature on leadership in Norway is available, but based on the analysis of Gjermundshaug, Seim and Berglund (2018), there seems to be a gap when looking at the skills for the development and innovation of a company. Rather than putting all focus on individual character traits of leaders, research shows that the importance of skills around what can be learned for the growth of the company should also be incorporated in order to increase productivity. A Norwegian study, conducted by Martinsen and Glasø (2013), two professors of the leadership department at the BI Norwegian Business School, confirms this theory by explaining that many managers in Norway do not have the profile or characteristics that match with effective management, based on international research. This indicates that Norway might face leadership challenges, simply because their current methods of profiling leaders might lead to efficient but ineffective results (Martinsen & Glasø, 2013).

Furthermore, a survey based on a selection of 801 Norwegians, by Gillian Warner-Søderholm and Annika Søderholm (2018), has shown that there appear to be regional differences in regard to the extent that a leader communicates with his subordinates to find solutions. The problem lies in the fact that managers seem to generalise the culture. The question then became: what should be expected in terms of differences? The survey indicates that in the north and west of the country leaders do not have to live up to the expectation of having very descriptive answers to subordinates, compared to the Oslo and Southern region, where accurate answers are the norm. After all, collectivism is higher in the north, compared to the Oslo region and individualistic leaders will be looked down on. The conclusion from the research is that certain models of management are not applicable in every region. Although differences are small, there can be consequences when generalising managing methods. By gaining knowledge about the different regions, differences are easier to be predicted and appreciated (Warner-Søderholm, 2010).

Rudi Kirkhaug: a Norwegian leadership scholar

For further research, a dialogue with Rudi Kirkhaug (9 October 2018), a professor and teacher at the University of Tromsö, Norway, who researches leadership and change in organisations, has been conducted. In our interview, he shared thought-provoking insights about the country's culture. Whether in a private company or in the public sector, a leaders' integrity is of utmost importance. Kirkhaug describes the word integrity by explaining that a leader should be trustworthy and also predictable in everything he or she does. He notes that in his experience, leadership is often based on trust. This could be described as the keystone of leadership in Norway. Leaders educate and train themselves in relationship trust, where they uncover that the best way for someone in charge is to reveal his or her weaknesses. Exposure on both sides, that is the leader revealing his or her believed weaknesses to the subordinates and vice versa, could catalyse gaining trust. He also explains his view of a leader in Norway having to lead differently in diverse situations. At points, instructions must be given. However, it is more normal for the domestic leader to be in the coaching position rather than the instructor position. He resumes by saying that in Norway, the leader stands behind his or her employees and supports them in their work. As Norwegian employees are very independent, they would only seek guidance, assistance or help when they need it.

Furthermore, the professor believes the common domestic mindset is that the organisation can tackle a change better in an immeasurably rapid changing world if everybody is involved in the situation. This is done by communicating one's thoughts and thus earning a say in the decision-making process.

Marith Silseth: a Norwegian cross-cultural trainer

Executive and leadership coach, Marith Silseth, shared her views on leadership in Norway during a Skype interview. She has extensive experience as a leader in the pharmaceutical industry for over 20 years and currently works as a leadership coach (Silseth, 11 October 2018).

She explains that the key to becoming a great leader is in inspiring your employees to do their best and work their hardest for the organisation. According to Silseth, hierarchy in Norway is low and organisations are flat. Although a manager does have a certain authority in the form of his or her position, employees are not afraid to talk about concerns and problems, since everyone looks at managers as if they were any other employee. The extent of this friendly relationship between managers and employees is a bit of a controversial subject for a lot of executives. This is because it is hard to tell employees when you are not pleased with their performance if you have a friendly relationship with them. Silseth thinks that it is very important when there is as little hierarchy as in Norway, to be able to maintain proper leadership boundaries when needed. It is also important to give positive and constructive feedback. This stems from the fact that it is imperative to still be able to guide employees at times when they can still improve. When asked about the importance of experience and knowledge compared to personal characteristics, Silseth clarifies, *"I used to say that all leaders can become better leaders, but not everyone can become a great leader"* (11 October 2018). To become a great leader, a person first needs to have an interest in leadership and think about why he or she wants to be a leader and how to become it. As a result, everyone can become better by practice and experience (Silseth, 11 October 2018).

In-country leadership best seller

Dagrun Dvergsdal, CEO of a Norwegian consultancy firm, specialised in leader and team development, has written one of the most sought-after academic books discussing the concept of leadership and how the trait can be acquired. It is titled *Expanding your leadership – a journey towards building character* (Visitoslo, 2018).

Local leadership book	
Title	*Expanding your leadership*
Subtitle	a journey towards building character
Author	Dagrun Dvergsdal
Publisher	Abstrakt forlag
Year	2014
ISBN	9788279353621

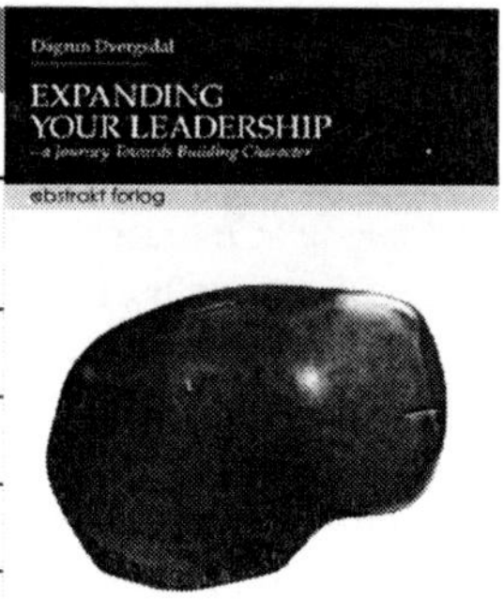

The main attraction of this publication is the fact that Dvergsdal fully appreciates that one is not born a leader but, with the correct guidance, can easily become one. She explains this by putting emphasis on the continuous process of building an individual's charm. Moreover, the book affirms that to stimulate individuals to develop into the best leaders they can be, it would be naive to assume that a generic, instrumental approach would suffice. The main aspects of character building that the author deems crucial for leadership success are the willingness to act, reflect and grow. Subsequently, the individual can acquire the skills necessary to project his or her vision and ignite the following of others (Dvergsdal, 2014).

Norwegian leadership YouTube review

A thought-provoking *Ted Talk* on Norwegian leadership gives a modest message. Norwegian psychologist Glenn Rolfsen (2016) challenges a vital part of leadership – the making a change within oneself, as the first step towards organisational success. Rolfsen points out the ongoing 'back-biting' that goes on in society. To interpret the word, one may call it 'talking bad behind each other's back'. He asks the audience which of them have witnessed this behaviour at their workplace in day-to-day life, and everybody raises their hand. The speech illustrates to the audience that there is an ongoing social phenomenon and that it is of no use for anybody to have 'back-biting' constantly recurring. He asserts, that when he had this thought, he instantly needed to step up as a leader and not talk in a negative manner about other people he knows, without their actual presence (Rolfsen, 2016).

Understanding hierarchy in Norway

When looking at hierarchy, Norwegians do not put much importance on power distance. Gibson defines Norway as an overall collectivistic country (1995). Knut Folmo, a Norwegian CIO and participant in the CCBS survey (2018), proclaims that the leadership pyramid is very low in Norway, implicating that the distance from managerial to subordinate levels on the work floor can be very short in the number of levels, and in terms of respect. Hence, it is not uncommon for a subordinate to exchange words and ideas with a manager and vice versa. While both parties should approach each other in a respectful and humble manner, the attitude between executives and their staff is very informal. The study of the CCBS survey (2018) has concluded that subordinates would hardly ever have to address their superiors by their title, *'Sjef'*, *'Direktør'* or *'Daglig leder'*. Less than a tenth of the respondents mention the need to address their respective leaders with their title. Furthermore, a CEO of an international consulting firm in Norway brought up an interesting point - there is only one exception when responding to whether Norwegians are supposed to address their leader by first name – the King. Correspondingly, Norwegian managers highlight that the country is ruled by an egalitarian society. One respondent explains that respect is earned, rather than assumed from a title.

Another response reads that Norwegians are oriented towards facts and tasks, not ceremonies (CCBS Survey, 2018).
Moreover, subordinates in Norway are encouraged to speak their mind with their superiors. This enables the leader to see different points of view, before coming to a decision. Employees tend to have a lot of freedom in setting their own work goals, while also deciding upon the way in which they fulfil their work-tasks most efficiently (Minelgaite & Stangej, 2017). Norwegian managers rely on the knowledge of their team members and place high importance on the development of their staff (Gibson, 1995). A large majority of the respondents indicate that leaders do not get superior office space or transportation to reflect his or her position (CCBS Survey, 2018). In addition, employees are expected to be team players. This is best described as having an energetic, approachable, participative and efficient work ethic (Minelgaite & Stangej, 2017). According to Trompenaars and Hampden-Turner (2001), Norwegians collectively separate between private and working life. When asked if they would help their boss paint their house, eighty per cent of the survey respondents disagreed. Managers asking subordinates for favours outside of the collective labour agreement is frowned upon. Outside of work, the boss does not have much authority (Trompenaars & Hampden-Turner, 2001).

How the Norwegians achieve leadership empathy

In order for a leader in Norway to receive empathy from his or her employees, their way of leading must be democratic. According to Kirkhaug (9 October 2018), this is a result of the democracy being embedded in the culture. Norwegian employees also tend to have a close relationship with their managers and look up to them for guidance, rather than directions. In terms of empathy, it appears that most of the respondents agree that the manager should actively spend time on the personal well-being of the team members. The superior is still supposed to be the one making the decisions. However, they should not expect to get appreciation from the employees, if they did not give them a say in the decision-making process as well (Kirkhaug, 9 October 2018).
To achieve empathy as a manager in Norway, it is vital to have experience and knowledge although it also essential to retain a friendly relationship with your personnel (Minelgaite & Stangej, 2017). Tollgerdt-Andersson (1993) also mentions the fact that employees expect of their superiors to be result-oriented and able to communicate these goals to their subordinates, in order for them to have a clear goal towards work.

In addition, it is crucial to have mutual trust between leaders and subordinates. Silseth, a Norwegian consultant specialising in leadership, emphasises that *"Trusting your employees is of utmost importance and the leader should not feel the need to supervise their work"* (11 October 2018).
According to Kirkhaug, leadership has become a paradoxical and complicated matter, and leaders need to be able to handle a wide variety of tasks and occurring problems. Therefore, leaders in Norway receive training and education on the subject. Without the proper knowledge in the profession, you will not achieve appreciation, nor be very successful in your field (Kirkhaug, 9 October 2018).

Pakistan

Roma Kisoenpersad, Marius de Best, Blawai Tariq, Arwin Naziri & Dania El Harmouch

"Vision without power does bring moral elevation but cannot give a lasting culture." This quote is from poet, philosopher and politician Muhammad Iqbal, also referred to as the 'spiritual father of Pakistan'. A citation that visualises the importance of leadership thought within the country. The Pakistani deeper culture puts its weight on numerous daily activities, as well as the way managers lead companies. *Islami Jumhurya Pakistan* (**اسلامی جمہوریہ پاکستان**), or the Islamic Republic of Pakistan, is highlighted in this chapter. With a population reaching over 200 million, the country is listed as one of the largest nations around the globe. The name 'Pakistan' was conceived in 1933 and means 'land of the pure' in Urdu, the official language. The country originated in 1947 as a result of the partition of British India. This detachment was accompanied by violence between Muslims, Sikhs and Hindus (Hussain, n.d.). Pakistan comprised the Muslim-majority areas of the Indian subcontinent, after which it developed as an independent country. The origin of Pakistan could be seen as rare among other Muslim countries in its relationship with Islam as it is the only country to have been established in the name of the Islam (Hussain n.d.).
The nation consists of various ethnic groups, each with their own culture and subcultures, but which are unified by common values like hospitality, trust and respect for elders. The core of the Pakistani ethos lies in respecting human feelings and strong family ties (Haleem, 2013). The nation's culture has a considerable influence when it comes to the practices in leading a group of people within an organisation.

How the Pakistanis characterise leaders

In Pakistan, leaders are expected to have a powerful presence within a team. Leadership in Pakistan is influenced by the familial system, which is characteristically hierarchical and personalised. This way, a leader becomes a symbol of influence and power. One could negatively affect stressful working environments by challenging employees with reward systems and personalised interaction within business affairs (Hussain, Ismail & Javed, 2017). More than eighty per cent of the business professionals that participated in the CCBS survey (2018) agree that leaders should encourage competition between their subordinates, in order to accomplish better results within the company. Research conducted by Mujtaba, Afza, and Habib (2011), concludes that attention is largely given to non-verbal aspects in conversations such as tone of voice, body language, eye contact and facial expressions. The CCBS survey (2018) participants agree that leaders should have a strong charismatic personality. On this topic, Bhatti (3 November 2018) also feels that in order to influence his or her employees, a leader should possess a charismatic personality. The research also reveals that Pakistani leaders are task-orientated and delegate in a direct manner, where trust and commitment are highly valued. Due to a highly scored uncertainty avoidance in Pakistan, employees are not tolerant of ambiguity and need guidance through clear instruction. In the business world, leaders desire obedience from their employees, whereas the employees expect their leader to be personally involved with them. *"To have been able to give my friend a few hours of happiness was worth its weight in gold. Those sharp suits on Wall Street will never understand such sentiments"* (Hashwani, 2017, p. 135). This is a quote from a business tycoon, who refers to collectivism in Pakistani business life.

Survey results and what local respondents say

Over seventy respondents have filled out a survey about leadership in Pakistan. The questioned professionals have a leadership occupation in different businesses or maintain similar professional activities. When looking at the degree of distance between leaders and subordinates, it becomes apparent that a personal distance between both parties is preferred (CCBS Survey, 2018). As Arfa Hussain, a project manager explains: *"Very few leaders actually lead. Most of them give orders here, which creates unfriendly nature in the organization"* (CCBS Survey, 2018). This shows that there is power distance present in the country, but it does not mean that there is absolutely no latitude in an organisation. For example, bending company rules to achieve desired results is accepted up to a certain level. Adil Rashid Qazi, a senior credit analyst, further supports this statement by saying: *"They may, but up to the extent that interest of the organisation is not jeopardized"* (CCBS Survey, 2018). Statistical analysis confirms what Qazi states; sixty per cent of the respondents agree on this topic (CCBS Survey, 2018). It shows that it is appreciated for people to show extra effort as long as it does not have a negative effect on the organisation. Since authorisation

is required for numerous events, sometimes it is necessary to neglect some rules in order to attain results.
Further research shows that leaders are advised to have a personalised way of communicating with their subordinates. Hashwani (2017) explains that his word is more important to him than his remuneration and that his highest reward is being able to look people in the eye. Actively spending time on the well-being of the team is a significant asset in Pakistani leadership. The vast majority of the CCBS survey participants agrees that managers should actively spend time on the personal well-being of the team members (CCBS Survey, 2018). Moreover, the Pakistani are highly competitive when it comes to career performance. This is reflected in the fact that eight out of ten professionals still feel that managers need to encourage some competition within their team to achieve better results for the company (CCBS Survey, 2018). Top management in organisations should be aware of what employees need in order to help them grow and be satisfied with their current position. This could easily be done by efficient collaboration and consultations on the necessities of performance (Abbas & Yaqoob, 2009).

Local leadership analysis

In-country literature review

Qaisar Abbas and Sara Yaqoob (2009) conducted research on the effect of leadership development on employee performance in Pakistan. In their analysis, Abbas and Yaqoob state that in today's organisations, leadership capability and requirements have a major effect on employee's performance in Pakistan. The study examines five factors of leadership development: coaching, training and development, empowerment, participation and delegation. These factors combined influence employee performance by 50 per cent. The rest of the employee performance is determined by other aspects and company tools, such as incentive programmes, motivational aspects and organisational trust.

Aisha Bela Malik (2018) investigated employee performance through surveys and also wrote about trust between business leaders and employees. Pakistan has faced historical corruption issues like illegal facilitation of payments and bribes within traditional leadership styles. Nowadays, doing the right thing is simple and happens to be one of the most valuable factors of leadership. In her article for *The Financial Daily*, Malik explains that today's employees desire transparency and independence due to their hard work and constant innovation.

According to Malik, future leaders are required to have a true, in-depth understanding of how to run a business, think broadly and transcend others in teamwork and communication.

Farooq Balooch: a Pakistani leadership scholar

Farooq Balooch (3 November 2018) has a master's degree in finance and economy and lectures on the topics of leadership and self-development. Balooch gained his experience in management during his entrepreneurial career, after establishing multiple enterprises. Since Balooch is familiar with the educational system in Pakistan, he feels that in the current situation, there is not enough attention directed towards moral values. The youth nowadays is only focused on being an individual top-performer. This encourages having a selfish attitude, an attribute that a leader should not possess. For adolescent individuals, the potential to be a leader in the future is already eliminated before such skills can be developed. As cited by Balooch, the Quran states: *"can the people with knowledge be equal, to those who have no knowledge?"* This means that without knowledge, one cannot become a good leader. According to the Islamic holy book, knowledge is a blessing. Balooch defines leadership as the art of inspiring and winning the hearts of people. For him, the best leadership style could be classified as transformational. It means that leaders should earn their respect instead of demanding it from subordinates, which is suitable for transactional leadership (3 November 2018).

Nadeem Bhatti: a Pakistani cross-cultural trainer

Nadeem Bhatti (3 November 2018) is a trainer in leadership and human resources and has spent more than forty-two years in the country's private business sector in Islamabad. He describes leadership as a vital phenomenon which is absolutely necessary for an organisation to successfully function. Additionally, he states that Pakistani leadership is developing towards an enhanced version of the current bureaucratic leadership style. Bhatti discloses the traditional Pakistani leadership style to be formed by a *'seth'* culture, which would translate as 'the boss is the most important asset in a team and that he should be satisfied and listened to'. Therefore, the top management decides about the key elements and no authority is granted to subordinates. In addition, Bhatti mentions that this places extreme pressure on employees, and it deters them from performing to their full potential. According to Bhatti, the leadership style in Pakistan has similarities with transactional leadership, where subordinates function under rewards and consequences.

In Bhatti's vision, an excellent leader requires integrity in every aspect, and he or she should work with the team instead of working above them. By acting in this way, leaders can create togetherness and efficiency rather than distance between their employees. This leads to a lack of motivation and job satisfaction. Bhatti believes that successful leadership consists of continuous employee training and knowledge of morals and strategy.

In-country leadership best seller

An in-country best seller on leadership is *CEO at 34*, written in 2014 by Faheem Sardar. Sardar has a respected name in brokerage and investment based in Islamabad. He obtained a Master's of Business Administration in Finance and Investments from Hamdard University in Karachi. He is also presently involved in training corporate governance and leadership skills at the Pakistan Institute of Corporate Governance. The author is the CEO of one of the faster-developing investment houses in Pakistan.

Local leadership book	
Title	*CEO at 34*
Subtitle	Managing and succeeding
Author	Faheem Sardar
Publisher	Profile Printing & Publishing
Year	2014
ISBN	978-969-9647-05-5

The book elaborates on the challenges one could face when starting a business in Pakistan. The writer describes the book as a set of guidelines on how to succeed in life, with specific reference to business life. People that are walking the path towards a management position will encounter different issues, and *CEO at 34* is written to help its readership in that perspective.

Pakistani leadership YouTube review

The following business leaders are just a few of the ones that define the business and leadership culture in Pakistan. It involves three modern-day leaders: Farees Shah - the country manager for one of the biggest online streaming services in Pakistan (VCast, 2018); Raza Pirbhai - the CEO of a popular fast-food chain

(School of Leadership, 2017); and, lastly, Kabeer Navi, who became CEO at a young age of a large micromanaging bank in Pakistan. For Shah, leadership styles within the diverse markets of Pakistan are characterised in a hierarchical way, based on mindset (VCast, 2018). In order to be a successful leader in Pakistan, one should have an open-door policy, which means that he or she should be accessible to all employees regardless of their hierarchical position in the company. This creates a personal relationship between a leader and his or her employees and fills the potential gap which is created once a leader is set above the other employees (VCast, 2018). Presenting yourself in high-class attire or being based in an attractive office location is not a necessity, since the most essential resources leaders can acquire are their employees (Navi, 2018). When leaders are able to empathise with their employees by having a humble mindset, the probability of having a well-put-together team of employees increases and so does the ability to guide infiltrates (Navi, 2018). Pirbhai adds that most leaders have started their careers from an unexpected position. Furthermore, leaders do not just simply pursue the path which is set out for them by a third party such as their family, which is a highly common principle in the Pakistani culture (School of Leadership, 2017).

As a leader, one should have the ability to recruit highly skilled employees who are capable of solving issues if they arise in the company. Navi also refers to those employees as 'the mamas', who are good pillars for a leader to build on due to their extraordinary capabilities. Having the ability to navigate and regulate your own career is an essential trait that all leaders must acquire. Since leaders have the ability to override employees, making appropriate choices and taking accurate measures should lie at the heart of what a manager does. Having an introverted personality as a leader can be a very defective trait since communication and empathy are essential for leaders in Pakistan (Navi, 2018). Creating a highly functional infrastructure in the company and having control over it can be challenging. However, this is fundamental for a company to operate successfully (VCast, 2018). Finally, Pirbhai notes that the most crucial thing a leader must be able to do in Pakistan is to dream big, set objectives and have an appropriate plan to reach those objectives (School of Leadership, 2017).

Understanding hierarchy in Pakistan

"The talk of management does not always match their walk" (Khilji, 2013). Within numerous organisations in Pakistan, the business culture could be described as a *seth* culture. Although it has multiple matching definitions, it refers to a highly

influential management top. Plenty of companies that are active in Pakistan are inherited or established by deep-rooted businessmen who summon their children to work for their company. When family members operate in the same organisation as their tribe, they often receive preferential treatments with the purpose of forwarding the company to them. This situation creates inflexibility, which results in fewer opportunities for young qualified talent to grow in a family-owned organisation (Razzaq, 13 November 2018). Furthermore, a communication gap between leaders and subordinates exists in lots of organisations since low autonomy is given to employees. Balooch (3 November 2018) agrees on this matter and states that power distance is largely present in the country's business culture. Leaders establish protocol and importance, and employees are expected to participate in what they tell them to do. It is unlikely for subordinates to provide feedback to their management during meeting sessions and afterwards since it will not be appreciated by the management top (Mujtaba et al., 2011).

Balooch also points out that: *"In the business world here in Pakistan, we have a lot of male dominance in all kinds of organisations - you will mostly see male bosses around you"* (3 November 2018). In most organisations, women are likely to face challenges with regard to male dominance. Female work is often not recognised and largely disregarded. Research shows that this is caused by cultural and economic reasons (Merkin & Shah, 2014).

Although disparity is visible, leaders tend to encourage their employees by convincing them that they have their best interest in mind. Special reward programmes are being held to increase job satisfaction and to ensure that employees will be loyal to the company (Razzaq, 13 November 2018).

How the Pakistani achieve leadership empathy

"Islam has taught me to see business as a social calling, not as an end in itself" (Hashwani, 2017, p. xv). With this quote, the writer clarifies the importance of social commitment for a successful business. In-group solidarity and a socialised culture, as well as building long-term relationships are highly emphasised by business leaders. It is advised to be thorough in communication towards one's subordinates, without destroying built-up relationships. Subordinates are expected to show docility and have a good balance between private and work situations (Mujtaba et al., 2011). In the interview conducted with Balooch, he states: *"The majority of our organizations don't understand this. The reason for this is the 'seth' culture, leaders don't treat their employees as human beings.*

They feel that they are the boss and do not have to do so" (3 November 2018). Respect towards leaders is central. However, leaders are obliged to meet requirements in order to achieve respect from subordinates. Some of the requirements are met when a leader is a visionary thinker and a powerful decision-maker (CCBS Survey, 2018).

In Pakistan, respect is an essential part of society. For example, aged leaders are more rapidly respected than younger leaders. Prof Faryal Razzaq (13 November 2018) illustrates this: *"Our culture places a lot of emphasis on respect. Young bosses struggle to get work done by elderly staff as the staff who are older than bosses expect to be respected and listened to."* This also corroborates the fact that leaders should have a personalised approach concerning communication with subordinates (Hussain et al., 2017). The Pakistani culture is recognised as a collectivistic culture. Therefore, loyalty overrules most social regulations and rules inside a company. Substantiated by Hofstede's theory, leaders must cherish strong, long-term relationships and be responsible for members of their group.

Perú

Jasper van Lente, Shirley Esquivel Nuñez, Yingjie Shen, Xiaowen Chen & Davis Koffie Uesugi

Peru is a sum of traditions, cultures and languages. It is like the Amazon River, which results from the union of several tributaries until it reaches its enormity. In a way Peru was created in a similar way; in the blood of present-day Peruvians indigenous, European, African and Eastern traces are to be found (PromPeru, 2018). *La República del Perú* is the birthplace of one of the first and most influential American civilizations: the Incas. Their empire extended to most of South America until the conquest by the Spaniards. Which resulted in a fusion of indigenous and Spanish culture that has influenced the country's art, mindset and even business behaviour (Favale, n.d.).

Peru is located in the western and central part of South America. Although Peru's official language is Spanish, Quechua (an indigenous language) is mostly used in the central and southern highland regions and is therefore considered the second tongue (Blácido, 2016). In Peru, language and communication are highly valued. Furthermore, long-term relationships play an important role and are key to successful business and social interactions (Ogliastri & Salcedo, 2018). Peru is rich in natural resources, which has led to a strong mining industry. In addition, the natural beauty of the country attracts an increasing number of tourists, bolstering the tourism sector. Another large sector is agriculture, resulting in Peru being one of the main suppliers of blueberries worldwide. Peruvians are very fond of food, and it is one of their important sources of pride. Peru's culinary revival embraces the country's modern and ancient gastronomic components (Pollan, 2018).

How the Peruvians characterise leaders

Peru has endured a lack of irreproachable public leaders over the last twenty years. To illustrate this point, former President of Peru, Alberto Fujimori ended up in prison convicted of criminal charges and corruption during his term in charge. It appears that the present political culture in Peru demotivates the Peruvians. Due to a lack of ethical leadership, subordinates have little confidence in potential leaders and their promises (Daly & Navas, 2015).

However, Peruvian mentality is changing. Access to training related to management and leadership has improved significantly. Hopefully, this will influence new leaders to come to light (Sanchez, 21 September 2018).
According to research conducted through the Esan University of Lima, there appears to be a noticeable connection between good leadership and the results of an organisation, since the concepts and activities linked to leadership create value in a company. According to Calderón, a leader manages to influence another person positively or negatively based on his or her skills and abilities; a leader is the engine, the person who is able to make a group achieve its maximum potential (Calderón, 15 October 2018).
Peruvians tend to turn a business relationship into a friendship, which is an ability that generates trust, an important leadership characteristic (Michiels, 19 September 2018). It is also an attribute that might have a positive impact for future leaders and for the population, to restore its belief in good leadership.

Survey results and what local respondents say

Our survey on Peruvian leadership accumulated over 75 responses from local and experienced professionals in Peru. First of all, Peruvians rate efficiency high. When it comes to a deadline, Peruvians will try their utmost to get the job done on time. Over 70 per cent of the respondents strongly agree that missing a deadline is seen as a failure, while merely one-sixth has the opposite opinion.
In order to enhance work efficiency, some people insist that competition is a trusted way to achieve goals. The majority of the participants believe that competition contributes to improved results, which in turn makes the workplace in Peru more active and competitive. Whereas nine per cent of Peruvian respondents seem to be opposed to internal competition.
Secondly, the larger part of the respondents admits that there is gender inequality in the workplace. On respondent sums it up as follows: *"Women have more family-type leadership than men"* (CCBS Survey, 2018), which results in a large difference between male and female leaders, not only in the status or situation but also in the way they lead a team. Finally, the way of addressing a manager proves that the relationship between employers and employees is changing and becoming more flexible and easy-going. In this survey, the mass majority of the employees are allowed to address their leader by his or her first name. One of the respondents, who is employed in a branch of Regulatory Affairs and Quality Assurance gives her supplementary explanation: *"Sobre todo en empresas transnacionales existe mucho el trato horizontal. En cambio, en*

empresas familiares peruanas, mayormente los empleados se dirigen con un 'señor' o 'señora' a sus lideres". According to the respondent, there are two options depending on whether it is a family business or not. Transnational companies tend to have a lot of horizontal treatment. In contrast, in Peruvian family businesses, employees address their leaders mostly as 'lord' or 'lady'.

Local leadership analysis

In-country literature review

In the study *The Influence of Personality Domains and Working Experience in Peruvian Managers' Leadership Styles: An Initial Study*, Fernando A. D'Alessio (2009), from the University of Phoenix, investigates the relationship that exists between the five personality domains, working experience and the three leadership styles of 500 managerial MBA students of leading business schools in Peru. An interesting factor of his study is that it has been conducted in already developed countries, but not yet in a developing country, such as Peru. D'Alessio focusses on how the aforementioned factors, influences leadership in Peru and the preliminary conclusions of the study indicate that life and work experience could play a role in the development of leadership behaviours. In addition, he states that certain personality domains are more influential, such as openness to experiences, and suggests that this domain should be looked into in more detail (D'Alessio, 2009). Professor Rolando Luque Mogrovejo (2015) comments in *Conferencia: Liderazgo político: el gran lector, la institucionalidad y la traición* about the complicated Peruvian political leadership and what influences the people who assume the role as leaders. He further discusses the manner in which they endeavour to achieve or fail to deliver. He points out the importance of those leaders who are indeed successful, their ability to function in a weak institution and how some leaders ignore the ideals that got them to office in the first place. Professor José Luis López Follegatti (2015) continues the point of leaders going against the ideals they propagated in *Conferencia: Liderazgo y sociedad en el Perú de hoy*. Instead, he proposes that there is a need for a powerful leader that would not change ideals due to a sudden change nor inconveniences, but would stick to them in the good and bad. Professor Follegatti mentions the huge social gaps in various sectors and economic progress hindered by corruption as the cause of some of the present problems. In conclusion, the work of both Mogrovejo and Follegatti provide a more detailed view of the political problems, which might give outsiders a better understanding of the current issues.

Lydia Arbaiza: a Peruvian leadership scholar

For this study, Lydia Arbaiza has been interviewed. She is a Peruvian Professor in Leadership and Organizational Behaviour, and Strategic Management at Harvard University. Over the past eight years, she has managed the direction of the institutional programmes for State and NGOs at Esan University. Professor Arbaiza has published seven books and contributed to numerous academic journals. To begin with, she expresses her personal views of the current Peruvian manager. She states, *"A Peruvian leader is the one who has a lot of facility to adapt to face complex contexts and is a person who exercises leadership in a flexible way"* (Arbaiza, 19 October 2018). As Peru is a developing and growing country, many management models are challenged to adapt and adjust themselves to the ever-changing circumstances. In her publications about how the leadership in Peru is changing, she points out that if there were a change in leadership, there might also be a change in the economy of the country. In addition, she proposes, in some detail, the tools she considers necessary to successfully lead a team. For example, great negotiating skills create conviction, and efficient ways on how to systemise and speed up work motivate team members to reach their goals. Additionally, she mentions that there has been significant progress, with the work on gender issues in Peru up to the present time. As a result, there now are more female managers rising up through the ranks. Fairness and equal opportunity are becoming an essential part of recruitment for middle and higher management (Arbaiza, 19 October 2018).

Pablo Lavado: former Vice-Minister and Economist

Pablo Lavado is a renowned Peruvian Economist and is a Professor of Economics at the Postgraduate school at Pacific University. He was also appointed as Vice-Minister of Services and Health.

In the interview we conducted, Professor Lavado emphasised the importance of trust in the Peruvian culture and its role in leadership and business. During the interview, he was asked whether trust is a major asset when doing business in Peru, to which he seems to agree. Lavado mentions that Peruvians are considered friendly, nice and welcoming when interacting, but when doing business this stance changes. To such an extent that distrust amongst new business partners is quite common, which implies that trust is not given easily. Therefore, he emphasises the high value of trust, meaning that much effort has to be put into gaining and establishing it. This is why he believes that creating trust when doing business in Peru is a good asset, especially due to the scarcity of it. Furthermore, when asked what the three vital things are to run a successful team in Peru, he lists (i) respectfulness, (ii) identifying each member's skill and (iii) knowing where and when to push your team or let them rest instead. Regarding the first point, respectfulness, this includes respecting the leader not just because of personal capabilities but also on how he or she treats and interacts with their subordinates. Respect should be mutual and will entail trust and confidence within the leader. Secondly, identifying the individual skills of each member will make a more efficient and well-organised team, by bringing out the highest capabilities in all of them. Finally, knowing when to let the team rest is important as well. This can occur, for example, by organising social events where the team can relax a little. This can also raise morale, which will help them to keep up the work they are doing, and it will let the team know that they are appreciated. Such activity will support the creation of trust and make the bond with the team stronger rather than just keeping the relations on a professional basis only (Lavado, 2 November 2018).

In-country leadership best seller

One of the best-selling books about leadership was written by the above-mentioned Lydia Arbaiza in 2017 and is called *Liderazgo y comportamiento organizacional* (Leadership and organisational behaviour). The book discusses leadership competencies and how to apply best-practices according to the characteristics and culture of an organisation. It is also noteworthy for highlighting key points in ensuring workers' welfare and anticipating issues which could impact on the employees' quality of life as well as job performance.

Local leadership book	
Title	*Liderazgo y comportamiento organizacional*
Subtitle	-
Author	Lydia Arbaiza
Publisher	Esan
Year	2017
ISBN	978-612-411-066-5

Peruvian leadership YouTube review

In the video, *Manejar Equipos de Alto Rendimiento*, Cesar Gamio gives a lecture on his experiences with leadership in Peru. In order to be a successful manager in Peru, it is important to define the goals of the company someone works for. Besides knowing the vision and mission of the company, it is crucial to define the specific goals of the group of employees as well. After the goals are defined, it is up to the manager to make sure everybody knows their own tasks and responsibilities. There appear to be three elements that define a manager. The first element is to have the skills and ability to do the job. The second element is to be realistic, to cope with the ups and downs. The final element is reliability, to be able to deliver on what has been agreed (Gamio, 2018).

In the video, *Los retos del liderazgo en una sociedad diversa y compleja como el Perú*, Alberto de Belaunde (2018) gives an address based on his experiences with leadership in Peru. De Belaunde is a lawyer and is one of Peru's youngest congressmen. He mentions that Peru is a conservative country and that this can influence the position of a Peruvian leader. The leading party, which is not the party of Alberto de Belaunde, has the majority. In the current culture, the leading party are the ones that make the final decision because of majority vote. Alberto points this out as a lack in the culture of leadership for a democratic country like Peru. He explains how to cope with frustration, and he points out that dealing with it is a key part of good leadership. Through experience Alberto self-learned two things regarding good leadership. Firstly, after working hard with a team for years and reaching a point where it actually starts moving forward, one may find that the reality is that you go two steps back. To reduce this relapse, it is important that leaders are always ready to defend to keep what they have and always develop further. Secondly, he experienced that it is easy to develop a cynical approach to employees. When there are problems and frustrations, it is hard for a leader to deal with. The dangerous thing about this is that it can increase cynicism. This can change your leadership approach in a bad way. He saw this happen a lot in the congress. The danger of getting cynical is that people forget the ideals and ambitions which got them in their position at the first place (De Belaunde, 2018).

Understanding hierarchy in Peru

Surprisingly, the hierarchy in Peru can be traced back to the Incan empire. Traces of this great civilisation are still noticeable in the present society. With globalisation and the dramatic emergence of the modern society, highly dissymmetric power relations fuelled unprecedented capital accumulation in Europe (Salas, 2012). Since Peru's history cannot be detached from the history of European colonialism, it is possible to see in modern Peruvian society, the effects of racism and nationalism. Initially, people in Peru were divided into different classes out of respect for their traditional values. One's power depended on someone's skills and wealth. People's loyalty to their leaders was derived from their deep trust in a leader's ability and moral quality. In addition to this, also the actual size of an organisation plays a role in the power play in Peru. It appears that large organisations tend to be more hierarchal and centralised than small organisations (Vargas, 14 October 2018). Regarding the hierarchy of the workplace, as mentioned before, the majority of the survey respondents strongly agree with the point that employees have to follow the established procedures, while only a few respondents believe that they still have some independence (CCBS Survey, 2018). Lastly, it is worth noting that leadership preferences in Peru are very much people-oriented, which is consistent with the literature review mentioned earlier.

How the Peruvians achieve leadership empathy

Peru is a relationship-oriented country. Strong informal and intrapersonal commitments are an essential part of business ethics in the Latin-American country. One should bear in mind that trust is a very important factor for Peruvians when it comes to empathy. As one of our survey respondents points out, *"Existe mucha empatía en muchos líderes en mi país, considero que la empatía permite consolidar equipos sacando lo mejor de cada miembro"* (CCBS Survey, 2018), which means it is generally believed in Peru, that empathy is an excellent tool used to build trust and close relationships. This applies when enhancing the efficiency of the whole team. In other words, Peruvians wish for leadership to be people-oriented and want their leaders to be able to collaborate well with their group members. In addition, Tim McIntosh, after having 28 years of working experience in Peru, claims in his book *How Peruvians define and practice leadership* that: *"responsibility for teams' effectiveness is not on the leader's shoulders but shared by the group. Final decisions should be left to the group and that the leader should view the group as a collective team"* (McIntosh, 2011). This is also why characteristics like transparency, being humble, setting an example and integrity are essential for leaders in Peru to succeed. All interactions and traits stated above all play into trust, in Peru. A leader can develop empathy with his team *"when managers can identify with the workers"* (Arbaiza, 19 October 2018). In general, leadership is very much associated with the character of the individual in question. If the managers are driven by self-interest, this would create distrust within the team. However, in Peru there have been numerous people in positions of power, who have favoured their own interests instead of the interest of the group or organisation in the past. Peruvian leaders commonly delegate authority incorrectly, by giving important decisions to unqualified personnel, which helps to serve the few rather than the majority and creates a conflict of interest (McIntosh, 2011).

Portugal

Martijn Atwater, Tiago Cabrita, Vania Vargas, Michel Bouman & Michael Spiegelhoff

Portugal, located in south-west Europe, bordered by Spain on the east and the Atlantic Ocean to the west, was founded in 1139. While this date does not necessarily place it among the ancient civilizations of this world, Portugal did not suffer from ever-changing borders like many other nations. Furthermore, the nation played a primary role during the Age of Discovery with its strong navy and famous *conquistadores* (Rodrigues & Devezas, 2007). The actions of both were immortalized by the words of the poet Luís Vaz de Camões: "*...Por mares nunca antes navegados passaram ainda além da Taprobana [...] E entre gente remota edificaram Novo Reino, que tanto sublimaram*" (...Between seas never sailed before they have passed beyond Taprobana [...] and among strangers built the New Kingdom, which they praise so much) (Camões, 1572). Portugal's influence can still be felt in the world today as Portuguese is the official language in seven countries, and the now Chinese territory of Macau and the Goa region in India (CPLP, 2018).
The predominant religion is Roman Catholicism with the mass majority of the population identifying as such. Portugal has been part of the European Union since the mid-eighties, and the national currency is the Euro. Being hit heavily by the most recent financial crisis, Portugal has seen increasing wealth levels and reducing unemployment figures for the past decade, outperforming countries like France and Finland (Instituto Nacional de Estatística, 2018; Statista, 2018). The leading sectors include a buoyant tourism industry, financial services and telecommunications while Portugal is the single largest cork producer in the world. Portugal's main trade partners are Spain, Germany and France. Portugal, however, is best known for its export products: Cristiano Ronaldo, port wine, *pastéis de Belém* and sunbathed beaches.

How the Portuguese characterise leaders

Before setting off to identify the main characteristics of Portuguese leaders, it is important to determine the cultural profile of the country. According to the findings in the GLOBE project, Portugal scores high on power distance, in-group collectivism and gender egalitarianism. Hofstede's (2001) high power distance score of Portugal indicates a high acceptance of the hierarchical order. High in-group collectivism is determined as the level of preference for closely-knit relations with unquestioning loyalty. Moreover, family affection, which so often is linked to south European countries, is confirmed, as Portuguese culture is extremely *afiliativo,* affiliative, and shows a low task-orientation (Alberto & Ferreira, 2007). This family affection is strongly affirmed by the survey results as more than 80 per cent of the respondents believe a manager is obligated to spend time on the well-being of the employees (CCBS Survey, 2018). Gender egalitarianism or *igualdade de género* holds significance in Portuguese society as mentioned in the GLOBE studies by Jorge Correia Jesuino (2008).

Based on the study conducted by João Alberto and Alexandre Ferreira (2007) for the *Universidade de Aveiro*, Portuguese culture shows low levels of assertiveness and is in the feminine dimension with a preference for quality of life, modesty and cooperation trumping achievement, material rewards and heroism in daily life. The two researchers also characterise the exceptional Portuguese leader as an inspirational figure, who is firmly attached to the team. This characterisation is also supported by the research of Maria da Costa Gonçalves (2008). In later research, it was concluded that the Portuguese lean towards a transactional leadership style. Wilson Gomes, EMEA Marketing Director and licensed at Harvard Business School, notes the importance of technical expertise for a leader. However, he demotes it to second in rank of importance as he believes the need of developing relationships with subordinates is more important than any other dimension or characteristic (Gomes, 2 November 2018). A leader in Portugal is diplomatic and cooperative, as well as a visionary with a hands-on attitude, often engaging with the team in administrative work. Modesty, pro-efficiency, conflict avoidance and auto-sacrifice are additional lower-tier traits appreciated by the Portuguese in their leaders (Alberto & Ferreira, 2007).

Survey results and what local respondents say

More than hundred Portuguese respondents filled in the CCBS survey. After analysing its data, there seems to be a large discrepancy between the different sectors in the country. As Pedro Tavares, a communication director and advisor to the Minister of Justice, notes, compared to the private sectors, governmental organisations adhere to the common theory and hierarchy: *"In many organisations, particularly Government, it's still a traditional leadership"*

(CCBS Survey, 2018). This statement is further highlighted by the comments from Maria Luísa Aldim, a consultant, who in her opinion believes that leadership models are globalising aided by social networks and digitalisation. The gap between the private and public sector can be explained by analysing the answers to the question if employees are expected to always follow procedures. Not surprisingly, close to 60 per cent found this to be true, while the other 40 per cent believe there is freedom to deviate from procedures (CCBS Survey, 2018). Secondly, while Jesuino (2008) found that gender egalitarianism holds significance, the respondents are divided about the chances for female staff to ascend to senior leadership positions. The camps are split into a group of 40 per cent who believe they do have an equal opportunity, while another 40 per cent believes this is not true. The remaining 20 per cent do not have a particular opinion on the matter and remains neutral. Furthermore, when asked if there is a style difference between men and women, Pedro Osório, an international business manager, argues that *"in some cases, women tend to be bossier, probably to show they are in charge due to their repressed personality"* (CCBS Survey, 2018). At the same time, a health services professional states that *"women have higher management skills and are better listeners because of the obstacles they had to climb to get to the top"* (CCBS Survey, 2018).
Lastly, the majority of the respondents agree that important meetings have to take place in the morning between 9:00 and 11:00. At the same time, about 40 per cent feel it is okay to confront staff during staff meetings to obtain targeted results. Moreover, more than 60 per cent of the leaders is open to criticism during meetings while just over 10 per cent believe this has to take place in a more indirect manner outside of meetings (CCBS Survey, 2018).

Local leadership analysis

In-country literature review

According to Milton Jorge Correia de Sousa and Dirk van Dierendonck, a leadership style that is gaining traction within Portugal is Servant Leadership. Accountability, stewardship, authenticity along with *"humility and standing-back"* can be critical in inducing the engagement-related feelings of vigour within high uncertainty conditions (Jorge Correia de Sousa & Van Dierendonck, 2014).
A case study by Maria da Graça Câmara Batista and her colleagues Furtado and Silva show how leadership is crucial in employee retention (Furtado, Batista & Silva, 2011). The authors believe that through different leadership behaviour and

the various expressions of styles such as persuading and sharing along with adaptability improves the staff retention rates.
Leadership is challenging enough; leading leaders poses its additional challenges according to Gomes and Yasin (2013). They conducted a study among project managers and found that the most common trait among these leaders were organisational skills and strategic thinking. However, there is also a minority that prefers features such as the desire for power, being individualistic and accepting the flow of others. However, both groups advocate for accountability, which is an aspect of being an effective leader (Gomes & Yasin, 2013).
Looking at traits for leadership, within Portugal, there is no greater example of charismatic leadership then Francisco de Sá Carneiro. Author José Pedro Zúquete in his paper *The flight of the eagle: The charismatic leadership of Sá Carneiro in Portugal's transition to democracy* reviews Sá Carneiro's influence on modern-day politics throughout his career. Zúquete analyses major aspects of Sá Carneiro's leadership style and, in particular, the development of the charismatic dynamics between the leader and his supporters through the 1970's (Zúquete, 2011).

Bernardo Almada-Lobo: professor at Porto University

Combining master's and PhD studies at Porto University, TU Eindhoven in the Netherlands, as well as MIT in Cambridge, USA, Dr Almada-Lobo carries vast experience in the field of leadership in Portugal. He notes that the way leaders share feedback in Portugal should be considered as this method is sometimes even used as a way of generating empathy with their teams to increase performance efficiency. Almada-Lobo remarks on this topic: "*whenever I'm criticising someone in a nice way, I'm raising the bar*" (2 November 2018). Furthermore, he emphasises the importance of setting up a plan, communicating clear deadlines, evaluating the time required and guiding the employee towards the agreed upon goal with a focus on how the manager can be of assistance. Additionally, Almada-Lobo further analyses how sharing feedback must be tailored to the current business environment, where multiple generations come together, and millennials begin to climb the leadership ladder. Moreover, the professor notes the uniqueness of each one of these millennials and how they are the organisation, instead of being part of the organisation. Lastly, it is important to realise that one approach does not fit all employees of an organisation and requires a personalised management style. To this end, Almada-Lobo notes that "*Transparency, rigorousness and pragmatism are important values [...]. In academia or research institutes the intellectual part of your job is also crucial; in those situations, people that are being led by you need to be convinced by your power of intellect"* (Almada-Lobo, 2 November 2018).

Wilson Gomes: a Portuguese marketing and communications specialist

Wilson Gomes has diverse cross-cultural work experience. He combines an engineering degree with a top-ranked General Management Program MBA from Harvard Business School. Gomes has leadership experience in Spain and Portugal and currently holds the position of EMEA Director of Marketing for Leica Biosystems. *"To be an effective leader, you have to invest time in developing the right relationship"* (Gomes, 2 November 2018). Gomes reflects on what makes a typical Portuguese leader; however, there are traits that he does not like about the Portuguese leadership style *"I found it to be quite rigid, formal and sometimes everything was complicated, or 'é complicado', as the Portuguese say"* (Gomes, 2 November 2018).

According to Gomes, this formality can be traced back to the way some professors treat their students, for example, by setting themselves far above the students. They provide the students with class material and expect them to read it without further guidance up until the exam: *"you have ten books, read them, show up for the exam, it is your problem"* (Gomes, 2 November 2018).

Nonetheless, he does see change coming as the younger generation is presented with more options in the work field and do not want or accept that the hierarchy is strictly top-down.

Lastly, he has some advice for young Portuguese students and professionals who aspire to become business leaders: *"Go abroad, travel extensively [...], you will be more visible to diversity and will understand better how to work more effectively with people"* (Gomes, 2 November 2018).

In-country leadership best seller

One of the best-selling books about leadership in Portugal was written by Odete Fachada in 2014 and is called *Liderança - A prática da liderança, a liderança na prática* (Leadership - the practice of leadership, leadership in practice). The writer studied psychology and is currently the director of *Odete Fachada Consultores, Lda.* Concurrently, she provides leadership training in Portugal as well as in countries like Brazil, Argentina, Guinea and Angola.

Local leadership book	
Title	*Liderança*
Subtitle	A Prática da Liderança A Liderança na Prática
Author	Odete Fachada
Publisher	Edições Sílabo
Year	2015
ISBN	978-972-618-777-6

Portuguese leadership YouTube review

To have a strong influence on people, leaders in Portugal should be able to win the hearts of the employees. There are various ways to achieve this goal, such as being an accessible leader, who is open for conversing with employees from all layers of the organisation. Furthermore, Portuguese leaders should be able to know how to listen to their employees. Listening is required to pick up pointers on project execution and receive feedback by captivatingly listening. When a leader uses this feedback and empowers the employee to execute on these ideas the chances of him or her winning peoples' hearts is increased significantly. A Portuguese leader should entrust his or her people with his or her knowledge and trust them with the execution of essential tasks. A good leader should also praise subordinates and to celebrate success (Monteiro, 2018).

As discussed by Caio Carneiro (2018), something that describes exemplary Portuguese leadership is the willingness to share all knowledge that the leader possesses with his or her followers. The best way to develop people is not to just be loud about personal accomplishments, but for leaders to show and share how they have become the leaders that they are today (Carneiro, 2018). All of these features combined can help to ensure a leader's position, and his or her coaching will elevate a group to reach a higher level of professionalism and achieve the mission of each company (Cortella, 2016).

Understanding hierarchy in Portugal

The main characteristic of business culture in Portugal is a relationship-based tradition. Unfortunately, bureaucracy is massive in Portugal, and thus conducting business relies heavily on interpersonal relationships to secure proper introductions and long-term goodwill (Lewis, 2006). These findings seem to be confirmed by Pedro Tavares, a communications director and advisor to the Minister of Justice who states: *"many organisations, particularly Government, it is still a traditional leadership, too hierarchical"* (CCBS Survey, 2018).
The *vínculo familiar,* or family-bond, has never faded over the centuries and remains as one of the core values for most Portuguese. These beliefs echo through in business, as Gomes put it: *"We are all a result of our circumstances, but I need to understand what those circumstances are. It allows you to understand better how people work, what drives them, how you can motivate them, it allows you to identify if they are going through a tough time"* (Gomes, 2 November 2018). The values are shaped by a strong patriarchy and the unmistakable influence of the *igreja católico romano* (Roman Catholic church). Moreover, the church did not only influence peoples' private lives, but also helped shape the hierarchical structure of Portuguese organisations, which is still visible today as age and seniority, or *antiguidade,* are highly respected. However, in recent years there has been a movement away from certain seniority criteria and, according to Maria do Rosário Palma Ramalho, the *"dismissal due to the elimination of work positions"* (*despedimento por extinção do posto de trabalho*) became easier (do Rosário Palma Ramalho, 2013).
Portuguese staff expects leadership and guidance from their superiors. Professor Almada-Lobo indicates that employees need feedback and clear guidance. Even if they are confident enough, they want a leader guiding them and helping them to understand how they can improve themselves (Almada-Lobo, 2 November 2018). Moreover, independent decision-making is not often seen, and staff members are given a distinct role (Franco & Gonçalo Matos, 2013). Additionally, the Portuguese corporate culture may be described as a *família*, with the leader being seen as a father figure combining the practices of attachment with subordination. However, compared with its peers Spain, France and Belgium (the Latin European cluster) (Ronen & Shenkar, 1985) the Portuguese results are moderate with employees reporting their organisation as flat rather than tall regarding hierarchy (Globe, 2007). At the same time, over 50 per cent of the respondents feel it is mandatory, or at least required at a regular rate, to address leaders according to titles or positions and just under 40 per cent

state it is necessary to use the surname rather than the first name of their leaders or *líderes* (CCBS Survey, 2018).

How the Portuguese achieve leadership empathy

First and foremost, a team recognises and appreciates a leader that is competent and knowledgeable. This is reflected in the survey results where organisational experience and technical competence are given as the primary qualities required for a leader (CCBS Survey, 2018). This will allow him or her to achieve a high-status position within that group. Additionally, the ability to support and communicate with the group can be extremely efficient when trying to gain their empathy, since the leader in Portugal is also a paternal figure which employees turn to in case of uncertainty. Professor Almada-Lobo points out *"The way you are able to communicate and understand your team beyond just the rational speech, being able to understand their emotions, can cause a positive impact in the business relationship"* (Almada-Lobo, 2 November 2018).

Furthermore, a Portuguese leader is more successful if he or she shows compassion towards the subordinates' professional and personal affairs, displaying truthful concern for their well-being (Globe, 2007). Additionally, according to the CCBS survey, more than 80 per cent of the respondents feel that a manager should actively spend time on the well-being of team members and more than 60 per cent do not feel they need to keep distance to maintain respect (CCBS Survey, 2018). This feminine attitude leads to an increase in commitment and accountability towards their tasks.
Such leader-subordinate relationships arise from high trust and friendship among the team members, as well as from mutual respect, stability and the clear communication of realistic goals and expectations. Gomes (2 November 2018) notes the importance of authenticity, passion and caring towards employees. Moreover, Alberto and Ferreira found in their study that the emotional involvement of a leader in his or her team proves to be efficient (2007).

The research by Alberto and Ferreira (2007) also supports the findings in the psychological analysis performed by Correia Jesuíno, Gouveia Pereira and Antero Reto (1993). They found that independently of the gender of the respondent, the most appreciated traits in a leader are competence, planning and organisation; support, consideration for the employee and acceptance; and communication and clarity of roles and objectives. Personality and fairness are traits which are also appreciated; however, they fall into a secondary plan (Alberto & Ferreira, 2007). The findings of Alberto and Ferreira are confirmed by the results from the survey, where traits such as competence, visionary and charismatic, expertise, and consensus or compromising scored high. As Luis Francisco, a general manager in the tourism sector, comments, it is important to have leaders *"that care for people"* (CCBS Survey, 2018).

Considering the ever rapidly evolving world of business, it is crucial for a leader to be flexible enough to understand and adapt to a new environment, as well as to constantly challenge the beliefs and attitudes towards team motivation and engagement (Almada-Lobo, 2 November 2018).

Senegal

Ties Visser, Dave Dekker, Leon Zeeuw, Kieran Taylor & Jeremy Alberts

Senegal owes its name to the Senegal River, which forms its borders to the east and the north. This West African country has a population of over 16.5 million. The CFA-Frank is used throughout Senegal and is also used in twelve of the former French colonies – and in one Spanish and Portuguese colony (Visser & Tolhurst, 2010). Senegal includes many ethnic groups and has no fewer than eleven national languages. Although Wolof and Fula are mainly used as spoken languages, Senegal's written language is predominantly French. This French influence started four centuries ago when the French established a trading post in Senegal and intensified when it became a French colony in 1854 (Carnes, 2012). Through the centuries, Senegal has a tragic history of slavery, which forcibly removed over thirty million West Africans from the continent. Something that concerned the strong and hardworking middle-class population and slavery negatively influenced the country's development. According to the United Nations Development Program, more than one-third of the population is still living below the poverty line in Senegal (Human Development Reports, n.d.). The country nevertheless is known to be one of the safest countries in Africa (Telegraph Travel, 2017). Religion is an important element in Senegalese culture, with 90 per cent of the population identifying as Muslim (Visser & Tolhurst, 2010). A perhaps related aspect of the culture is *hospitality*. The Senegalese population even believes this to be a national trait. For instance, Senegal's national football team is known as the *Lions of Teranga*, which means the 'protectors of hospitality' (Fenton, 2016).

How the Senegalese characterise leaders

In Senegal, employees generally believe that their superiors have been chosen for their position because of experience and subject knowledge. As in other hierarchical cultures, managers often adopt a more paternalistic attitude towards their employees. Leaders may demonstrate concern for an employee's well-being that actually goes beyond the workplace. There is no clear dividing line between work and private life.

Thioune (18 October 2018) puts this more clearly: *"you can be the best leader in the world but if you come to Africa you have to understand the social behaviour and the social mindset."* This is essential if you desire to be a successful leader in Senegal as a good leader should be involved if his or her employees may have an issue in their work or even a family issue. *"It is all about being a social partner. As a leader, you want to be recognised as almost a family member"* (Thioune, 18 October 2018).

In Senegal, people frequently speak using hints and allusions. Thus, leaders in Senegal are expected to use implicit or diplomatic communication. To give an example: making direct eye contact during a greeting or throughout conversation could brand someone as being arrogant. For this reason, the Senegalese tend to lower their gaze while in conversation, especially when speaking with someone that is more senior than themselves, whether in age or position. Senegal has inherited French commercial traditions and legal procedures. Leaders will respect a person if they have a high title and if it is displayed prominently on a business card. Gold embossed business cards are highly regarded, for instance.

Survey results and what local respondents say

Senegalese employees tend to break rules when things begin to become urgent. This is due to the fact that planning is not very common in Senegal. Rules are rarely found in many business sectors. *"Things are very loose and sometimes done purposely, in order to keep people adaptable"* (CCBS Survey, 2018). Rules are constantly changing in Senegal to whatever is convenient for the business or its employees. A CCBS survey respondent affirms this: *"Employees usually break the rules when things get urgent because of a lack of forecasting or planning"* (2018). Deadlines are often missed due to this issue, and in fact, it is expected that tasks will not be completed on time.

The survey shows that a *"certain part of the population is not ready to understand and agree to be evaluated upon their performance and get a matching function"*. Senegalese expect to receive promotion based on their seniority at a company and on how they are perceived by colleagues rather than their performance. The survey also shows that once a leader's business is fully functioning, *"[he] or she tends not to be there, daily operation of the business is left to a partner or associate"* (CCBS Survey, 2018). However, when the business owner is present, it is usually for short periods of time, and this time is normally used for quick back to back meetings. As stated by a consultant, and managing director in Dakar (16 October 2018), it is not uncommon for a leader to be working from elsewhere, whether this may be abroad or at the comfort of his own home. *"The most important thing is to get the job done"* (Thioune, 18 October 2018).

Local leadership analysis

In-country literature review

Leaders in Senegal can be described as having an ability to set a clear goal, put mechanisms in place to meet it and the determination to get people to join this goal (Oumar Fedior, 2014; Financial Afrik, 2014).

The Senegalese tend to use 'soft power' to achieve leadership towards different cultures (Bodian & Kelly, 2018). This can be explained as *"non-material capabilities such as reputation, culture, and value appeal that can aid the attainment of a state's objectives"* (Viotti & Kauppi, 2013, p. 207).

According to "La chronique du Coach Kader", teams in Senegal prefer to be led by someone who has the ability to listen. On the other hand, criticising colleagues is not appreciated and not easily forgiven (Wade, 2016). They prefer a leader who cares for the employees like they are part of their family.

Business in Senegal is hierarchical; however, open-minded supervisors can also be found. Some younger and more upcoming leaders, who have studied abroad, utilise a less hierarchical leadership style and understand that others can come up with good ideas. However, this might clash with the traditional style. *"What you have to understand is there are two different working styles in Senegal, one of which is very traditional. The second is young people who have experience in France, United States or in Canada and they have a different mindset"* (Thioune, 18 October 2018). If there is a conflict in the company, it can often get out of control. This is due to the fact that there is a lack of respect between the two styles of leadership. For example, Thioune notes that: *"[i]n the newer style of leadership, family and brotherhood is not as important"* (18 October 2018).

Mamadou Khabib Salla: a Senegalese leadership scholar

An interview with a Senegalese businessman living in Dakar. He is a consultant at business cabinet CEREP, and president of an NGO, Afrique Solidarité. He has been leading five businesses and has several degrees in management and entrepreneurship. In addition, Salla has also written leadership modules and methods. These are available in Africa, and Salla teaches his courses to people wanting to start their own enterprise. During an interview, Salla shared his experience with Senegalese leadership.

Salla explains that it is important for a good leader to gain experience in all kinds of fields, in order to build a leadership style that is adaptable in any area of work: *"You must be able to work with any person and lead them easily in the right way desired,"* and to this end, *"leadership is achieved by experience acquired from different fields"* (Salla, 14 October 2018). This view is echoed by another expert that was interviewed for this study, Thioune (18 October 2018). Experience and understanding your employee as well as having a good relationship is key to being a good leader in Senegal.

More young, upcoming people can be found leading a team. However, these are mainly the well-educated ones, with again the aforementioned experience. Women can be found in any kind of field, which is a major difference from ten years ago. *"We have great and well-educated women running enterprises, doing business, travelling around the world, giving courses, speaking at conferences, forums and representing our country"* (Salla, 14 October 2018). In some cases, women are even preferred for leadership roles over men. Some difficulties can arise for leaders if they have to lead a new team of people, due to trust issues. Trust is a very important aspect in Senegal, as mentioned before, and team members and employees need to know that they can trust in their leader's capabilities. Sharing information between men and women will only be a problem for a traditional leadership style, but as a whole, Senegal is moving forward and everyone is becoming equal, according to Salla (14 October 2018).

A Senegalese cross-cultural trainer

Our source is a consultant, co-founder and managing director of a company that helps people to conduct business in Senegal. The company specialises in helping expats to settle in and understand the country's culture, and also offers cultural training. In a Skype interview, the (anonymous) consultant shared experience on typical Senegalese leadership traits.

Deadlines tend to be very flexible in Senegal: *"Deadlines don't really exist"* (16 October 2018), and when they are set, they are rarely adhered to. Senegalese get started on a task when they have the time for it. There are many factors involved, and this is the main reason why Senegalese cannot give an accurate time of completion. There are even expressions in the local Wolof language: *"It's done, when it's done, when you rush you will end up making the wrong decision"* (16 October 2018). This makes it difficult for foreign businesses to come to do business in Senegal.

Traditional leaders usually are not in the office since they are usually busy gaining external contacts for the company. This makes a leader more of a figurehead. The supervisor at the office will then be the one in charge of daily business in the office. When the leader is in the office, a lot of people will want to meet with him or her, and it will prove difficult to schedule a meeting. Meetings will last around fifteen to thirty minutes with each colleague, and it is a very quick in and out process. In Senegal, there is no open-door policy; the door to the office of the person in charge will usually be closed. *"You can't just come in, even if it's urgent and even sometimes you knock and they don't answer and that just means they don't want to see you"* (16 October 2018).

In-country leadership bestseller

A book recommended to us by bookshop *Librairie Aux Vents*, located in Dakar, is *Le Top Manager.* It is one of the best-selling local books on leadership, written by author Madou Sylla. Madou is the founder of Prime Dash and affiliate companies. Prior to this, Sylla was the CEO at Systems and Solutions International Group (SSIG), a management consulting firm. Sylla holds a Bachelor of Science in Economics from Shepard University and a Master's in Business Administration (MBA) from Marshall University (Sylla, 2017). Published in July 2013, the book offers an insight into the business world, helping its readership to conquer challenges that all leaders face.

Local leadership book	
Title	*Le Top Manager*
Subtitle	Systèmes & État D'esprit pour diriger avec succès
Author	Madou Sylla
Publisher	Adolé Akpabie
Year	2017
ISBN	978-0692898512

Senegalese leadership YouTube review

Most Senegalese leadership YouTube videos are available in French. Mademba Aliou Fall (2017) talks about leadership from the perspective of the Senegalese army. Senegal, as a whole, is known for developing leadership at junior ranks and then working their way up through the army. In the seventies, the army began to change its leadership style to start working from the bottom to top leadership. The bottom-up strategy is successful because the top ranks are able to look ahead, leaving the ranks below to manage the ranks below, and so on. *"Bottom-up strategy is very efficient. The boss can be the boss, the workers can be the workers"* (Fall, 2017).

Badou Kane (2014) is a professional speaker from Senegal whose topics include, amongst others, leadership in Senegal. He gives consideration to the concept that leaders are no true leaders unless they have suffered hardship. *"Champions want to quit, losers quit"* (Kane, 2014). This catch-phrase acknowledges that even champions desire to stop, yet they have the endurance and determination to keep going. In the end, what is important is that a person does not quit if he or she ever wants to be a success. Whereas, the so-called losers will quit, simply because they cannot handle the hardship they are experiencing.

Understanding hierarchy in Senegal

Our anonymous source (16 October 2018) explained to us that there are two main leadership styles in Senegal. The traditional style is used mostly by the older generation, 45 and plus. This generation is very much part of the French style which applies a very top-down hierarchy. Under this leadership style, employees do not really ask questions or make suggestions. *"[The leaders] make all the decisions, they sign all the papers, they sign all the cheques, they sign everything and any signature goes straight to the top. They don't delegate very well"* (16 October 2018). The new style is mostly used by leaders under the age of 45 who have often studied abroad in the US or in Europe. These types of leaders have moved away from the top-down hierarchy and are more aware of collective and democratic 'horizontal' leadership styles. According to Hofstede (n.d.), the power distance in Senegal is very high, meaning that everyone is not equal. For example, the less educated expect to be told what to do by people who are better educated. Authority is concentrated in the hands of a few highly-placed people, and older people or 'elders' are held in high regard. Relationships demand an exchange of intimate information at all times. This is essential in the Senegalese culture as it makes it possible to form a bond between people. 'Small talk' before and after meetings is greatly valued and expected. However, when it comes to criticism, it is worth noting that within the Senegalese culture one is not accustomed to discussing problems with someone in public. People instead prefer to be approached in private to discuss the matter in order to avoid humiliation (McDade & Spring, 2005). The Senegalese mostly indicate that misunderstandings originate from insufficient communication. When it comes to communicating with superiors, it is important to avoid constant eye contact as this can be seen as arrogance or a sign or superiority. Dressing professionally is also taken seriously by the Senegalese (Hofstede, n.d.). The 'boubou' is a traditional dress particularly worn on Fridays when going to the mosque.

How the Senegalese achieve leadership empathy

A highly-regarded leader in Senegal will possess a range of different qualities. Problem-solving, open-mindedness and the ability to listen are important characteristics as leaders in Senegal will have many colleagues surrounding them that will come to them for guidance. It is important to have experience in different kinds of fields, as mentioned by Salla (14 October 2018). Senegalese leaders achieve leadership empathy by proving and then maintaining these characteristics (McDade & Spring, 2005). Furthermore, a leader in Senegal achieves leadership empathy by upholding respect for colleagues despite any issues that may exist. Any issues or conflicts would be addressed in private so that it could not be overheard by any other colleagues. Therefore, reiterating the importance of respect displayed by leaders towards their colleagues, which further demonstrates their use of leadership empathy.

When first meeting somebody from Senegal, it is advised to show an interest in the country and culture. Moreover, from a relationship point of view, it will be appreciated when adequate time is taken to inquire about the health and welfare of family members or friends. Senegalese leaders utilise this conversational tool to achieve empathy. It is not uncommon for greetings to last a long period of time; however, greetings and small talk are very important. *"Senegalese leaders manage their employees not hard, but with friendship if they are working the correct way"* (Salla, 14 October 2018). Finally, the Senegalese build strong relationships with whomever they are in contact with, whether it may be a colleague or customer. *"I have to understand the mindset of my colleagues and try to build a confident relationship between us"* (Thioune, 18 October 2018). Therefore, portraying another way in which leadership empathy is achieved.

Korea (Rep. of)

Mohammed el Bouhdifi, Jasmijn van Beekum, Saman Aziz, Kristiane Ochaeta & Jiyeon Seo (서지연)

The Republic of Korea (ROK, South Korea, 대한민국), has rapidly evolved into a modern technological paradise. A place where efficiency thrives in the dance moves of K-pop megastars, to the success of the multinational *chaebols*. Seoul, otherwise known as the city that never sleeps, has garnered a reputation for being alive with activities at any hour of the day. Restaurants, *jjimjilbang* (bathhouses), *noraebang* (karaoke houses) and other establishments are open twenty-four seven. Because of their vibrant lifestyle, Koreans live by the slogan: *pali pali (빨리빨리),* which literally means '*quick-quick*' in English. A coffee break does not exist in the Korean dictionary, but a *toppokki* and a coffee for on the road is a common find.

While the country is three times smaller than its overseas neighbour, Japan, the current population is over fifty million people; with almost half of the population living in one of the five major cities: Seoul, Busan, Incheon, Daegu and Daejeon (Kostat, 2017). That South Korea has changed over the last two decades has been affirmed by Jeong (2015) who notes that South Korea has shown a remarkable economic boom, which has been described as the Miracle of the Han River. After the Second World War, the ROK was one of the poorest countries in the world. However, with governmental interference, economic planning and the cooperation of citizens it overcame its dark period. This so-called 'Asian Tiger' is now one of the largest economies in the world (Kim & Park, 2003).

In recent times, citizens of the ROK have been characterised by a blend of tradition and modernity, which includes eating kimchi, drinking a glass of soju, listening to *k-pop* and looking at their Samsung smartphones while using kakaoTalk *(카카오톡).* In the past decade, the Koreans have been taking a more prominent position in the Western World. Hae-Joang (2005) notes that the 'Korean Wave' (the rapidly growing global interest in Korean culture) is growing every day with the help of technological inventions. Despite this rapid growth, the Korean population still values its old culture, family traditions and being status-conscious.

How South Koreans characterise leaders

South Korean leadership is based on an ongoing commitment to serve the public interest (Jang, 2000). This commitment acts as a moral foundation, which influences the ideals of South Korea's political leaders. Past presidents have focussed their strong leadership skills on the idea of the Korean ethos: hard work and self-reliance (Kwon, Kim, Lee & Yi, 2011).
The prioritisation of public welfare over individual liberties is a testament to South Korea's ongoing commitment and has proven successful with the country having one of the world's leading economies (Kwon et. al, 2011). The Korean ideology for leadership is based on liberal democracy, nationalism and Confucianism (Jang, 2000). The combination of these three elements indicates that Korean people are involved and care for one another. According to Heekyung Jo Min (2015), leaders in South Korea are compared to the head of a family or clan and are viewed as a familial figure by employees. According to Dr Jeong Park (17 October 2018) and Daniel Cho (17 October 2018), qualities that define a good leader include organisational experience, exceptional listening skills and coordination skills. Leadership in South Korea is unique in its use of a top-down management style. In a standard top-down business hierarchy, employees are required to unquestionably obey orders given by their superiors. However, managers in South Korea ensure that their business plans are communicated to each employee and make an effort to convince their subordinates of the viability of each plan (Kim, Lee & Lee, 2013). Mutual trust between the manager and employee is vital to success. This trait is based on the Confucian ideology of *inhwa (융화)*, where employees are expected to remain loyal to their superiors and managers are expected to maintain a certain level of protection and respect (Kim et. al, 2013). However, it is important to note that a leader is sometimes defined as being in the centre of a situation, surrounded by his superiors, colleagues and subordinates, rather than being above them (Baik, Seo, Koo & Kim, 2010). This gives a whole new perspective on how Koreans view leadership. In line with this is the *kibun*. Koreans follow the way of the *kibun (기분)*, which translates to a mood or feeling of balance and good behaviour (Lee, 2011). In the business environment, all employees are required to respect the *kibun* of another person. Providing feedback in a positive manner also sustains the balance of *kibun* by preserving the harmony of the employer/employee relationship.

Relationships in the Korean culture are formed on the basis of *we-ness (우리 의식)*. This concept is based on emotions, *Jeong (정)*, rather than a business transaction (Shim, Baik & Kim, 2014). *Jeong* is the feeling of affection, concern, understanding, loyalty, warmth and an emotional connection to someone or something (Seoulsync, n.d.). In Korean businesses, this results in decision-making processes taking longer because all parties need to consider each individual opinion. South Korean leaders show a great deal of care and respect for their corporate environment and enjoy the reciprocated benefits of those positive practices from their employees.

Survey results and what local respondents say

The following analysis of the 2018 CCBS survey provides a Korean perspective on the concept of leadership. Over fifty Korean respondents with an academic or professional background completed this survey. According to the results, three main aspects stood out: work ethics, criticism and role models.
More than half of the respondents do not change their management decisions easily. This statement is reinforced by several anonymous respondents who mentioned that a leader has to be a powerful decision-maker. The survey also shows that high work pressure is notable, with more than half of respondents stating that "*missing a deadline is more or less seen as a failure*" (CCBS Survey, 2018).

Criticism also presented itself as a huge factor. More than half of the leaders would rather hear criticism from their team in an indirect manner outside a staff meeting (CCBS Survey, 2018). Employees usually address criticism after a meeting in a respectful way, as not to damage the *kibun* of their leader. According to the survey, leaders also feel that they should spend time on the personal well-being of their co-workers (CCBS Survey, 2018).
For South-Korean employees it is essential to have a role model within the workplace. This is further supported by CFO, Inchil Chung (2017), who states: "*we use titles for every position*". Survey respondents overwhelmingly agree that it is imperative for a leader to have an academic title on their business card. A large majority of the respondents believes that a team member must not address their boss by his or her first name. Therefore, the majority of the respondents address their boss with their proper title (CCBS Survey, 2018).

Local leadership analysis

In-country literature review

In the book *초격차 넘볼 수 없는 차이를 만드는 격* (*Super Gap*), written by Kwon Oh-Hyun (권오현), former CEO of Samsung 권오현 (2018), the author states that the three virtues of leadership should include integrity, humility and generosity. According to Bae Myung-bok, who works at JoongAng Ilbo, the three virtues can be explained in the following way: *"Integrity is the ability to make objective judgments and be frank in discussions regardless of one's own position."* He defines humility as a readiness to learn from anyone and being courteous to others, while generosity refers to *"the attitude of not choosing unlawful means or expediency for personal interests"* (Bae, 2018).

The book, 한국형 리더십 (*Korean Leadership*) written by 백기복 (2017) discusses Korean leadership from a global perspective. He mentions that the Korean leadership style considers both cultural specificity and human universality. Cultural specificity lies in the unique characteristics of Koreans, called *jeong* (정). Korean leadership differs from global leadership on two fronts. The first is that Korean leaders should be able to place themselves in the shoes of their subordinates and co-workers (백기복, 2017). Being able to do so means that a leader is armed with self-affirmation, passion and is able to be harmonious with those around him or her. This leads to the development of a warm mutual relationship. The leader is responsible for the performance of duties, leading the way and adopting new initiatives. The second difference is that South Korean leaders are not only expected to know how to act positively but also to know how to get there. Thus, they must have knowledge of the negative aspects that can occur and how to deal with them effectively (백기복, 2017).

Dr Jeongbae Park: a Korean leadership scholar

Dr Jeongbae Park (박정배) is a professor at Hanyang University and also the CEO of Orbit Co. When describing Korean leaders, he explains that leadership is mainly based on personality. Some leaders choose a more commanding or controlling stance, while others choose to recreate familial relationships within the workplace. However, he states that: *"according to the times and atmosphere, the demands for leadership are slightly different, you can focus on communication or external networking skills or professional skills"* (Park, 17 October 2018). The business atmosphere is constantly changing as a result of these demands. In order to function effectively as a manager, the communication competency is the most necessary skill, followed by job expertise and a problem-solving ability. He elucidates that *"communication is essential to [understanding] the other person"*, which corroborates with the previously mentioned point that Korean leaders place a great deal of effort into the relationships with their employees. Park compares the manager/employee relationship in South Korea to that of a military platoon leader and his infantry. In larger corporations, the business hierarchy still operates in a systematic manner, with a strong command system as the driving force. While start-up companies are becoming more prominent, they may choose to adopt a horizontal or meritocratic management system, which deviates from the norm. Due to the existing vertical integration business structure, leaders are viewed in a complex manner, whereby they are expected to possess all the capabilities necessary to lead, but they are still thought of as being too authoritarian. However, Park voices that this mode of thought is played out, which lends proof to the continuously changing business landscape.

Park (17 October 2018) describes the Korean economy as having a mixed Western influence, stemming from the United States and Europe. Conducting business in South Korea differs from its influenced style, due to the strict regulations that are currently in place. These principles have contributed to the remarkable growth that South Korea has achieved in less than a century. What sets the country apart from others is its development of a well-educated workforce, one that continues to produce sound infrastructure and advanced communication and business systems. *Kibun* plays a large role in maintaining the high level of professionalism that Koreans are acquainted with. By taking into consideration the time, place and occupation that surround the nuances of communication, situations can be dealt with in a streamlined manner. Concerning challenges that foreigners might face in the South Korean workforce, the most common obstacle is the power struggle between managers and their subordinates. South Korea continues to make great strides in each facet of its development as a country, and while old-fashioned practices might still exist, the old and the new coincide in harmony with each other.

Daniel Cho: a Korean with a leadership position

Daniel Cho (조성훈) is the Director of Samsung Electronics Europe Logistics B.V. in the Netherlands. His day-to-day activities include managing the supply chain and logistics processes of Samsung Electronics Europe Logistics B.V., a subsidiary of Samsung Electronics Co. Ltd. which is responsible for supplying customers in Europe with Samsung products.

The main discrepancy that Cho has noticed between the Netherlands and South Korea is the working culture. South Korea has a culture of consideration, which means that people do not rely on a social system to protect them, unlike the Netherlands. In the Netherlands, there are rules and regulations in place that can help take care of obstacles that an employee might face. In Korea, people rely more on the consideration of the individual instead of a social system. Because of all the systems in place, the Netherlands has a higher percentage of gender equality than South Korea (Cho, 17 October 2018).
Korean employees are accustomed to handling fast-paced orders from higher management. In comparison to Western culture, Koreans do not communicate as much and are more task-focused. He is reminded of the saying "*It is said that the West learns freedom of speech and Korea learns the importance of silence*" (Cho, 17 October 2018). In the Korean culture, it is important to listen without any interruption while in the Netherlands and Western Europe, there seems to be a culture where employees are constantly voicing their opinion, even if this opinion is not well-thought-out. Since Koreans do not speak much in a workplace environment, it is imperative to listen well. A Korean employee will generally not speak unless he or she has something important to contribute to the conversation. Korean employees often do not make adjustments by themselves, and managers need the ability to anticipate the needs of the employees and coordinate their opinions.
The manager/employee relationship in the past was a boss-subordinate relationship. However, Korea has changed a great deal in the past decades, and nowadays, employees demand to be treated with respect as the younger generation will not accept the boss-subordinate relationship without respect, regardless of the remuneration offered. This can be viewed as an adaptation of Western culture. The Korean culture is changing to look at employees at an individual level rather than as a part of a larger group. The goal is to recognise achievements and to communicate as individuals.
Cho (17 October 2018) believes that leaders should choose their positions carefully because they have the natural ability to lead and are hardworking and not because of money or good connections.

In-country leadership bestseller

Nanjung Ilgi (난중일기) or War Diary of Yi Sun-sin is the personal diary of Admiral Yi Sun-sin (이순신). It highlights the admiral's daily life during the Japanese invasions of Korea (임진왜란). Admiral Yi Sun-sin is a well-respected man in Korea, and this book brings his great teachings about leadership to modern management. In this book, Yoontae Kim (김윤태), who has been teaching leadership for over 15 years as the CEO of Change Consulting, casts his expertise and analytical capabilities in a different light. He elaborates that Admiral Yi Sun-sin accurately grasped the missions and not just the tasks that needed to be completed. A leader who understands company missions well, beyond just task management, can leverage an organisation (Kim, 2018). This book summarizes Yi Sun-shin's history in order to compare it to the present day. It analyses the essence of leadership that Yi Sun-Shin, the hero of Korea, used and introduces the way to be a great leader.

Local leadership book	
Title	*리더십, 난중일기에 묻다*
Subtitle	조직을 세우고 팀원을 성장시키는 자기경영 리더십
Author	김윤태
Publisher	성안당
Year	2018
ISBN	9788931582031

Korean leadership YouTube review

South Korea is hailed as a wonder within the world of economics, due to its rapid success in developing a functioning, modern economy over the past 60 years (Yonsei University, n.d.). The country's leaders have played a large role in the development of its economy and continue to do so nowadays.

The management style in South Korea is harmony-oriented. The video, "Management Styles of Philippines, South Korea, and Japan", states that "*CEOs in South Korea are mostly owner-managers, who are also founders of the company, or descendants of founders*" (Guippe, 2017). This shows that Korean companies prefer to keep tight-knit relations within the organisation. The video reiterates that "*managers respect their workers, and that they care about the work and life of their employees*" (Guippe, 2017), and also sheds light on common practices of Korean leaders.

In her TedTalk, Yeonhee Kim (October 2013) describes factors which make the Korean leaders of multinational companies successful. Through her analysis of South Korea's three major *chaebols*: Samsung, Hyundai and LG, Kim explains that the success of these companies relies on the fact that they go against the grain of what is traditionally taught in business schools (Kim, 2013). They are able to achieve this by hiring local senior talent to lead the company. By ensuring that leaders are Korean, the interaction among different levels of hierarchy within the company becomes virtually seamless as ideas are easier to translate, due to everyone sharing the same language and work ethic. Kim emphasises that local leadership is paramount to success because decision-making is streamlined when everyone understands cultural norms and expectations (Kim, 2013). This understanding is based on senior leader's personal experiences of growing up in South Korea's fast-evolving economy, which makes Korean global leaders more open and flexible, and thus makes adaptation to changing demands easier (Kim, 2013).

Understanding hierarchy in Korea

An important aspect of Korean hierarchy is family names and wealth. This is visible in Korean c*heabols (재벌)* where large conglomerates are owned by South Korean families. According to Rowley and Bea (2003), a *cheabol* can be described as "*an octopus with many tentacles*" (p.189). In these companies, there is a family-like corporate environment. According to Chung, Lee, and Jung (1997), employees see the workplace as a second home. This means that colleagues are involved in personal activities, but it is also expected that employees work hard and show respect to the company. Cho and Yoon (2001) note that in the Korean labour market a strict hierarchal structure is followed where seniority is heavily respected. Job divisions depend on experience, education and years of service. Strict title recognition is crucial to determine the appropriate title for colleagues by complete name and function. According to the CCBS survey, more than ninety per cent of the respondents state that it is unacceptable to address leaders by their first name (CCBS Survey, 2018). Power distance is also visible in the way Koreans greet each other. The juniors with lower power must bow to senior colleagues in order to show respect (Lee, 2012). Additionally, gender inequality in the workforce is a controversial topic in South Korea. As the CCBS survey shows, more than half of the respondents disagree that women have equal access to senior leadership positions (CCBS Survey, 2018). Most working women put their careers on hold when they have children, making re-entering the workforce a challenge (Kim, 1996). This fact is illustrated by one of the respondents: "*women tend not to promote in her company, because when women become mothers, they have to raise their child and it results in career discontinuity*" (CCBS Survey, 2018).

How the Koreans achieve leadership empathy

Bearing in mind that Korea is being influenced more and more by other cultures, their traditions and social status are still a huge part of everyday life (Greaves, 30 March 2018). In the business world, Koreans try to remain polite, friendly and thoughtful. Leaders avoid reprimanding their subordinates in public so as to preserve face for both parties. The results of the CCBS survey show that almost eighty per cent of the respondents agree that the manager should actively spend time on the personal well-being of their employees. Seog Joo Wong states that "*If you are a good leader with ingenuity, charisma, and a caring mind for your employees, they will like and follow you as their uncle or father*" (CCBS Survey, 2018). This also emphasises the paternalistic role that is undertaken by leaders. On the other hand, a leader expects their subordinates to be dedicated to their work and to remain open to new ideas. Many Koreans are creative and love to show initiative when given the opportunity (Inanlou & Ji-Young, 2017). Furthermore, it is expected that subordinates follow pre-established procedures (CCBS Survey, 2018). Another way for leaders to achieve empathy is through sharing a mutual sense of humour. At the end of the day, it is important to have balance which combines both business and social aspects in order to maintain respect in a Korean working environment (Kim, Lee, Wong & Shan, 2016).

Sri Lanka

Lea Alejandrino, Efrim van Barneveld, Anna van den End, Vay Melis & Nicky van der Zwaan

With its teardrop-shaped island that is around 29 times smaller than Indonesia, Sri Lanka is based in the Indian Ocean and is home to approximately 21 million habitants. The island itself provides a lot of natural resources, such as graphite, limestone, clay, phosphates and mineral sands. Most of Sri Lanka's terrain is low, with mountains in the south-central interior. Sri Lanka was first colonised by the Netherlands and Portugal, but later belonged to Britain. It was during the British colonial period that English, one of the three official languages along with Sinhala and Tamil, was introduced (De Silva, 1981). Around six decades ago, Sri Lanka became politically independent and is now seen as a lower middle-income country, with a society that is considered feminine. Two decades later, a civil war broke out due to earlier conflicts between the Sinhala-Buddhist majority and the Sri Lankan Tamil minority (Gombrich, 1990). Sri Lanka is inwardly-oriented and based on growth in non-tradable sectors. Although in the past the economy has known restrictive trade policies and prominent anti-export biases, prospects for the island seems promising.

How the Sri Lankans characterise leaders

To begin, the perspective of gender roles with Sri Lankan leaders is rather interesting. As Chandrakumara, De Zoysa and Manawaduge (2009) state, almost three-quarters of Sri Lankan leaders are men. However, that does not mean that Sri Lankan men hold no respect for women, as several females have led the country in the past (Statista, 2018). This shows that women are quite capable of leading and managing in Sri Lanka, with the respect of Sri Lankan men. Chandrakumara, De Zoysa and Manawaduge (2009) also show that over half of the leaders in Sri Lanka tend to be between 30 and 50 years old.
It is uncommon to have a younger leader in a company as leaders are expected to have experience. "*You have to have good experience in the field. You have to have leadership qualities, you have to be assertive. You have to have a certain, a persona of a leader. People look up to those traits*" (Wickramanayake, 1 November 2018). Leaders should be well-educated and preferably possess

several elements of charisma (Chandrakumara, De Zoysa & Manawaduge, 2009). Moreover, the CCBS survey (2018) gives an indication of the traits a leader should have, with close to a third of the respondents indicating that technical competence, organisational experience and market expertise are desirable leadership traits. In keeping with what was discussed earlier, Sri Lankan professionals give more value to its leaders' knowledge and skills rather than their gender or seniority (CCBS Survey, 2018).
When characterising Sri Lankan leaders, it is also important to realise that Sri Lankans do not only apply Asian traits of management philosophy, but also Western traits. This is evident in the fact that Sri Lankan managers maintain distance from their co-workers, but their reward system is based on individual achievement (Nanayakkara, 1999). It is not hard to understand this idea, as many multi-national Sri Lankan companies shine their light on leadership. Besides different exterior culture, Sri Lankan leadership styles also differ depending on the type of organisation and its personal culture (CCBS Survey, 2018).
Generally speaking, managers in Sri Lanka are dependent on others, take little risk and do not like to change the situation or status quo (Chandrakumara, De Zoysa & Manawaduge, 2009). As most respondents in the survey indicate, decisions will not be changed very easily (CCBS Survey, 2018). This is evident in the work style of one of Sri Lanka's richest businessmen - Dhammika Perera, who has been active in the business sector from 1987. His strategy is to own the business and make decisions based on the mathematical models he created himself. His analyses are detailed, meaning he goes through all the information and plans before reaching a decision, yet he still relies on professionals for day-to-day operation (Amarasinghe, 2011).

Survey results and what local respondents say

Approximately forty Sri Lankan professionals have shared their views about leadership in their country in the CCBS Survey (2018). Primarily, the respondents are convinced that leaders should encourage competitions within the team in order to achieve better results. Although a minority of the respondents agree with Dilantha Kahandawala, a quality leader in productions, that a *"[w]orking culture of collaboration among the team members is always better than creating a competition between them"* (CCBS Survey, 2018). At the end of the day, the final decision as to whether one should encourage collaboration or competition within a group lies in the hands of the management. Regarding decision-making, most participants agree that once management has made its decision, it cannot be easily changed. In Sri Lanka, authority is often used to control followers, as one professional explains: "*There is almost no questioning of your superior. [It is] very much a 'Yes Sir, No Sir, 3 Bags full Sir'* attitude towards leadership" (CCBS Survey, 2018). The employees are expected to do their tasks according to the prescribed procedures and within the deadline that is set by the management. Therefore, it is not surprising that the majority of the managers view missing a deadline as a failure.

Furthermore, most respondents believe that there is a significant difference in leadership styles between men and women. According to a professional in the banking sector: "*When it [is time] for decision making men are stronger and brave compared to women*". Additionally, the survey shows that the majority agree that a good leader should have organisational experience. As a local professional, Chandi Perera, explains: "*It depends on one's education, qualifications, family tree and the level of self-confidence*" (CCBS Survey, 2018). Besides this, most respondents convey that leaders get working space and transportation that match their position. In other words, a high position in a company reflects a high level of luxury in Sri Lanka. Also, adding one's academic title on business cards and email is very important according to almost half of the professionals. Considering that almost a quarter of the professionals are neutral on this matter, there is a slight indication that Sri Lankans want to showcase their status in visible ways (CCBS Survey, 2018).

Local leadership analysis

In-country literature review

Dr Erabaddage Ayoma Gayathri Sumanasiri, of the University of Sri Jayawardenepura, conducted research on creating sustainable businesses in complex environments. For this, 821 managers were studied using factor analysis and structural equation modelling. Sumanasiri found that the main factors of sustainable leadership in Sir Lanka were the leader's prioritisation of stakeholders and employee engagement (Sumanasiri, 2016). In a similar study, Jask Jayakody conducted a survey amongst 53 managers who are reading for MBA degrees and wrote an article about charismatic leadership in Sri Lankan business organisations. His work concludes that leaders' sensitivity to their subordinates' needs has less effect than a leader's rhetorical skills when it comes to forming charisma. The article explains that charisma is what sets leaders apart from others (Jayakody, 2008). Furthermore, Ambalam Pushpanathan, a senior lecturer at the Vavuniya Campus of the University of Jaffna, interviewed successful female entrepreneurs from different kinds of businesses. She then wrote an article about different leadership styles amongst women, and from that shows that task-leadership has a significant negative relationship with profitability (Pushpanathan, Ramesh & Nimalathasan, 2012).

Navodinee Wickramanayake: a Sri Lankan cross-cultural trainer

Navodinee Wickramanayake, originally from Sri Lanka, is the founder and executive director of *The Better Tomorrow Movement*, a social start-up that leverages international collaborations. Wickramanayake also won the Queen's Young Leaders Award. In the interview, different topics were discussed, starting with the impact of Sri Lankan history on current leadership models. Wickramanayake explains that the civil war of the past does not influence today's business culture. Regarding gender roles, she notes that women in Sri Lanka are able to reach the top, but should be prepared to show some male traits and to also deal with sexism. She adds that next to being assertive, the most important characteristic of a leader is experience in the working field. Sri Lankans should normally own diplomas to enter the business environment, but once employed, experience and knowledge become much more important. Regarding empathy and staff well-being, she expresses that in her experience, Sri Lankan leaders care deeply about their subordinates and that employer-employee relationships tend to be quite informal: *"In most cases [supervisors] know about your family and the family will maybe come to like the company Christmas party, and you know, the New Year party. You get to meet people's families and you get to know people"* (Wickramanayake, 1 November 2018). It is worth noting, that this can strongly differ depending on the type of organisation. Lastly, Wickramanayake points out that the caste system no longer applies in modern Sri Lanka.

In-country leadership bestseller

In 2018, Rozaine Cooray and Dr Pujitha Silva published the book *RockStars: growing stellar performers in organizations*. Cooray is an organisational psychologist, whereas Silva works as a biomedical engineer and life coach. Together they presented the book as a brainchild of their joint efforts. Promised to be an inspirational book for a wide audience, *RockStars* was both new and refreshing. It became a transformational leadership book and a best seller in Sri Lanka. It is based on the P3 Growths Coaching Model, which Silva created himself, and it takes a holistic approach towards development and improvement. As a result of Silva being a native English speaker, the book is written in English as well. In addition to the book, *RockStars*, the authors also supply the Rockstar

Programme. During this, Silva and Cooray personally help companies to grow, with help of the theories in their *RockStars* book.

Local leadership book	
Title	*RockStars*
Subtitle	Growing stellar performers in organizations
Author	Rozaine Cooray, Dr. Pujitha Silva
Publisher	Independently published
Year	2018
ISBN	978-171-773-710-6

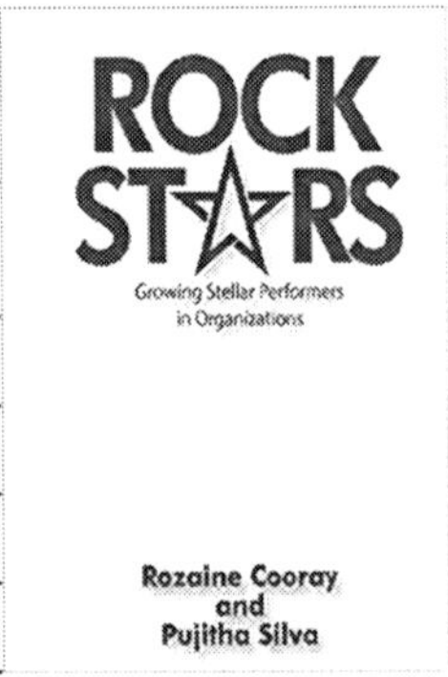

Sri Lanka leadership YouTube review

On 24 October 2017, a TEDxColombo talk on the matter "Can leadership be taught?" was uploaded on Youtube. In this video Vidusha Nathavitharana, founder of High5 Consultancy and Training, provides his perspective on what it takes to become a leader. When he was asked whether leadership can be taught, it brought him to the conclusion that from just talking, you cannot create a leader. Nathavitharana (2017) points out that leadership is of a collectivistic nature: *"It's not the programme itself, but it's getting everyone involved. Leadership is collectivistic and so is creating leadership"*.

He also emphasises the importance of inner confidence when it comes down to becoming a leader, and in the end, he believes that leadership cannot be taught. Despite this harsh conclusion, he does not imply that he and his company are unnecessary in the area of training leaders: *"Our role is to facilitate the learning of leadership, but very importantly: transforming them into leaders"* (Nathavitharana, 2017).

Understanding hierarchy in Sri Lanka

For years Sri Lankans were used to the fact that a person's role, status and social order in business are defined by the caste of your family. In actual fact, this no longer applies to modern corporate Sri Lanka (Wickramanayake, 1 November 2018). However, Sri Lanka is still known for its high power distance, which means that less powerful members of institutions and organisations within this country expect and accept that power is distributed unequally (Hofstede Insights, n.d.). Surprisingly, this acceptance does not always mean that Sri Lankans maintain only formal relationships with the more powerful members of their society. On the contrary, employer and employee relationships are quite informal leaning to familial. Keep in mind that in terms of keeping personal distance between leaders and employees, opinions might differ depending on the organisation's culture, but in general, it is not unusual if a leader shows personal interest in his or her employees (Wickramanayake, 1 November 2018).

Equally important as power distance when it comes down to understanding hierarchy is the definition of gender roles. Sri Lanka has been the first country with a female leader back in 1960, and since then there have been several terms when a woman was leading the country (Statista, 2018). Therefore, acceptance of the hierarchy does not mean that hierarchy must be led by a man. Nevertheless, women should be prepared to deal with a lot of sexism on their way to the top: *"So sexism is very much prevalent in Sri Lanka. I am not going to sugar-coat that. It is very much prevalent"* (Wickramanayake, 1 November 2018). Given that Sri Lanka has a high power distance, it would not be exceptional to assume that Sri Lankans care about and look up to status, but the survey shows that this is not the case. The majority of the respondents believe that it is not necessary for a leader to maintain a personal distance from their employees to achieve the right level of respect (CCBS Survey, 2018). However, roughly the same number of participants believes criticism can be given directly to a leader in staff meetings (CCBS Survey, 2018). Thus one can conclude that although unequally distributed hierarchy is expected and accepted, people do not really look up to status. To further support this, the majority are of the opinion that leaders can be addressed by their first name (CCBS Survey, 2018).

How the Sri Lankans achieve leadership empathy

A collectivistic culture has always been present in Sri Lanka (Fernando, 2007). Therefore, caring for one another is very normal in everyday life. This way of living has had, and still has, a great influence on how Sri Lankan leaders interact with their followers. According to one respondent, *"Ethics and morals in leadership [are] based on our culture and spiritual beliefs"* (CCBS Survey, 2018). Generally, it is expected for leaders to care for their subordinate's well-being and needs, and for subordinates to expect that of their managers (Jayakody, 2008). Almost all of the respondents are convinced that leaders should actively spend time on their staff's well-being (CCBS Survey, 2018), and as Dilantha Kahandawala mentions: *"The leader should always be in touch with each team member"*. Indeed, Wickramanayake explains that in most cases managers know about their employees' family. She also conveys that, in her experience, asking personal questions is valued by Sri Lankans, and she therefore believes that it is important to *"[a]sk personal questions, [be] invested in your employees [and have] a genuine interest in their well-being*" (1 November 2018). Furthermore, Wickramanayake states that due to the relatively close work relationship between managers and their staff in private sectors, there is a more informal working environment. However, to give a nuance on this matter, she suggests that this closeness certainly depends on the culture of each company and that superiors and subordinates in a corporate sector, for example, have a closer relationship in comparison to the more hierarchical public sector companies.

Keeping the collectivistic culture in mind, Sri Lankans also expect a great verbal indirectness and politeness from their managers. It is of the utmost importance that leaders in this country avoid hurting their employees' feelings and try to minimise their imposition (Amarasinghe, 2011). Surprisingly, the results of our survey prove to us that there is a contrast between Sri Lankan leaders' and staff's point of view on this matter. To illustrate, almost half of the professionals that filled out the survey imply that they do not prefer to hear criticism in an indirect manner (CCBS Survey, 2018). Additionally, Wickramanayake mentions that employees in corporate sectors are encouraged to immediately contact supervisors regarding issues and are even allowed to have direct access to top management (1 November 2018).

Ukraine

Olga Maciejewska, Stijn Wichary, Sunny Byun & Vlaa Zhybalko

Once part of the Soviet Union, Ukraine (Україна) is today the second largest country in Europe. Kyiv (Київ) is the capital city of the country. Just like its neighbouring countries, Russia and Belarus, Ukraine uses the Cyrillic alphabet. With respect to Ukrainian culture, the locals are known for their generosity and keenness towards building relationships. Once a relationship is formed, it is common to be spoilt by an overwhelming amount of food and drinks when invited to dinner. Ukrainians' fondness for building relationships is also apparent in the business environment.
The country has an emerging free market using its local currency - Ukrainian hryvnia (₴). Thanks to its nutrient-rich soil, Ukraine cultivates large amounts of grain. Even Ukraine's national flag represents the common agricultural landscape of the country; the yellow bottom part symbolises the fields of wheat whereas the blue top half represents the blue sky above. The vast majority of Ukrainians aged between 19 and 25 are enrolled in universities with many of them pursuing technological and science studies. Thanks to such a preference, Ukraine has become one of the countries with the largest number of IT developers and technicians in the World (Aridi, 2017).

How Ukrainians characterise leaders

The definition of an ideal leader (лідер) in the Ukrainian business culture might come across as harsh and surprising to people raised in countries with a lower power distance score. The analysis of a research study conducted by Kliuchnikov (2014) shows that Ukrainian leaders should be authoritarian in order to effectively manage their subordinates. Vadim, a CEO in the IT sector admits: *"In Ukraine, if you are a leader, you have to get as much control as possible: time tracking, micromanagement, strict deadline control. If you don't do this, you fail"* (CCBS Survey, 2018). Consequently, the respondents of Kliuchnikov's (2014) study argue that a strict attitude is not perceived negatively in Ukraine but is, in fact, viewed as a positive way to create the feeling of security and promote employees' respect. The occurrence of such a phenomenon stems from a belief that a strong leader is a guarantee of protection for his or her followers as an authoritarian leader takes full responsibility for his or her absolute decisions and their results. In addition, a successful Ukrainian manager must be an all-knowing specialist or risk losing his or her subordinates' respect. One of the respondents in Kliuchnikov's (2014) study illustrates the importance of maintaining this faultless image as a foundation for building a manager's authority. The respondent notes that if the leading manager makes professional mistakes, it will lead subordinates to consider the manager as unworthy to be in charge. On the other side of the spectrum, a successful leader in Ukraine is described as charismatic and able to build family-like relationships with subordinates. Kliuchnikov (2014) argues that a manager in Ukraine should not only be strict towards employees to be successful but should also be able to show humaneness, empathy and care.

Moving away from expectations to reality, based on Klichnikov's (2014) research, it appears that there are three main types of managers in Ukraine: the 'General Director', the 'Cowboy' and the 'Rational Merchant' (Möllering & Stache, 2007). The 'General Director' type is described as a manager who still works like in the old Soviet times: inefficiently and by personal command. The second common archetype of a leader is the 'Cowboy', depicted as a manager who takes advantage of the lack of reliable rules in Ukraine or who follows the spirit of the free market and capitalism excessively. The lack of reliable rules in Ukraine is confirmed by Arsen Popelnyuk, the chief economist of Techcorp. Popelnyuk claims that it is a well-known fact that Ukrainian law is not one hundred per cent efficient, and within different sectors of the market, some managers take advantage of the lack of reliable rules (Popelnyuk, 11 October 2018).

The third and the most recently formed type of a leader is the 'Rational Merchant'. This type represents a manager with better knowledge about how capitalism and the free market work. Such managers are often to be found within Ukraine's younger generation that distances itself from the old Soviet legacies and embraces the Western business culture (Möllering & Stache, 2007).

In addition to the different management types, it is also possible to identify different corporate traditions among Ukrainian businesses.

Fuxman (2004) distinguishes Ukrainian firms with two prevalent management styles: the *Enforcement* and the *Encouragement* Management style.

The enforcement management style uses fear of losing certain benefits of a job to improve employee efficiency and is mainly used by managers within domestic organisations that are economically unstable (Fuxman, 2004). In contrast, the encouragement management style uses motivation to enhance the efficiency of employees and is widely used by managers of foreign firms, who are relatively more secure in their jobs. These differences between the behaviour of domestic and foreign firms in Ukraine is confirmed by an experience of Pavel, a Ukrainian general director, who notes: *"I am managing an EU branch in Ukraine and I see a big difference from other [purely] Ukrainian companies [with] regard to the management"* (CCBS Survey, 2018). While it is possible to differentiate these styles among Ukrainian firms, many of them operate through a combination of both encouragement and enforcement managerial styles (Fuxman, 2004).

Survey results and what local respondents say

The Cross-Cultural Business Skills Survey (2018) has collected responses of over forty Ukrainian managers. One of the most outstanding results in the survey clearly indicates that Ukrainian managers are expected to actively contribute to their subordinates' personal well-being. Iryna Voloshchenko, working in the IT sector, shares the following opinion about the current Ukrainian business culture: *"Teamwork is in need of developed emotional intelligence and absence of [an] abuse of micromanagement"* (CCBS Survey, 2018). Similarly, the respondents do not support the managers keeping a personal distance from their employees, which is in contradiction to Ukraine's high score in Hofstede's power distance dimension. These contradictory opinions might be the result of the generational shift and the changing approach to authority. What is more, the survey results reveal a rather confrontational nature among Ukrainian leaders. The vast majority of respondents claim that Ukrainian leaders prefer to hear criticism in a direct manner during a meeting. Similarly, the managers are also allowed to confront their subordinates in order to obtain targeted results. One of the CCBS survey (2018) respondents describes local Ukrainians as more straightforward and less polite. The professional also observes that they care more about profit than the business culture. In a like manner, in-company competition is highly encouraged by the managers in order to boost team morale (CCBS Survey, 2018).

The CCBS Survey results prove that in Ukraine, rules are rules. When asked about following established procedures, more than half of the respondents indicate that they expect their team members to proceed with settled agreements. Additionally, in Ukraine, missing a deadline is viewed as a failure by the majority of respondents. On top of this, bending the rules to achieve better results is also frowned upon. Many of the respondents note that the rules might be changed in some particular cases, but only with prior consultation and permission from a leader. These responses once again confirm the authoritarian structure of Ukrainian business culture. "*There is a strong top-down hierarchy in Ukraine. More so than in Western-Europe*", notes a Ukrainian managing director in the retail sector. This is also illustrated through the respondents' top choice of leadership figure: the powerful decision maker. Equivalently, one-third of the responses show that the leader should have a strong charismatic personality. Despite the authoritarian business culture, a large number of Ukrainian managers do not consider their academic title on a business card to be important. Similarly, local leaders do not feel the necessity of having respectable office space and transportation to match their positions.

There are some noteworthy opinions found in the survey regarding gender equality in Ukraine. Over the half of respondents claim that there is a difference between female and male managers in Ukraine, especially in terms of power display. As one general manager in the IT sector puts it: "*Women are normally more autocratic than democratic because otherwise it might be hard for them to achieve their goals*" (CCBS Survey, 2018). This opinion is supported by a few other voices that also suggest that female managers need to put in more effort to prove that they are in the right position. The reason behind this is that female managers might often feel distrusted and disrespected by their male subordinates, which in turn might make them either too emotional or too tough. Other respondents explain the managerial differences invoking a psychological construct of the two genders, suggesting that women are naturally more emotional and sensible. Nevertheless, there also appeared many contradictory opinions, which unambiguously argued that there are no real differences between male and female managers as "*It depends on a person, not on gender*", according to Dr Prof Tetyana Vasilyeva, Director of Oleg Balatskyi Academic and Scientific Institute of Finance in Ukraine (CCBS Survey, 2018). Concerning the balance of the two genders in managerial positions, Popelnyuk states that in Ukraine, there are still more men in high positions than women: "*In Ukraine, from an early childhood, men are instilled with the idea that they are more suitable for this kind of job than women*". Of course, there are exceptions, but the majority of Ukrainian managers remain male.

Local leadership analysis

In-country literature review

The Ukrainian market is facing challenges that it has never encountered before. An associate professor of Kyiv National Economic University, Denys Lifintsev (2016), argues that there is an undeniable need for cross-cultural management skills in Ukraine; these skills are needed in order to fully exploit the emerging opportunities that come from an EU-Ukrainian Association Agreement. In his analysis, Lifintsev (2016) draws attention to the process of globalisation and the weakening national currency as factors resulting in the rise of many international business possibilities for Ukraine. For Lifintsev, the country finally has a chance to become part of, what he calls, a civilized world, but there is a series of preconditions that need to be met first. The author argues that the mentality of Ukrainians needs to change and open up to a global mindset as Ukrainian managers currently have little to no knowledge on how to manage an international team or establish business relationships with other cultures (Lifintsev, 2016). The understanding of another culture is not an obstacle, but a competitive advantage when doing business. Ukrainian Master's student, Dereko (2017), explains that Ukrainians prefer to do business with people they know and trust. Therefore, they pay close attention to building relationships with their business partners. The writer advises hiring Ukrainian interpreters to avoid any cross-cultural miscommunication to those who are unfamiliar with such a way of working. Dereko (2017) further claims that Ukrainians can come across as tricky business partners to people born in different cultures. For example, when Ukrainians know that there is a deadline, they may try to delay the project in an attempt to force their business partners into making approvals. Occasionally, they might even threaten to end relationships that they have already established in order to get favoured results. Petrenko's (2016) article confirms Dereko's (2017) theory, arguing that Ukrainian leaders are often hesitant to do business with people from significantly different cultures. The author explains that in the eyes of Ukrainians, such a business would require a thorough understanding of cultural diversity and leverage skills, which the majority of Ukrainian managers simply lack (Petrenko, 2016).

Denys Lifintsev: a Ukrainian leadership scholar

In the interview, a Ukrainian associate professor and an author, Dr Denys Lifintsev (Денис Ліфінцев), shares his views on the present and future of

Ukrainian business culture (Lifintsev, 7 November 2018). The interviewee has previous experience in the Ukrainian corporate environment, and he currently teaches management and cross-cultural communication at the Kyiv National Economic University.

Lifintsev describes a good Ukrainian leader as a person with excellent oratory and communication skills. In addition, a leader would be someone who is able to inspire and motivate his or her co-workers. By the same token, Lifintsev describes how exceptionally important it is for a manager to possess a great amount of knowledge and to be an absolute expert in their field, in order to gain trust and respect from the Ukrainian team (Lifintsev, 7 November 2018).

According to Lifintsev, the collapse of the USSR had a significant influence on the Ukrainian business culture. Nowadays, the managers are more open and readier to embrace the Western managerial style than their predecessors. The young Ukrainian leaders are keen to implement the more democratic approach within their team: "*Modern managers are trying to be more oriented on building strong corporate culture, on forming a good climate and building a good atmosphere in their companies, not just giving orders or behaving like kings.*" (Lifintsev, 7 November 2018). He also mentions that the majority of the Ukrainian managers are still male, but that this has been progressively changing in the past couple of years. He notes, "*The number of female leaders is growing. Day by day, we see more and more interesting female leaders*" (Lifintsev, 7 November 2018). The associate professor admits that there is no significant difference between male and female managers as it is more about the personality and the way they learnt to manage people. One is more democratic and the other is more authoritarian. But at the end of the day, it all depends on the person, not on gender.

After years of professional experience and observing the changing Ukrainian market, Lifintsev expresses very positive premonitions about the future of Ukrainian leadership as it is becoming more Western-orientated and democratic (Lifintsev, 7 November 2018).

Arsen Popelnyuk: a Ukrainian manager

Arsen Sergeevich Popelnyuk (Арсен Сергійович Попельнюх) is a chief economist in the company Techcorp (Техкор) located in Poltava, Ukraine. The company produces components for drilling rigs that are used for the extraction of oil and gas. In the interview, Popelnyuk shares many interesting views on Ukrainian leadership, gender differences and the influence of the former Soviet Union on management style. The Techcorp Chief Economist defines a good leader as a person who stands out from the crowd and is able to drive their teams to the limit of potential in order to reach specific goals within the organisation. When you approach a real Ukrainian leader, it is apparent that "*Бажання вдосконалюватися сильніше ніж страх поразки*" (The desire to develop is stronger than the fear of loss) (Popelnyuk, 11 October 2018). The influence of the former Soviet Union on Ukrainian management style is still apparent. Many people who have experienced the Soviet Union as working adults are still in charge of many organisations across Ukraine and are still using the same old Soviet methods to manage their employees. Popelnyuk observes that as there are still many managers using the old Soviet way and not being open to modern management styles, Ukraine has not been able to fully develop and progress as a country. However, on the positive side, together with the managers of the younger generation, the situation has been rapidly changing. An increasing number of young and Western-oriented professionals with their own ideas and methods are taking over important positions within the country. They are capable of listening to their employees' opinions and are open to taking them into account, even if the person's position is lower in the internal organisational hierarchy (Popelnyuk, 11 October 2018).

In-country leadership best seller

Local leadership book	
Title	*Різнобарвний менеджмент (Multi-coloured management)*
Subtitle	Еволюція мислення, лідерства та керування (Evolution of thinking, leadership and management)
Author	Валерій Пекар (Valeriy Pekar)
Publisher	Фоліо (Folio)
Year	2015
ISBN	978-966-378-410-6

Pekar (2015) is a president of Euroindex, an entrepreneur, a teacher at Kyiv-Mohyla Business School and the author of over 250 articles on management. His recent book, *Різнобарвний менеджмент* (Multi-coloured management), became a local best seller for leadership. The writer's book describes the evolution of organisations and large social systems, which in the professional literature are called the 'Integral Dynamics'. The book gives the readers an insight into the leadership styles and managerial cultures and provides the tools to change them. *Multi-coloured management* is a book designed for professionals who strive to develop their management skills and improve their businesses (Pekar, 2015).

Ukrainian leadership YouTube review

The founder and CEO of the Ukrainian Leadership Academy, Roman Tychkivskyy, argues that one can be born a leader or become one. The CEO explains that life is defined as a movement and each subsequent action has specific consequences. In a like manner, the more effectively the leader works on self-improvement, the better he or she will become in managing people. Tichkivskyy (2017) believes that leaders need to perceive themselves not only in the context of their individuality but also as a member of a certain community. He adds that a leader is responsible for his actions today, which determine his effectiveness tomorrow. Tichkivskyy is convinced that a good leader should be characterised by the four fundamental qualities: knowledge, skills, attitude and values. Unfortunately, the traditional school does not teach these qualities, which will surely be essential on the career path of any future Ukrainian leaders. One can only become a good leader by putting a lot of self-effort into reading books, practising leadership or finding a mentor. Only through such self-development can one be committed to the ultimate growth of his country and the future generation (Tichkivskyy, 2017).

In a personal interview, Gerashchenko (2016) claims that a good leader must be able to distinguish changes within a company that arise from development. He further explains that development is always a change, but a change is not always development. Subsequently, he adds that in order to develop leadership qualities, a person should begin to think in a certain way. Gerashchenko (2016) admits that a system is needed for development – a system that will allow improvements of certain cognitive pathways and which, in turn, will lead to more effective actions. The interviewee further notes that there are three criteria that are important for development: regularity, accuracy and a clearly defined goal. In addition, Gerashchenko (2016) argues that leadership thinking can be developed by anyone as it is in everyone's nature since their birth, but due to the influence of external factors in life, this thinking might get very deformed. Ultimately, it does not matter in what kind of sphere you are in, but people need to get out of their comfort zone to develop. Although this might seem risky or even scary, a real leader should feel comfortable with the challenge of facing their personal discomfort and working on their deformations of thinking (Gerashchenko, 2016).

Understanding hierarchy in Ukraine

There is a popular saying in Ukraine that goes: *"Два пани - три гетьмани"* which translates as: Among two men you will see three kings. According to a Tatar-Ukrainian associate professor, this saying perfectly illustrates the nature of dominant archetype in the Ukrainian philosophy of leadership (CCBS Survey, 2018). The authority and positions are well respected amongst Ukrainian employees and are essential to maintaining a healthy work environment. Hofstede's findings strongly support this statement as the country has scored an astounding number of 92 in its power distance dimension (Hofstede Insights, n.d.). Uliana Vovchuk, a marketing manager in the digital sector, points out that it is especially the stereotype of age, which is still very much present in the Ukrainian business environment (CCBS Survey, 2018). She notes that you can get a glimpse of how important age still is in establishing the hierarchical ladder, especially when travelling around the country and doing business with smaller local companies (CCBS Survey, 2018). Nevertheless, Kliuchnikov's study (2014) reassures that Ukrainians highly value a strong hierarchical work setting and work the most efficiently under a paternalistic type of leadership. However, as it was mentioned before by Lifintsev, the approach to authority has been changing gradually in recent years due to a generational shift (7 November 2018). Natalya, the Leadership Development Centre Coordinator, notes in the survey; *"I observe the tendency to reduce the gap between managers and subordinates, especially with processes of globalization. Leadership becomes more open"* (CCBS Survey, 2018). Subsequently, Dereko (2017) adds that the younger generation is still loyal to authority though, at the same time, does not hesitate to seek new and interesting options beyond the stereotypical structures.

As established before, Ukrainian leaders prefer and are expected to keep a distance between them and their followers in order to remain in their position of power. There is no place for friendship in the boss-subordinate relation as it could make Ukrainian employees feel more relaxed and think that they can get away with lower quality work. Additionally, it is also perceived as unprofessional and as a weakness in a leader (Kliuchnikov, 2014). Nevertheless, a relationship between a manager and an employee is expected and necessary to a certain extent. It appears to be clear that the paternalistic style of leadership in Ukraine has its two sides: the harsh one, which requires 'the father' to be powerful and strict, and the soft one, which allows him to be caring and protective of his 'children' - the employees. This working structure, according to Kliuchnikov's research (2014), appears to be the most effective and efficient in the Ukrainian business culture.

How Ukrainians achieve leadership empathy

In the harsh and highly competitive Ukrainian market, empathy plays an important role as a foundation of building a positive environment that makes the employees feel valued, which helps them to reach their full potential (Holtzman, 2009). Dmitry Yatsyshyn, the CEO in a brand marketing agency, supports this statement by sharing his opinion on the topic: "*I think that good conditions for staff [form] the key to success for any company*" (CCBS Survey, 2018). In order to survive in a competitive environment and enhance employee effectiveness, Ukrainian business leaders are required to focus on building and managing effective workplace relationships (Holtzman, 2009).
Understanding and openness to different perspectives of the team members seem to be another highly important factor in establishing leadership empathy in Ukraine. Such an approach benefits the employees by giving them an opportunity to grow professionally and, in turn, builds employees' loyalty towards their leaders. Kliuchnikov's (2014) study shows that a certain degree of freedom given to the employees has a positive impact on their motivation and attitude towards the work. Managers who are able to respect and accept the point of view of their subordinates, rather than forcing their own opinions, will not only build stronger work relationships but also increase the effectiveness of the overall collaborations. Ukrainian employees prefer to work with such leaders and tend to trust and support them. In addition, with such managers employees are encouraged to contribute to the work even more (Kiluchnikov, 2014).

One of the respondents of Kliuchnikov's (2014) study adds: *"The first thing that motivates people to work is the personal relationship that they may have with their leader"*. Director in Economics and Management, Dr Prof Tetyana Vasilyeva, underlines the importance of such an attitude: *"For a successful teamwork, it is necessary to build good personal relations with the members of the team"* (CCBS Survey, 2018). Hence, understanding the employees' needs to grow and be heard can help managers in Ukraine to take any required actions and empower their team members to reach their full potential.

Another way of building a positive dynamic with Ukrainian employees is by showing them trust. One of the Ukrainian employees in the interview with Kliuchnikov (2014) puts it this way: *"When a leader tells you that he trusts you one hundred per cent, you invest all of yourself into the job that you do."* In an ideal scenario, in which a skilful manager provides his skilful subordinates with a detailed manageable work plan description and informs them what is required to be done, there is nearly nothing that can go wrong. The exception here might be the motivational level and possibility that the employees would not have enough drive to accomplish the task. Therefore, a good Ukrainian manager should give his followers a little degree of freedom and trust that they will successfully accomplish what is expected. This would encourage an employee to be more motivated and creative, which generates more innovative solutions and brings more productivity to the work processes. Consequently, this improves business efficiency (Holtzman, 2009).

Kyiv references were kindly provided by Dr Denys Lifintsev (Денис Ліфінцев)

Uruguay

Sven Dooijeweerd, Robbin Hegeman, Kylian Kherbache, Bastian Lamers & Jossy Valenzuela

Uruguayan historian and novelist Eduardo Galeano states: *"On the map, surrounded by its large neighbours, Uruguay seems tiny. But not really. We have five times more land than Holland and five times fewer inhabitants"* (Britannica, 2018, par. 1). Uruguay, officially named the Oriental Republic of Uruguay, is a sovereign state located in the south-eastern region of South America. Uruguay currently has an estimated population of approximately 3.5 million inhabitants. The majority of the population lives in the capital Montevideo, which is also the only large city containing about half of the population of the entire country. The remaining inhabitants are spread out over approximately thirty smaller towns across the country. The combination of open space and low population density has brought Uruguay many opportunities for economic development.
Uruguayans are mainly of European origin. Most inhabitants are descendants of European immigrants from two centuries ago, mainly originating from Italy and Spain, as well as, to a much lesser extent, from France and Britain.
The majority of the inhabitants of Uruguay is middle class. The extremes between wealth and poverty that are existent in most of the other South American countries are absent. Education in Uruguay is easily accessed and compulsory for nine years. In addition, education is free through post-graduate studies. This has resulted in Uruguay having one of the highest literacy rates in South America at almost a hundred per cent.

How the Uruguayans characterise leaders

Fernando Iruleguy, a professor at Universidad de Montevideo, explains more precisely in an interview how the Uruguayans characterise leadership. He describes the qualities that a leader requires in a country such as Uruguay. *"A good leader needs to be humble, educated, fair, a doer instead of a thinker, a risk taker and someone getting involved in activities"* (Iruleguy, 7 April 2018). There is not a specific leadership type in Uruguay; there are simply diverse leadership styles in the different work environments, such as national and international companies (Sapelli, 28 March 2018). A leader needs to be a caring person, concerned about the well-being of the employees. One should engage employees in conversations about their personal life. In Uruguay, leaders are open and do not hide their private lives. It is important for a leader to present him or herself as a real human being, such as a closely related person - a father, a brother or a friend (Iruleguy, 7 April 2018). Because Uruguay is a small country, there exists closer relationships between leaders and employees than in, for example, Brazil or Argentina. Guillermo Feria agrees with the above statement: *"First of all to be professional you need to know what you are doing. Secondly to get to know the people you are working with. Not only them but maybe also the family"* (Feria, 23 October 2018). Viriginia Gravinia, a philosophy student, did a thorough research analysis for her PhD in leadership characteristics in Uruguay. The results of the discriminant analysis identify two variables. A positive attitude and values toward innovation and creativity and a leadership behaviour that is characterised by a combination of intellectual stimulation, management by exception (passive), and laissez-faire scales as the highest discriminating variables between two groups (Gravina, 2013).

Managers of companies in Uruguay have to be able to handle the difficulties arising from the ever-changing market, which is quite unpredictable. Managers, although their intention is to work on long-term strategies, have to continually change their tactics in response to the fast-changing circumstances (CCBS Survey, 2018). A manager needs to have access to the right political connections. It is through strong networks that he or she is able to positively represent the company on the market. *"A manager needs to be knowledgeable and passionate within all Latin countries; people need to see a strong leader"* (Casaretto, 15 October 2018). Also, while managers need to have authority, it is just as necessary for them to have the ability to be merciful.

Survey results and what local respondents say

In order to gather more detailed information about leadership in Uruguay, an online survey has been conducted among more than forty experts with a certain involvement in leadership and/or management. Nearly all respondents agree that missing a deadline is equivalent to failure. This shows that Uruguayans strongly believe in meeting set targets. A similar conclusion could be drawn from the fact that over three-quarters of the respondents agree that when a manager makes a decision, it will not be changed very easily - meaning that whatever a manager decides is commonly final (CCBS Survey, 2018).

Secondly, the majority of the respondents believe that the relationships between a leader and his or her subordinates should be informal. The statement about whether it is important to address leaders according to their titles or positions was found to be never or hardly the case by most respondents. It is universally agreed upon that employees can address their leader by his or her first name. However, the president of a significant local enterprise indicates that there is a certain degree of nuance associated with this: *"It really depends more on age difference and how long you know the person than on position. In general people call each other by their first name"* (CCBS Survey, 2018). Also, Uruguayans unanimously agree that a manager should actively spend time on the personal well-being of employees (CCBS Survey, 2018). This proves that leadership empathy plays a large role in the Uruguayan work environment. A respondent even states the following: *"Empathy might be the most important skill for a leader because he/she can understand you and how you work and therefore take out the best of you"* (CCBS Survey, 2018).

Thirdly, a balance between formal and informal behaviour at the Uruguayan workplace is generally determined by company culture. As retrieved from the survey, it mainly depends on the specific company culture. Generally, in newly-founded businesses, a more informal style is shown. This is contrary to larger and elder organisations, where a more formal style is present. Thus, it is desirable to research the company culture in advance so that unwanted and awkward situations can be averted.

Finally, the difference in positioning based upon gender is not equal in Uruguay, according to the survey respondents. More than half of the respondents agree that men and women do not have equal access to senior leadership positions. Many respondents point out that it is, in fact, more difficult for a woman to gain access to a management position. However, if they do gain this access, people are generally positively impressed. When asked if a difference between the leadership styles between men and women exists, a partner working in professional services says: *"Yes, in general women are more engaged with staff morale and pursuing better involvement of the company with the community. They tend to be somehow more resilient and less spasmodic in their decision making"* (CCBS Survey, 2018).

Local leadership analysis

In-country literature review

The book Management, leadership and entrepreneurship in Latin America the land of opportunity – the real leader in the global economy by Dr Librado Enrique Gonzalez gives a thorough explanation about the current situation of management, leadership and entrepreneurship in Uruguay. For Gonzalez, Uruguayan people seem to be uniting for the right causes and every day the country is bearing witness to more emerging leaders, who will be the future guides of the nation (Gonzalez, 2014). After a rough history, Uruguay is at a good stage of development since it displays all the signs of an emerging nation. For management in Uruguay, it is imperative that things go smoothly so that a common goal can be achieved. Therefore, the management within an organisation is perhaps the most vital entity and contains the power to 'make' it or 'break' it in Uruguay (Gonzalez, 2014).

Dr Alvaro Marcelo Moerzinger Pagani: Uruguayan Ambassador

In view of his professional background as a PhD holder in International Relations, an interview was conducted with Dr Alvaro Moerzinger Pagani at the Embassy of Uruguay to the Netherlands in The Hague, to understand his perspective on leadership in Uruguay. In addition to being an academic, Pagani is currently the ambassador of Uruguay in the Netherlands. Pagani is an expert in the field of cross-cultural business management, with his extensive years of experience in different countries such as Colombia, Canada, Hong Kong and now the Netherlands. During the interview, was discussed that a Uruguayan leader needs to have moral management and also excellent people skills. Pagani states: "*The first most essential thing in one person, to know how to work with the people. To conquer the market, you need to have a very clear target*" (Pagani, 11 November 2018). Having a human touch and being genuinely interested in the well-being of the employees is also key to success. Positive feedback is essential, according to Pagani. "*The people feel good. I work hard. I spend many hours, but I have the support of my boss. People, and always I try to compensate, you know, with money, with the travel, with a gift*" (Pagani, 11 November 2018). According to Pagani, the overall situation in Uruguay improved when President Jose Mujicia decided that education should be free for primary school, high school and even university (Pagani, 11 November 2018).

Guillermo Feria: a Uruguayan entrepreneur

Feria is an entrepreneur with a visionary strategy. He holds a degree in business management, teaches planning and evaluation of investment projects at the Catholic University of Uruguay. In addition, he leads QGLATAM, an SME of approximately ten employees. According to Feria, to be a good Uruguayan leader, a person must have characteristics that vary depending on the industry and the number of people to be supervised. The type of company matters too; in a high-tech software company, for example, you need to be a good professional, have high intellectual capacity and get to know the people you work with, their family and feelings. If one works with less qualified people, they need to see their leader as a reference, not only as a person with lots of knowledge and experience, but also as an individual they can trust (Feria, 23 October 2018). Trust is key for this lively culture. The same goes for teamwork. It is expected from a manager not only to lead by authority but also by building a connection with his or her team. When it comes to working together, there is no clear hierarchal distinction, although, there are people who can take decisions and others that must obey them. This distinction does not take away the fact that managers can sit together at the same table with their personnel and enjoy lunch. This reflects the down-to-earth mentality of a true Uruguayan leader.

In-country leadership bestseller

No Más Pálidas is a book on Uruguayan leadership, written by Enrique Baliño and Carlo Pacheco. After 22 years of experience as General Manager and President at IBM Uruguay, Enrique Baliño founded his own company, which provides strategic consulting services for other companies. He wrote a book, sharing his experience along the way (BCC Conferenciantes, n.d.)

Local leadership book	
Title	*No Más Pálidas*
Subtitle	Quatro actitudes para el éxito
Authors	Enrique Baliño & Carlos Pacheco
Publisher	CreateSpace
Year	2010
ASIN	B0049B2FL8

In English, the title translates as: No more *Pale* - four attitudes for success. The term *'pale'* is used to describe the way, in which people in Uruguay and Argentina tend to complain about everything all the time. Baliño sees a successful leader as someone who is positive and a team player. Leaders are exceptional yet normal persons, who continuously work on improving themselves and take responsibility for their actions (No Más Pálidas, n.d.). In addition, a managing director comments: *"*No mas Pálidas *is about how a leader needs to focus on those variables or problems that the organization can actually change or affect and there is absolutely no sense in allocating resources or spend time in those problems that the organization cannot change (e.g. exchange rate, world prices, etc)"* (CCBS Survey, 2018)

Uruguay leadership YouTube review

One of the interesting leaders in the world is Jose Mujicia. Wedged between two enormous and powerful neighbours, Uruguay has always struggled to get noticed. But now, their charismatic president has put the country on the map because, in a world of bland politicians, Mujica stands out from the crowd. He lives a simple, austere life, still gets around in his old VW Beetle, and shows zero interest in the trappings of high office. He is like every leader should be - humble, good towards the poor and not taken over by money and power. Political expert Adolfo Garcé states: *"Sometimes I think that he escaped from a book! A very old book!"* (Dateline, 2014). Mujica will be remembered as the poor president of Uruguay. The honest and authentic President of Uruguay. Mujicia donated almost all of his salary to charity, and instead of buying a private jet for parliamentary flights, he bought an air ambulance helicopter to help the people in need.

Understanding hierarchy in Uruguay

In Uruguay, there are certain inequalities in the different fields in the workplace. First of all, compared to other countries, Uruguay has a relatively high score when it comes to hierarchical order within a company, according to Hofstede Insights (n.d.). Pagani states that *"I work with them directly and they work with the rest of the team"* (11 November 2018). With "them" Pagani means a select group of people, consisting of two to three persons. In this way, the communication within the company will be easy-going, quick and will save time but will also maintain a hierarchical culture within the company.

On the other hand, Feria (23 October 2018) claims that a hierarchical sphere is not really noticeable on the work floor, but the difference between decision makers, takers and executives is. In a Uruguayan hierarchical company culture, subordinates expect to be told what to do by those with a higher rank.
Thirdly, when doing business in Uruguay, this is normally done with a manager or someone of a high rank in the company, according to Burleson, Zhou, Mawji, Herrera and Masrour (2018). Most co-workers will think it is disrespectful to answer a question that is not addressed to them. Burleson et al (2018) agree in this and say in a recent study: *"When performing customer service in these countries, we would need to ask opinions or do business with only their managers or bosses and not get any opinions from the workers because they may not answer you or think that it is disrespectful"*. It is also a way of politeness towards the person asking the question. In this way, they will get the correct answer to their question. Even though Uruguay has a strong hierarchical corporate culture, the relationship between subordinates and leaders is nevertheless robust, and they do have interests in each other's well-being.

How the Uruguayans achieve leadership empathy

Uruguayan leaders use empathy to improve relationships with their colleagues and achieve the best possible result within the company. A standard Uruguayan manager can be very respectable at his or her job and validate his or her position in the hierarchy through previous training and experience. However, this is not enough. To succeed as a leader, it is necessary to lead and generate bonds of trust with the team members (AméricaEconomía, n.d.). As explained by Feria (23 October 2018), without responsiveness, a leader will not be successful. They must engender *confianza*, or trust, which is the equivalent of a moral contract that seals the relationship of an employee with his superior.
Moreover, as claimed by Fedra Feola, Country Manager of Great Place to Work, in Uruguay there are many companies in which managers focus on attaining what organisations want, and these managers are the ones who end up generating a good work climate. Feola evaluates the characteristic of leadership, the development of skills and abilities, not only technical but emotional. (GPTW, n.d.). A company might have the best benefits, but if the front-runners do not lead their people with a certain quality, and if they do not care and communicate well, they will not get the support of their employees (Elobservador, 2017).

Bibliography

Bibliography

Abbas, Q., & Yaqoob, S. (2009). Effect of leadership development on employee performance in Pakistan. *Pakistan Economic and Social Review*, 47(2), 269–292.

Abderrahmane, A. (2017). *تأثير الرتبة الوظيفية للعامل الجزائري على اتجاهه نحو القيادة النسوية*. Retrieved from https://www.asjp.cerist.dz/en/article/53029 on 6 November 2018.

Acoustical Society of America. (2014). *The science of charismatic voices.* Retrieved from https://phys.org/news/2014-10-science-charismatic-voices.html on 19 September 2018.

Aguilera, G.C. (2018). E-mail interview. 12 November.

Ai, S. (2006). School leadership and management in Cambodia: National culture and its impacts on leading educational changes. *Journal of International Cooperation Studies,* 13(3). Retrieved from http://www.research.kobe-u.ac.jp/gsics-publication/jics/shoraku_13-3.pdf on 9 November 2018.

Aimar, C., & Stough, S. (2007). Leadership: does culture matter? Comparative practices between Argentina and United States of America. *Academy of Educational Leadership Journal*, 11(3).

Aktouf, O. (1994). *Traditional management and beyond: A matter of renewal.* Morin, Montreal.

Aktouf, O. (2002). *La stratégie de l'autruche: post-mondialisation, management et rationalité économique.* Montréal: Éditions Écosociété.

Aktouf, O. (2009). *Management and Organization.* Retrieved from https://books.google.nl/books?id=pppMDwAAQBAJ&pg=PA489&lpg=PA489&dq=omar+aktouf+leadership&source=bl&ots=Tz926GDC-P&sig=zOGum5GhSP-R8NZHe0QY4uwQOhQ&hl=nl&sa=X&ved=2ahUKEwia76Ccu8feAhVPhRoKHc-PCw8Q6AEwDXoECAQQAQ#v=onepage&q=aktouf&f=false on 12 November 2018.

Alberto, J., & Ferreira, A. (2007). *Concepções de Liderança Excepcional em Portugal.* Aveiro: Universidade de Aveiro. Retrieved from https://ria.ua.pt/bitstream/10773/1506/1/2007001117.pdf on 2 October 2018.

Alejandro, D., & Carlos, F. (1970). *Essays on the Economic History of the Argentine Republic.* New Haven, CT: Yale University Press.

Alfaomega. (n.d.). Retrieved from https://www.alfaomega.com.mx/default/catalogo/profesional/administracion/liderazgo-y-motivacion-de-equipos-de-trabajo-9a.html on 5 November 2018.

Ali, A. H., & Schackleton, V. J. (1990). Work related values of managers: A test of the Hofstede Model. *Journal of Cross-Cultural Psychology,* 21(1), 109-118.

Almada-Lobo, B. (2018). Personal interview. 2 November.

Amarasinghe, A. (2011). *A comparative analysis of facework strategies of Australians and Sri Lankans working in Australia.* Retrieved from https://pdfs.semanticscholar.org/df4b/1567fd025318c3d80891cceb8695194da297.pdf on 12 October 2018.

Amarasinghe, U. (2011, July 7). Dhammika Perera: Awakening the Giants. *Business Today.* Retrieved from http://businesstoday.lk/article.php?article=3549 on 5 October 2018.

Amazon. (2017). *Why great leaders are catalysts.* Retrieved from https://www.amazon.com/gp/product/B0733H16X2/ref=dbs_a_def_rwt_hsch_vapi_taft_p1_i0 on 12 October 2018.

AméricaEconomía. (n.d.). Retrieved from https://mba.americaeconomia.com on 5 November 2018.

Amoako-Agyei, E. (2009). Cross-cultural management and organizational behavior in Africa. *Thunderbird Int'l Bus Rev*, 51, 329-339. doi:10.1002/tie.20270.

Amoako-Agyei. E. (2018). *Into Africa: 4 Business strategies for global companies seeking economic growth & social impact.* Retrieved from http://gigarelifestyle.com/business-and-finance/into-africa-4-business-strategies-for-global-companies-seeking-economic-growth-social-impact on 11 November 2018.

Amwele, H. N. (2013). *An empirical investigation into the factors affecting the performance of SMEs in the retail sector in Windhoek, Namibia* (Doctoral dissertation).

Andajani S., Hadiwirawan O., & Sokang, Y. A. (2016). *Women's leaderships in Indonesia: Current discussion, barriers, and existing stigma*. Retrieved from https://www.researchgate.net/publication/301543446_Women's_Leaderships_in_Indonesia_Current_Discussion_Barriers_and_Existing_Stigma on 22 September 2018.

Anonymous (2018). Skype interview. 16 October.

ANSA. (2017). *Four Italian cities among world 100 most-visited sites.* Retrieved from /www.ansa.it/english/news/2017/11/07/ansa-four-italian-cities-among-world-100-most-visited-sites_2d30f6d0-0181-4d1e-9aa0-1088f5c9f5d9.html on 5 November 2018.

Antlov, H., & Cederroth, S. (1994). *Leadership on Java: Gentle hints, authoritarian rule*. Surrey, UK: Curzon Press Ltd.

Apriani, F. (2009). The influence of competence, motivation, and leadership on work effectiveness. *Business and Bureaucracy Journal of Administrative and Organizational Sciences*, 13-17.

Arbaiza, L. (2017). *Liderazgo y comportamiento organizacional.* Retrieved from https://www.esan.edu.pe/publicaciones/libros/2017/liderazgo-comportamiento-organizacional/ on 22 October 2018.

Arbayza, L. (2018). Video interview. 18 October.

Aridi, A. (2017, November 17). Can Ukraine transform itself into an innovation-driven economy? [blog post]. Retrieved from https://blogs.worldbank.org/psd/voices/can-ukraine-transform-itself-innovation-driven-economy on 27 September 2018.

Ashraf, J., & Ghani, W. I. (2005). Accounting development in Pakistan. *The International Journal of Accounting*, 40(2), 175–201.

Askanews. (2018). Sonia Lenza - Italia sopra la media Ue per numero di donne leader in azienda [video file]. Retrieved from https://www.youtube.com/watch?v=gV3owQaS1eQ on 23 September 2018.

Background Note: Ethiopia. (2004). *Background Notes on Countries of the World: Federal DemocraticRepublic of Ethiopia* (pp. 1–7). Retrieved from http://search.ebscohost.com.rps.hva.nl:2048/login.aspxdirect=true&db=buh&AN=12807790&site=ehost-live on 4 October 2018.

Bae, M. (2018). *What is leadership?*. Retrieved from http://koreajoongangdaily.joins.com/news/article/article.aspx?aid=3054756 on 23 October 2018.

Baik K., Seo, J., Koo, J., & Kim, J. (2010), 한국형리더십, *Korean Academy of Management,* 18(4), 33-69.

Baikadi, S. B. (2016). Ordered thinking versus disordered doing: A study of entrepreneurial role stress in the Ethiopian business environment. *Journal Of Economic Development, Management, IT, Finance & Marketing*, 8(2), 24-53.

Baikadi, S. B. (2018). Telephone interview. 24 October.

Baker, C., & Campbell, M. (2013). *Context matters: An Ethiopian case study. Adapting leadership development methods to serve different cultures. Center for Creative Leadership.*

Balooch, F. (2018) Personal interview. 3 November.

Baltrimienė, R. (2005). Cultural dimensions of Lithuania and its relative position in the context with other European countries. *Tarptautinės mokslinės praktinės konferencijos pranešimų medžiaga. Karjeros konsultantas tarpkultūrinėje Europos erdvėje*, 11-17. Retrieved from https://www.smk.lt/uploads/archyvas/mokslas/karjera/renata_baltrimiene.pdf

Bandyopadhyay, S., Humavindu, M., Shyamsundar, P., & Wang, L. (2009). *Benefits to local communities from community conservancies in Namibia: an assessment.* Retrieved from http://search.ebscohost.com/login.aspx?direct=true&db=buh&AN=45048479&site=eh ost-live on 13 September 2018.

Bayiley, Y., & Teklu, G. (2016). Success factors and criteria in the management of international development projects. *International Journal Of Managing Projects In Business*, 9(3), 562-582. doi: 10.1108/ijmpb-06-2015-0046.

Becker, R. (2009). Mayan language planning for bilingual education in Guatemala. *International Journal of the Sociology of Language*, 1989(77), 93-116. doi:10.1515/ijsl.1989. 77.93.

Ben, P. (2018) Skype interview. 11 November.

Bennington L., & Habirb A.D. (2003). *Human resource management in Indonesia.* Retrieved from http://citeseerx.ist.psu.edu/viewdoc/download?doi=10.1.1.621.168&rep=rep1&type=pdf on 24 September 2018.

Benon-be-isan Nyuur, R., Ofori, D. F., & Debrah, Y. (2014). Corporate social responsibility in sub-saharan africa: Hindering and supporting factors. *African Journal of Economic and Management Studies*, 5(1), 93-113. Retrieved from https://search.proquest.com/docview/1520636975?accountid=130632 on 20 September 2018.

Berberiàn, S. (2018). *El liderazgo es para presidir y no para ocuparse*. Retrieved from https://www. prensalibre.com/opinion/opinion/el-liderazgo-es-para-presidir-y-no-para-ocuparse on 10 October 2018.

Berhanu, K., & Poulton, C. (2014). The political economy of agricultural extension policy in Ethiopia: Economic growth and political control. *Development Policy Review*, 32(2), 197-213. doi: 10.1111/dpr.12082.

Bertani, M. (2015). *Famiglia e politiche familiari in Italia. Conseguenze della crisi e nuovi rischi sociali: Conseguenze della crisi e nuovi rischi sociali.* FrancoAngeli.

Bhatti, N. (2018) Telephone interview. 3 November.

Blácido, R. (2016). *La situación del quechua en el Perú y su inclusión en el sistema educativo*. Lima: Universidad de Lima.

Bobbio, A., Dierendonck, D. V., & Manganelli, A. M. (2012). Servant leadership in Italy and its relation to organizational variables. *Leadership*, 8(3), 229-243. Retrieved from https://journals.sagepub.com/doi/abs/10.1177/1742715012441176?journalCode=leaa on 18 September 2018.

Boccucci, L. (2014). Catch Leadership TEDxTrento. [video file]. Retrieved from https://www.youtube.com/watch?v=KAA7WxQh5lc on 23 September 2018.

Bodian, M., & Kelly, C. L. (2018). Senegalese Foreign Policy: Leadership Through Soft Power from Senghor to Sall. In *African Foreign Policies in International Institutions* (pp. 327-351). Palgrave Macmillan, New York.

Booysen, L. (1999). A Review of challenges facing Black and White women managers in South Africa, *Southern African Business Review*, 3(2), 15-26.

Bossen, L. (1982). Plantations and labor force discrimination in Guatemala. *Current Anthropology*, 23(3), 263-268. doi:10.1086/202829.

Boudreaux, K., & Nelson, F. (2011). Community conservation in Namibia: Empowering the poor with property rights. *Economic Affairs*, *31*(2), 17-24. Retrieved from http://search.ebscohost.com/login.aspx?direct=true&db=buh&AN=60960257&site=eh ost-live on 13 September 2018.

Bourgoin H. (1984). *L'Afrique malade du management*. Paris: J. Picollec.

Boyatzis, R. E., & Ratti, F. (2009). Emotional, social and cognitive intelligence competencies distinguishing effective Italian managers and leaders in a private company and cooperatives. *Journal of Management Development*, 28(9), 821-838.

Braun, E. (2016). ExecuNet - People First Leadership: A Conversation with [video file]. Retrieved from https://www.youtube.com/watch?v=Pgp-Ml7pqOI on 12 October 2018.

Britannica. (2018). *Uruguay | History, Geography, & Facts.* Retrieved from https://www.britannica.com/place/Uruguay on 2 October 2018.

Brown, I. (2000). *Cambodia*. Oxford, UK: Oxfam.

Budhwar, P., & Mellahi, K. (2006). *Managing Human Resources in the Middle East.* Retrieved from http://iranrahbord.com/wp-content/uploads/2017/11/HRM-in-Middle-east.pdf on 2 October 2018

Buisseret, D. J., Black, C. V., Ferguson, J. A., & Bryan, P. (2018). *Jamaica - History, geography, & points of interest.* Retrieved from https://www.britannica.com/place/Jamaica#ref54491 on 27 September 2018.

Burleson, R., Zhou, P., Mawji, A., Herrera, G., & Masrour, S. (2018, July). *Comparing Cape Verde, Usa, and Uruguay*. Presented at the Institute for Global Business Research Conference. Retrieved from https://www.igbr.org/wp-content/uploads/2018/07/2018-Internet-Conference-Proceedings.pdf#page=61 on September 2018.

Bush, T., Purvis, M. & Barallon, L. (2009). Leadership Development in Small Island States. In Lumby, J., Crow, G. M., & Pashiardis, P. (eds). *International Handbook of the Preparation and Development of School Leaders*. Routledge.

Business Leaders Malta. (2013). Business Leaders Malta Conference 2013 [video file]. Retrieved from https://www.youtube.com/watch?v=2HS3UhmKyFA on 11 October 2018.

Business Leaders Malta. (2014). Business Leaders Malta 2014 - Growth+ [video file]. Retrieved from https://www.youtube.com/watch?v=VldttP2KYso on 11 October 2018.

Buttini, P. (2014). *Città dei Capi*. Ipsoa.

Calderón, O. (2018). Telephone interview. 15 October.

Carneiro, C. (2018). Os 5 Princípios da Liderança [video file]. Retrieved from https://www.youtube.com/watch?v=cP-_pIGbnwI on 14 October 2018.

Carnes, N. (2012). *Al-Maghreb, the Barbary Lion*. iUniverse: Bloomington.

Carroll, S. J., & Gannon, M. J. (1997). *Ethical dimensions of international management*. Thousand Oaks, CA: Sage.

Casadellibro. (n.d.). Retrieved from https://www.casadellibro.com/libro-liderazgo-y-motivacion-de-equipos-de-trabajo/9788473564922/1131194 on 1 November 2018.

Casaretto, R. P. (2018). Skype interview. 15 October.

Cassar, V. & Cortis, R. (2004). Perceptions of and about women as managers: Investigating job involvement, self-esteem and attitudes. *Women In Management Review*. 20. 149-164. 10.1108/09649420510591834.

Cassar, V. (2017) Transformational leadership and work attitudes, comparing explanatory frameworks. *Leadership and Development Journal*, 38(5), 646-661.

Cassar, V. (2018). Skype interview. 4 November.

Catania, G. (2013). *The relationships between age and intrinsic and extrinsic motivation in workers in a Maltese cultural context*. Retrieved from https://www.researchgate.net/publication/294728794_The_relationships_between_age_and_intrinsic_and_extrinsic_motivation_in_workers_in_a_Maltese_cultural_context on 20 October 2018.

CCBS Survey. (2018). *Leadership around the world Survey*. In SurveyMonkey online: Amsterdam University of Applied Sciences.

CDRI. (2009). Youth situation analysis in Cambodia: Challenges, perception and opportunities for youth. *Cambodia Development Review*, 13(1). Retrieved from https://cdri.org.kh/wp-content/uploads/cdr09-1e.pdf on 28 September 2018.

Chandrakumara, A., De Zoysa, A. & Manawaduge, A. S. (2009). *Leadership styles and company performance: the experience of owner-managers of SMEs*. Presented at the 4th International Asian Academy of Applied Business Conference in Makati City, The Philippines.

Chaney, L., & Martin, J. (2011). *International business communication*. Upper Saddle River, N.J.: Prentice Hall.

Cherry, K. (2018). *Intrinsic Motivation*. Retrieved from https://www.verywellmind.com/what-is-intrinsic-motivation-2795385. Consulted on 20 October 2018.

Chhoeun, T., Sok, P., & Byrne, C. (2008). Citadel of woman: Strengthening female leadership in rural Cambodia. *Gender and Development*, 16(3), 535-547. Retrieved from https://wwwjstororg.rps.hva.nl:2443/stable/pdf/20461301.pdfrefreqid=excelsior%3A50ca35f2706922b8764711726448c68a on 9 November 2018.

Chhokar, J. S., Brodbeck, F. C., & House, R. J. (2007). *Globe: Culture and Leadership Around the World*. London: Lawrence Erlbaum Associates.

Cho, D. (2018). Interview. 17 October.

Cho, Y. H., & Yoon, J. (2001). The origin and function of dynamic collectivism: An analysis of Korean corporate culture. *Asia Pacific Business Review*, 7(4), 70-88. Retrieved from: https://www.tandfonline.com/doi/abs/10.1080/713999116 on 07 November 2018.

Chopik, W. J., O'Brien, E., & Konrath, S. H. (2017). Differences in empathic concern and perspective taking across 63 countries. *Journal of Cross-Cultural Psychology, 48*(1), 23-38. Retrieved from http://journals.sagepub.com/doi/pdf/10.1177/0022022116673910.

Chung, K. H., Lee, H. C., & Jung, K. H. (1997). *Korean management: global strategy and cultural transformation.* Berlin: W. de Gruyter.

Constitutional Council. (2010). *The Constitution of the Kingdom of Cambodia.* Chapter III, Art. 31. Retrieved from http://www.wipo.int/edocs/lexdocs/laws/en/kh/kh009en.pdf on 28 September 2018.

Conton, W. (1966). *The African.* London: William Heinemann.

Cortella, M. S. (2016). Gestão de Pessoas. Liderança e Coaching [video file]. Retrieved from https://www.youtube.com/watch?v=923F4HxB6u4 on 23 October 2018.

Country Reports - Ethiopia. (2018). *Ethiopia Country Monitor.* Retrieved from http://search.ebscohost.com.rps.hva.nl:2048/login.aspxdirect=true&db=buh&AN=13045598&site\=ehost-live on 9 October 2018.

Country Reports. (2018). *Namibia.* Retrieved from http://search.ebscohost.com/login.aspx?direct=true&db=buh&AN=130461438&site=e host-live on 13 September 2018.

Country Watch. (2018). *Norway, 2018 Country Review.* Retrieved from http://www.countrywatch.com/Intelligence/CountryReviews?CountryId=129 on 12 October 2018.

CPLP. (2018). *Declaração Constitutiva da Comunidade dos Países de Língua Portuguesa.* Retrieved from https://www.cplp.org/id-3869.aspx on 22 October 2018.

Craig, W. (2017, September 20). Why a Strong Employee/Employer Relationship Is Important. *Forbes.* Retrieved from https://www.forbes.com/sites/williamcraig/2017/09/20/why-a-strong-employeeemployer-relationship-is-important/#1af9d32664d9 on 13 September 2018.

Cucculelli, M & Micucci, G. (2008). Family succession and firm performance: Evidence from Italian family firms. *Journal of Corporate Finance,* 17-31. Retrieved from https://www.researchgate.net/publication/314899450_Family_Succession_and_Firm_Performance_Evidence_from_Italian_Family_Firms on 6 October 2018.

D' Alessio, F. (2009). *The influence of Personality Domains and Working Experience in Peruvian Managers' leaders Style: An initial Study.* (pp. 12-32). Lima: Pontificia Universidad Católica del Perú. Retrieved from https://papers.ssrn.com/sol3/paper.cfm?abstract_id=1479672.

D'Achille, P., & Patota, G. (2016). *L'italiano e la creatività: marchi e costumi, moda e design.* Goware & Accademia Della Crusca.

D'Iribarne, P. (2014). *Le Management Africain Introuvable.* Retrieved from https://www.researchgate.net/publication/278777245_Le_management_africain_introuvable on 9 November 2018.

D'Alessio, F. (2008). The influence of personality domains and working experience in Peruvian managers' leadership styles: An initial study. *Journal of CENTRUM Cathedra,* 1(1), 13-33.

Daly, J. & Navas, D. (2015). *Corrupcion en el Perú.* Lima: Pontificia Universidad Católica del Perú. Retrieved from http://vcentrum.pucp.edu.pe/investigacion/wps/pdf/CERES_WP2015-07-0007.pdf on 23 October 2018.

Danbolt, I.L. (2016). *All about Business. Nordic Women on Boards and in Leadership.* Nordic Council of Ministers.

Darmanin, A. (1992). *Developing Leadership Skills: A training manual for leaders.* Hamrun, Malta: Media Centre.

Darmanin. (2007, June 3) Leadership in Maltese organisations. *Times of Malta.* Retrieved from https://www.timesofmalta.com/articles/view/20070603/opinion/leadership-in-maltese-organisations.15718 on 4 October 2018.

Dateline, S. B. S. (2014). The Poorest President [video file]. Retrieved from https://www.youtube.com/watch?v=YFSmaztcP4c on 11 October 2018.

De Belaunde, A. (2018). *Los retos del liderazgo en una sociedad diversa y compleja como el Perú*. Conferencia ILA 2018 [video file]. Retrieved from https://www.youtube.com/watch?v=4lsg_DG9q6g&t=514s on 23 October 2018.

De Bruyn, G. (2015). A leadership metaphor? TEDxWindhoek [video file]. Retrieved from https://www.youtube.com/watch?v=JUI_vl_GE6U on 11 October 2018.

De Renzo, F. (2005). *Dialetto*. Retrieved from http://www.treccani.it/enciclopedia/dialetto_percent28Enciclopedia-dei-ragazzipercent29/ on 22 September 2018.

De Silva, K. M. (1981). *A History of Sri Lanka. California,* United States: University of California Press.

Del Monte, A., & Papagni, E. (n.d.). *The Determinants of Corruption in Italy: Regional Panel Data Analysis*. Retrieved from https://pdfs.semanticscholar.org/4e41/98b7f605f896142f1b2ab6c172f3621dc77c.pdf on 4 October 2018.

Dereko, A. (2017). *Leadership and management styles in Ukraine*. Retrieved from http://ir.kneu.edu.ua/bitstream/2010/21784/1/355-359.pdf on 13 September 2018.

Derr, C. B., Roussillon, S., & Bournois, F. (eds.). (2002). *Cross-cultural approaches to leadership development*. Greenwood Publishing Group.

Dhatt, R., Theobald, S., Buzuzi, S., Ros, B., Vong, S., & Muraya, K. et al. (2017). The role of women's leadership and gender equity in leadership and health system strengthing. *Glob Health Epidemiol Genom,* 2(8). Retrieved from https://www.ncbi.nlm.nih.gov/pmc/articles/PMC5870471/ on 9 November 2018.

Diliani, D. S. (2016). *Identifying the Leadership Effectiveness of the Executive Leaders in Indonesia*. Retrieved from https://search.proquest.com/docview/1881121210?rfr_id=info%3Axri%2Fsid%3Aprimo on 18 September 2018.

D'Iribarne P. (2009), *L'épreuve des différences : l'expérience d'une entreprise mondiale*, Paris: Seuil.

Diskienė, D., Marčinskas, A., & Stankevičienė, A. (2010). Leadership attitudes in Lithuanian business organizations: Evidence and perspectives. *International Journal of Leadership Studies*, 5, 283-304.

Do Rosário Palma Ramalho, M. (2013, November). Portuguese labour law and industrial relations during the crisis. Governance and Tripartism Department International Labour Office. Retrieved from https://www.fd.unl.pt/docentes_docs/ma/DCM_MA_27484.pdf on 2 November 2018.

Dormagen, J.V. (2008). *"Il Duce" and other fascist senior staff: contribution to a sociology of charismatic domination.* Retrieved from https://www.cairn-int.info/article-E_RHMC_553_0035--il-duce-and-other-fascist-senior-staff.htm on 18 September 2018.

Drucker, P. F. (n.d.). *La gerencia de empresas*. Retrieved from https://books.google.nl/books?id=I6GaAgAAQBAJ on 4 November 2018.

Du Toit, P. (n.d.). *About*. Retrieved from http://www.pennydutoit.com/ on 21 October 2018.

DuBrin, A. J. (2001). *Leadership: Research findings, practice, skills (3rd ed.)*. Boston: Houghton Mifflin.

Duncan-Price I. & Hamilton R. (2015). "I am a PowHERhouse" - Women & Leadership in Jamaica: Politics and Business [video file]. Retrieved from https://www.youtube.com/watch?v=4nBKwuAJGNk on 03 November 2018.

Dvergsdal, D. (2014). *Expanding your leadership*. Oslo: Abstrakt Forlaget.

Earuyan Solutions. (2017, 30 July). Dearth of women's leadership in Ethiopia - Seminar 3. Capital Hotel Addis Ababa.

Earuyan Solutions. (2018, february). Seminar series report: The dearth of women's leadership in Ethiopia. Retrieved from https://www.awib.org.et/currency/focus/item/1169-the-dearth-of-women-s-leadership-in-ethiopia-seminar-series-report-report.html on 1st November 2018.

Ekern, S. (2011). The production of autonomy: Leadership and community in Mayan Guatemala. *Journal of Latin American Studies*, 43(1), 93-119. Retrieved from http://www.jstor.org.rps.hva.nl:2048/ stable/23030585 on 2 October 2018.

Elobservador. (2017). *Sepa cuáles son los mejores lugares para trabajar en Uruguay*. Retrieved from https://www.elobservador.com.uy/nota/sepa-cuales-son-los-mejores-lugares-para-trabajar-en-uruguay-20171122500 on 13 September 2018.

Emergo (n.d.). *Team*. Retrieved from http://emergo.com.na/team/ on 31 October 2018.

Esterhuysen, P. (2013). *Africa A to Z: Continental and Country Profiles, third edition* [Book]. Retrieved from https://books.google.nl/books on 2 October 2018.

Euromonitor. (2018). *Namibia: Country Profile.* Retrieved from //www.portal.euromonitor.com/portal/?Aeb3kDJaDQkBs%2b8BdDQsvw%3d%3d on 13 September 2018.

Euromonitor. (n.d.) *Malta: Country Profile*. Retrieved from http://www.portal.euromonitor.com/portal/analysis/tab on 28 September 2018.

Eurostat. (2018). *Women in the EU earned on average 16 percent less than men in 2016.* Retrieved from https://ec.europa.eu/eurostat/documents/2995521/8718272/3-07032018-BP-EN.pdf/fb402341-e7fd-42b8-a7cc-4e33587d79aa on 18 September 2018.

Expat Focu.s (2018). *Malta business culture.* Retrieved from http://www.expatfocus.com/expatriate-malta-business-culture on 4 October 2018.

Fall, M. A. F. (2017). Leadership from the Bottom Up [video file]. Retrieved from https://www.youtube.com/watch?v=_XqCEeWyVYE on 03 November 2018.

Favale, R. (n.d.) *El Imperio Inca*. Barcelona: Universidad de Barcelona. Retrieved from http://www.comercioexterior.ub.edu/latinoamerica/lecturas07_08/Incas/elimperio_inca.pdf on 20 October 2018.

Fedior O. (2014). *Emergence: Quel leadership pour le Sénégal?* Retrieved from http://reussirbusiness.com/emergence/emergence-quel-leadership-pour-le-senegal/ on 12 October 2018.

Fenton, S. (2016). Teranga. *The Little Baobab*. Retrieved from http://thelittlebaobab.com/teranga/ on 11 October 2018.

Feria, G. (2018). Skype interview. 23 October.

Fernando, M. (2007). *Spiritual Leadership in the entrepreneurial business.* Massachusetts, USA: Edward Elgar Publishing.

Ferraro, C. (2013). *Il passaggio generazionale nell'impresa familiare. Analisi del fenomeno e aspetti valutativi: Analisi del fenomeno e aspetti valutativi.* Published by FrancoAngeli.

Fiedler, F. (1967). *A theory of leadership effectiveness.* New York: McGraw-Hill.

Financial Afrik (2014) *Quel type de leadership pour l'émergence économique et sociale du Sénégal?* Retrieved from https://www.financialafrik.com/2014/08/26/quel-type-de-leadership-pour-lemergence-economique-et-sociale-du-senegal/ on 12 October 2018.

Flamholtz, E.G. (1986). *How to make the transition from entrepreneurship to a professionally managed firm.* San Francisco: Jossey-Bass

Floris, P. (2008). *Leadership e change management. Leadership: non il successo di un singolo ma la forza di un gruppo.* Published by Franco Angeli.

Follegatti, J.L.L. (2015). Conferencia: Liderazgo y sociedad en el Perú de hoy (pp29-39) In Caravedo Molinari, B. (2015). *Es posible el Liderazgo en el Perú actual. Problemas y perspectivas en la política, empresa y sociedad Peruana*. Universidad del Pacifico. Retrieved from http://repositorio.up.edu.pe/bitstream/handle/11354/972/CaravedoBaltazar.pdf?sequence=1&isAllowed=y on 22 October 2018.

Forrest, J. B. (1999). Namibia's post-apartheid agricultural bureaucracy restructuring: The agricultural extension service, 1990-1996. *The Journal of African Policy Studies*, 5(1), 33-52. Retrieved from https://search.proquest.com/docview/61753507?accountid=130632 on 13 September 2018.

Franco, M., & Gonçalo Matos, P. (2013). *Leadership styles in SMEs: a mixed-method approach.* New York: Springer Science+Business Media.

Frese, M., Brantjes, A., & Hoorn, R. (2002). Psychological success factors of small scale businesses in Namibia. *Journal of developmental Entrepreneurship*, *7*(3), 259-282. Retrieved from http://search.ebscohost.com/ on 25 September 2018.

Furtado, L. C. d. R., Batista, M. d. G. C., & Silva, F. J. F. (2011). Leadership's impact on turnover and career abandonment intention: The Azorean hospital nurses case. *Hospital Topics*, 89(3), 51.

Fuxman, L. (2004). Emerging trends in Ukrainian management styles and the challenge of managerial talent shortage. *International Journal of Commerce and Management*, 14(1), 28-43. Retrieved from https://search-proquest-com.rps.hva.nl:2443/docview/212839945?accountid=130632 on 13 September 2018.

Gallas, D. (2018). *Why confidence in Argentina's economy is dwindling*. Retrieved from https://www.bbc.com/news/world-latin-america-44107630 on 29 September 2018.

Gamio, C. (2018). Manejar Equipos de Alto Rendimiento [video file]. Retrieved from https://www.youtube.com/watch?v=JC_Zxucj-Il on 16 October 2018.

Gani, D. S. (2004). Leadership in Indonesia: A case for managing relationship within organizations. In *Leading in High Growth Asia: Managing relationship for teamwork and change* (pp. 195-209).

Gatt, M. (2016). *Emotional intelligence and effective leadership: Considerations of managers in the Maltese business society.* Retrieved from https://www.um.edu.mt/library/oar/handle/123456789/15582 on 20 October 2018.

Gebremariam, G. W., & Delesa, T. M. (2014). Assessment of leadership in practices and effectiveness in Ethiopian universities. *Journal of Research in Commerce & Management*, 5(7), 52-59.

Gerashchenko, V. (2016). Як стати лідером? [Video file]. Retrieved from https://www.youtube.com/watch?v=G_T1MYNftJ0 on 2 November 2018.

Ghislieri, C., & Gatti, P. (2012). Generativity and balance in leadership. *Leadership*, *8*(3), 257-275. Retrieved from https://journals.sagepub.com/doi/abs/10.1177/1742715012441177?journalCode=leaa on 18 September 2018.

Gibson, C. B. (1995). An investigation of gender differences in leadership across four countries. *Journal of International Business Studies*, *26*(2), 255-279.

Giovanni, L. (2018). Zoom interview. 13 October.

Gjermundshaug, T. M., Seim, I., & Berglund, R. (2018). *Innovative ledere: En casestudie av norske lederes innovative ferdigheter.* Retrieved from https://brage.bibsys.no/xmlui/handle/11250/2565529 on 12 October, 2018.

Global Affairs Canada. (2018). *Country Insights - Guatemala*. Retrieved from www.international.gc.ca/cil-cai/country_insights-apercus_pays/ciic_gt. aspx?lang=eng on 2 October 2018.

Global growing. (2017). *Fact 7.* Retrieved from http://global-growing.org/en/content/fact-7-about-three-quarters-african-population-live-less-2-half-population-less-125-day on 15 October 2018.

Global Security. (2017). *Conga-Brazzaville – Politics.* Retrieved from https://www.globalsecurity.org/military/world/africa/cg-politics.htm on 13 October 2018.

Globe Project. (2016). *Global leadership & organizational behavior effectiveness.* Retrieved from https://globeproject.com/results/countries/ITA?menu=list on 17 September 2018.

Globe Project. (2016). *Indonesia.* Retrieved from https://globeproject.com/results/countries/IDN?menu=list on 5 October 2018.

Globe. (2007). *Leadership and culture in Portugal.* New Jersey, London: Lawrence Erlbaum Associates.

Gombrich, R. F. (1990). The Bod hi Pfija. In R. F. Gombrich, R. Gombrich, & G. Obeyesekere (eds.), *Buddhism Transformed: Religious Change in Sri Lanka* (pp. 384–390). Delhi, India: Motilal Banarsidass.

Gomes, C. F., & Yasin, M. M. (2013). Managing public sector projects in Portugal: Meeting the challenge through effective leadership. *Journal of Leadership, Accountability and Ethics*, 10(2), 113-122.

Gomes, Wilson (2018, 2 November). Leadership in Portugal with a marketing and communications specialist.

Gonçalves, M. N. (2008). *Estilos de Liderança - Um estudo de auto perceção de enfermeiros gestores*. Porto: Universidade Fernando Pessoa.

González, C. D. (2017). Management en Argentina: Culture and an innovative perspective. *Palermo Business Review* 15(45). Retrieved from https://search-proquest-com.rps.hva.nl:2443/docview/1949474412?accountid=130632 on 2 October 2018.

Gonzalez, L.E. (2014). Uruguay management, leadership and entrepeneurship style. In L. E. Gonzalez (Ed.), *Management, Leadership and Entrepreneurship in Latin America The Land of Opportunity (pp. 326–333).* Retrieved from https://books.google.nl/on 13 September 2018.

Gooden, D.J & Preziosi, R. (2011). *Cultural values and management behaviour in the United States, Jamaica, and the Bahamas.* Retrieved from https://www.researchgate.net/ on 11 October 2018.

GPTW. (n.d.). Retrieved from http://www.greatplacetowork.com.uy/mejores-empresas on 18 October 2018.

Grandday. (2010). *Hofstede Analysis High Context vs. Low Context cultures Business Etiquette.*

Gravina, V. (2013). *Investigating leadership characteristics and attitudes toward creativity according to agency context for agriculture extension agents in Uruguay* [Book]. Retrieved from https://docplayer.net/58356572 on 13 September 2018.

Greaves, A. (2018). Skype interview. 30 March.

Grigoreva, A. (2017). *Effects of Cultural Components on Business in Italy.* Thesis. Saimaa University of Applied Sciences. Retrieved from on 18 September 2018.

Grobler, A., & Singh, M. (2018). Leadership in southern africa: A regional afrocentric hierarchical taxonomy. *Insight on Africa*, 10(2), 169-193. Retrieved from http://dx.doi.org/10.1177/0975087818772236 on 14 September 2018.

Guechtouli, W., & Guechtouli, M. (2011). *Innovation et [entrepreneuriat] en Algérie: quelles barrières culturelles?* Retrieved from https://www.researchgate.net/publication/320041553_Innovation_et_entreprenariat_en_Algerie_quelles_barrieres_culturelles on 12 October 2018.

Guippe, A. (2017). Management Styles of Philippines, S. Korea, and Japan [video file]. Retrieved from https://www.youtube.com/watch?v=qqj3A0MaI34 on 15 October 2018.

Hae-Joang, C. (2005). Reading the "Korean Wave" as a sign of global shift. *Korea Journal, 45*(4), 147-182. Retrieved from http://citeseerx.ist.psu.edu/viewdoc/download doi=10.1.1.640.4468&rep=rep1&type=pdf on 07 October 2018.

Hainsch, C. (2018) Skype interview. 17 October.

Haleem, S. (2013). *The Essential Guide to Customs & Culture - Pakistan*. London, United Kingdom: Kuperard.

Hashwani, S. (2017). *The Truth Always Prevails: A Memoir*. Lahore, Pakistan: Jumhoori Publications.

Hatum, A. (2006). The influence of national business environment as shaper of organizational action. *Management Research*, 4(3), 155-168. Retrieved from http://dx.doi.org.rps.hva.nl:2048/10.2753/JMR1536-5433040302 on 27 September 2018.

Hays, J. (2008). *Land and Geography of Indonesia*. Retrieved from http://factsanddetails.com/indonesia/Nature_Science_Animals/sub6_8a/entry-4078.html on 2 October 2018.

Hendon, D. W., Hendon, R. A., & Herbig, P. (1999). *Cross-cultural business negotiations.* [Books24x7 version] Retrieved from Books23x7: http://common.books24x7.com.rps.hva.nl:2048/toc.aspx?bookid=7390. on 1 October 2018.

Hernandez, S. (2018). Interview with Sonia Hernandez - The new CEO of Vodafone Malta [video file]. Retrieved from https://www.youtube.com/watch?v=fHqD3gPVfQs&t=113s on 11 October 2018.

Hoffmann, B. (2010). *The relationship between emotional intelligence and leadership among middle managers in Namibia* (Doctoral dissertation).. Retrieved from http://repository.unam.edu.na/bitstream/handle/11070/539/hoffmann2010.pdf?sequence=1 on 25 September 2018.

Hofstede Insights. (n.d). *Country comparison.* Retrieved from https://www.hofstede-insights.com/country-comparison/ between 3 October and 2 November 2018.

Hofstede, G. (1983). The cultural relativity of organizational practices and theories. *Journal of International Business Studies*, 14(2), 75-89. Retrieved from doi:10.1057/palgrave.jibs.8490867 on 12 October 2018.

Hofstede, G. (2001). Culture's consequences: Comparing values, behaviors, institutions, and organizations across nations. Thousand Oaks, CA: Sage Publications.

Hofstede, G., Hofstede, G. J. & Minkov, M. (2010). *Cultures and organizations: software of the mind, third edition*. [Books24x7 version] Retrieved from http://common.books24x7.com.rps.hva.nl:2048/toc.aspx?bookid=142700 on 10 November 2018.

Holtzman, I. (2009). *РОЛЬ МОТИВАЦІЙНОГО МЕХАНІЗМУ В СИСТЕМІ УПРАВЛІННЯ ПЕРСОНАЛОМ*. Retrieved from http://eprints.zu.edu.ua/11632/ on 5 October 2018.

House, R. J. (2014). *Culture, leadership, and organizations: The GLOBE study of 62 societies*. Thousand Oaks, CA: SAGE Publications.

Hughes, C., & Un, K. (2011). *Cambodia's economic transformation*. Copenhagen, DK: NIAS Press.

Human Development Reports. (n.d.). Retrieved from http://www.hdr.undp.org/en/indicators/153706 on 13 April 2018.

Humavindu, M. N., & Stage, J. (2013). Key sectors of the Namibian economy. *Journal of Economic structures*, *2*(1), 1.

Hussain, G., Ismail, K. W., & Javed, M. (2017). Comparability of leadership constructs from the Malaysian and Pakistani perspectives. *Cross Cultural & Strategic Management*, 24(4), 617–644.

Hussain, R. (n.d.). Pakistan - Oxford Islamic Studies Online. Retrieved from http://www.oxfordislamicstudies.com/article/opr/t236/e0616 on 11 November 2018.

Inanlou, Z., & Ji-Young, A. (2017). The effect of organizational culture on employee commitment: A mediating role of human resource development in korean firms. *Journal of Applied Business Research*, 33(1), 87-94. Retrieved from http://dx.doi.org.rps.hva.nl:2048/10.19030/jabr.v33i1.9869 on 11 March 2018.

INSPIRED.Cambodia. (2017, June 22). *Toastmasters: Leadership Community Club* [Video file]. Retrieved from https://www.youtube.com/watch?v=wlvtqCaLnmw on 11 October 2018.

Instituto Nacional De Estatistica. (2018). Estatísticas. Retrieved from http://www.ine.gov.mz/estatisticas on 20 October 2018.

International Medical Travel Journal. (June, 2010). *Malta Targets Medical Tourism*. Retrieved from https://www.imtj.com/news/malta-targets-medical-tourism/ on 28 September 2018.

Irawanto, D. W. (2011). An analysis of national culture and leadership practices in Indonesia. *Journal of Diversity Management (JDM)*, 4(2), 41. Retrieved from https://doi.org/10.19030/jdm.v4i2.4957 on 23 September 2018.

Iruleguy, F. (2018). Skype interview. 7 April.

ISA, International Strategic Analysis. (2018). *Country: Italy*. Retrieved from https://www.isa-world.com on 13 September 2018.

ISM University (2016). *ISM Vadovų magistrantūra – Šiaurietiškas lyderis: Bjornar Lund* [Video file]. Retrieved from https://www.youtube.com/watch?v=ezSyhxd8V7I on 19 October 2018.

ISM University. (2013). *Former President of Lithuania Valdas Adamkus on leadership and education* [Video file]. Retrieved from https://www.youtube.com/watch?v=4yzs5NjyjaI on 19 October 2018.

Isolabella, C., & Kaneklin, C. (1997). *Immagini emergenti della leadership nelle organizzazioni*. Vita e Pensiero.

Istat. (n.d.). *Strutture produttive*. Retrieved from http://noi-italia.istat.it/index.php?id=3&tx_usercento_centofepercent5Bcategoriapercent5D=10&tx_usercento_centofepercent5Bactionpercent5D=show&tx_usercento_centofepercent5Bcontrollerpercent5D=Categoria&cHash=17c921a97e9803953bd95788a3f54d8a on 22 September 2018.

ITA, The International Trade Administration. (2017). *Republic of Congo – market overview*. Retrieved from https://www.export.gov/article?series=a0pt0000000PAtYAAW&type=Country_Commercial__kav on 13 October 2018.

Jang, D.J., (2000). The Characteristics and Moral Grounds on Political Leadership in Modern Korea. International Leadership Association Annual Meeting, November 3-5, 2000, Toronto, Canada. Retrieved from: http://www.hawaii.edu/intlrel/pols605c/leadership/Modern%20Korea/jang.htm on 4 October 2018.

Jasinavičius, N. (2017). *Nuo amato prie verslo*. Lithuania: Kopa

Javidan, M. (2004). Performance orientation. In M. Javidan, R.J. House, P.J. Hanges, P.W. Dorfman, & V. Gupta (Eds.), *Culture, Leadership and Organizations: The GLOBE Study of 62 Societies* (pp. 241).

Jayakody, J. (2008). Charismatic leadership in Sri Lankan business organizations. *Journal of Management Development*, 27(5), pp. 480-498. Retrieved from https://www.emeraldinsight.com/doi/abs/10.1108/02621710810871808 on 12 October 2018.

Jeong, G. (2015). *Miracle on the Han River: A Regression Analysis of the Effect of Chaebol Dominance on South Korea's Economic Growth*. (Undergraduate Honours Thesis).

Jesuíno, J. C, Pereira, O. G., & Reto, L. A. (1993). *Características dos Gestores de Topo: Uma Abordagem Qualitativa.* Lisboa: ISCTE - Instituto Universitário de Lisboa. Retrieved from https://repositorio.iscte-iul.pt/bitstream/10071/14363/1/Característicaspercent20dospercent20Gestorespercent20depercent20Topopercent20-percent20Umapercent20abordagempercent20qualitativa.pdf on 22 October 2018.

Jesuino, J. C. (2008). Leadership and Culture in Portugal. In J. S. Chhokar, F. C. Brodbeck, & R. J. House, *Culture and Leadership Across the World* (p. 596). New Jersey: Lawrence Erlbaum Associates.

Jesuino, J. C. (2013). Leadership and culture in Portugal. In *Culture and Leadership Across the World* (pp. 617-656). Routledge.

Jordan, S. C. (2016). *The Two Main Languages of Jamaica - Alpha Omega Translations.* Retrieved from https://alphaomegatranslations.com/foreign-language/the-two-main-languages-of-jamaica on 27 September 2018.

Jorge Correia de Sousa, M., & van Dierendonck, D. (2014). Servant leadership and engagement in a merge process under high uncertainty. *Journal of Organizational Change Management*, *27*(6), 877-899.

Kabasakal, H., Dastmalchian, A., Karacay, G., & Bayraktar, S. (2012). Leadership and culture in the MENA region: An analysis of the GLOBE project. *Journal of World Business*, *47*(4), 519-529.

Kane, B. (2013). Leaders and Leadership [video file]. Retrieved from https://www.youtube.com/watch?v=S0UopAu_gmo on 15 October 2018.

Kaneklin, C. & Isolabella, M.C. (1997). *Immagini emergenti della leadership nelle organizzazioni.* Vita e Pensiero.

Karbaum, M. (2015). The Dynamics of Social Change in Cambodia: Moving away from Traditionalism? *Internationales Asienforum,* 46(1), 243-253.

Katilienė, R. (2018). Personal interview. 9 November.

Katilienė, R., & Bakanauskienė, I. (2012). Expression of spiritual leadership in Lithuanian businesses. *Organizacijø Vadyba: Sisteminiai Tyrimai*, (64), 53-67.

Kent, A. (2003). Recovery of the collective spirit: The role of the revival of Buddhism in Cambodia. *Department of Social Anthropology,* 8. Retrieved from https://www.lir.gu.se/digitalAssets/809/809980_WP8Kent.pdf on 28 September 2018.

Khilji, S. E. (2013). Chapter 7: Human resource management in Pakistan. In P. S. Budhwar, & Y. A. Debrah (Eds.), *Human Resource Management in Developing Countries* (pp. 102–120).

Khodja, L., Fekkan, F., & Sofiane, A. (2018). *More women entrepreneurs in Algeris* [video file]. Retrieved from https://www.youtube.com/watch?v=84FcSAWYLlg on 12 October 2018.

Ki-Bok, B. (2017). 한국형 리더십 : 세계를 이끄는 신바람 다이내믹스. Retrieved from https://book.naver.com/bookdb/book_detail.nhn?bid=12153332

Kim, A. E., & Park, G. S. (2003). Nationalism, Confucianism, work ethic and industrialization in South Korea. *Journal of contemporary Asia*, *33*(1), 37-49.

Kim, S. K. (1996). " Big companies don't hire us, married women": exploitation and empowerment among women workers in South Korea. *Feminist studies*, *22*(3), 555-571. Retrieved from https://www.jstor.org/stable/3178130?seq=1#metadata_info_tab_contents on 07 October 2018.

Kim, T. Y., Lee, D. R., & Wong, N. Y. S. (2016). Supervisor humor and employee outcomes: The role of social distance and affective trust in supervisor. *Journal of Business and Psychology*, *31*(1), 125-139.

Kim, T., Lee, J., & Lee, J. (2013). Do interpersonal relationships still matter for turnover intention? A comparison of South Korea and China. *The International Journal of Human Resource Management,* 24(5), 968-971. Retrieved from http://web.b.ebscohost.com.qe2a-proxy.mun.ca/ehost/pdfviewer/pdfviewer?vid=1&sid=b1da10c0-bee9-4baa-a08a-d01c7ff28030%40pdc-v-sessmgr03 on 02 November 2018.

Kirkhaug, R. (2018). Personal interview. 9 October.

Kliuchnikov, A. (2014). *A cross-cultural study of effective leadership attributes in Ukraine and Russia.* Regent University.

Kostat. (2017). *2017 Population and Housing Census.* Retrieved from http://kostat.go.kr/portal/eng/pressReleases/8/7/index.board on 07 October 2018.

Kwon, H., Kim, T., Lee, J., & Yi, I. (2011). "Mixed Governance" and welfare in South Korea. *Journal of Democracy,* 22(3). Retrieved from: https://muse-jhu-edu.qe2a-proxy.mun.ca/article/444763

Lago, R. (2018). Telephone interview. 22 October.

Laksamana. (2018). Personal interview. 8 November.

Largosen, S. (2002). Quality management in Europe: a cultural perspective. *The TQM Magazine*, 14(5), 275-283.

Lasky, J. (2001). How to be culturally correct in South America. *Secured Lender*, *57*(3), 38-38.

Lavado, P. (2018). Telephone interview. 2 November.

Lawrence, P.D. (2018). Skype interview. 8 November.

Ledgerwood, J., & Un, K. (2002). *Cambodia in 2002: Decentralization and its effects on party politics.* Regents, United States: University of California Press Journals.

Lee, C. Y. (2012). Korean culture and its influence on business practice in South Korea. *The Journal of International Management Studies*, *7*(2), 184-191.

Lewis, R. D. (2006). *When cultures collide: leading across cultures, third edition.* [Books24x7 version] Retrieved from http://common.books24x7.com.rps.hva.nl:2048/toc.aspx?bookid=13710 on 9 October 2018.

Lifintsev, D. (2016). Cross-Cultural Management as an objective need for Ukrainian companies. Retrieved from https://www.researchgate.net/publication/301689618_Cross-Cultural_Management_as_an_objective_need_for_Ukrainian_companies on 6 November 2018.

Lifintsev, D. (2018). Skype interview. 7 November.

Linstead, S. (2009). *Management and Organization.* Retrieved from https://books.google.nl/books/about/Management_and_Organization_2e_EBOOK.html?id=pppMDwAAQBAJ&printsec=frontcover&source on 10 November 2018.

Lopéz, M. (2008). Globe: Culture and leadership around the world, Argentina. London: Lawrence Erbaum Associates.

Luiss, I. R. (2008). *Generare classe dirigente. Una sintonia positiva da ritrovare con il paese.* Milano: Il Sole 24 Ore.

Mabbett, I., & Chandler, D. (1995). *The Khmers. The Peoples of South-East Asia and the Pacific.* Oxford, US: Blackwell Publishers.

Madjdi, N. (2011). *Les déterminants du style de leadership qui contribuent au transfert des connaissances. Etude de cas: l'entreprise de l'Algérie poste (l'agence de M'sila)* (Doctoral dissertation, Université Mohamed Khider-Biskra).

Malik, A.B. (2018, 23 June). Developing economic leadership in Pakistan. *The Financial Daily*. Retrieved from https://thefinancialdaily.com/developing-economic-leadership-pakistan/ on 8 November 2018.

Mallen, M. (2011). *Effetto D: Se la leadership è al femminile: storie speciali di donne normali.* Franco Angeli.

MaltaProfile. (2017) *Banking Sector Profile*. Retrieved from https://maltaprofile.info/article/banking-2018 on 28 September 2018

Manzega. (2018*). Les dérives de l'Etat postcolonial en République démocratique du Congo(Broché).* Retrieved from http://www.editions-harmattan.fr/index.asp?navig=catalogue&obj=livre&no=60312 on 24 October 2018.

Marri, L.D.A., & Mallen, M. (2013). *Effetto D. Se la leadership è al femminile: storie speciali di donne normali: Se la leadership è al femminile: storie speciali di donne normali.* Franco Angeli.

Marshall, M., & Stokes, R. (2018). *Tradition and the Veil: Female Status in Tunisia and Algeria.* Retrieved from https://www.jstor.org/stable/pdf/160437.pdf on 2 October 2018.

Martin, J. S., & Chaney, L. H. (2012*). Global business etiquette: a guide to international communication and customs, second edition.* [Books24x7 version] Retrieved from http://common.books24x7.com.rps.hva.nl:2048/toc.aspx?bookid=45432 on 10 November 2018.

Martin, N. (2013). Edward Seaga, the Jamaican Visionary. *The Caribbean Current.* Retrieved from https://thecaribbeancurrent.com/edward-seaga-the-jamaican-visionary/ on November 2018.

Martinsen, Ø. L., & Glasø, L. (2013). *Lederes Personlighet: HVA Sier Forskningen?* Retrieved from https://brage.bibsys.no/xmlui/bitstream/handle/11250/222347/Martinsen_Glaso_Magma_052014.pdf?sequence=1&isAllowed=y on 12 October 2018.

Marturano, A., Oriani, R., & Quaglino, GP. (2009). *Crescere al futuro. Leadership e continuita d'impresa oltre la crisi.* Milano: Il Sole 24 Ore.

Massimo, L. M., & Massimo, R. (2011). *Leadership e team building di successo.* Maggioli editore.

Matondo, J. P. M. (2012a). A comparative study of five cross-cultural dimensions: Chinese construction companies in Congo. *African Journal of Business Management*, *6*(42), 10655-19664.

Matondo, J. P. M. (2012b). Cross-cultural values comparison between Chinese and Sub-Saharan Africans. *International Journal of Business and Social Science*, *3*(11).

Mavuanda. (2017). *Why are there 2 Congo's instead of being united as one Congo nation?* Retrieved from https://www.quora.com/Why-are-there-2-Congos-instead-of-being-united-as-one-Congo-nation on 2 October 2018.

Mayorga, J. A. G. & Codoñer C. M. (2008). *La Paradoja del Liderazgo Autocratico*. Retrieved from https://www.scribd.com/doc/143805378/La-Paradoja-del-Liderazgo-Autocratico-LIBRO-pdf on 11 November 2018.

Mbigi, L. (1995). *Ubuntu. The spirit of African transformation management*, Randburg: Knowledge Resources.

McDade, B. E., & Spring, A. (2005). The 'new generation of African entrepreneurs': networking to change the climate for business and private sector-led development. *Entrepreneurship & Regional Development*, *17*(1), 17-42.

Mcintosh, T. (2011). *Leadership Peruvian style: How Peruvian define and practice leadership*. Bloomington: iUniverse.

McKenna, A. (2017). Namibia. Retrieved from https://www.britannica.com/place/Namibia on 25 September 2018.

McNamara, V. (2015). Cambodia: From Dependency to Sovereignty - Emerging National Leadership. *Journal of International and Comparative Education,* 4(2). Retrieved from https://ejournal.um.edu.my/index.php/JICE/article/view/2741/5186 on 20 October 2018.

Merkin, R. S., & Shah, M. (2014). The impact of sexual harassment on job satisfaction, turnover intentions, and absenteeism: findings from Pakistan compared to the United States. *Springer Plus*, 3(1), 215.

Meyer, E. (2014). *The culture map: Breaking through the invisible boundaries of global business*. Public Affairs.

Mezrig, A., & Bouguesri, S. (2017). The role of human resource management practices in increasing the level of employees satisfaction in Algerian companies. Indian *Journal of Commerce and Management Studies*, *8*(1), 82. Retrieved from http://www.scholarshub.net/ijcms/vol8/issue1/Paper_13.pdf on 15 October 2018.

Miahouakana, M.J.P. (2008). L'ethnicité, un obstacle au développement économique des pays Africains, *Journal Le Chemin*, 5, 5.

Micallef, J. (2015). *Strategic management in small businesses: The role of managers' previous experiences and educational background* (Bachelor's thesis, University of Malta). Retrieved from https://www.um.edu.mt/library/oar//handle/123456789/5607 on 11 October 2018.

Michiels J. (2018). Telephone interview. 19 September.

Miembazi-Massamba, R. C. H. (2017). Research on the Impact of Organizational Commitment on Job Satisfaction between China and Congo-Brazzaville. *Journal of Research in Business, Economics and Management*, *8*(3), 1444-1450. Retrieved from http://scitecresearch.com/journals/index.php/jrbem/article/view/1054/745 on 15 October 2018.

Min, H. J. (2015). The subtleties of effective leadership in South Korea. *Human Capital Leadership Institute*. Retrieved from https://hcli.org/articles/subtleties-effective-leadership-south-korea on 23 October 2018.

Minelgaite, I. & Littrell, R. F. (2018). Country's preferred leader behaviour profile: Does cultural homogeneity matter? *Journal of Contemporary Management*, 23 (1), 1-27. Retrieved from https://doi.org/10.30924/mjcmi/2018.23.1.1 on 12 October 2018.

Minelgaite,I., & Stangej, O. (2017). *Nordic leadership & the Big picture: insights from the Nordic Boost Initiative.* Retrieved from https://doi.org/10.13140/RG.2.2.12205.90089 on 14 October 2018.

Mitiku, A. A., Hondeghem, A., & Troupin, S. (2017). Administrative leadership: Understanding the preferred leadership roles of the Ethiopian civil service managers. *African Journal of Economic and Management Studies*, 8(3), 366-394.

Mogrovejo, L. R. (2015). Liderazgo político: el gran lector, la institucionalidad y la traición (pp. 11-29). In Caravedo Molinari, B. (2015). *Es posible el Liderazgo en el Perú actual. Problemas y perspectivas en la política, empresa y sociedad Peruana.* Universidad del Pacifico. Retrieved from http://repositorio.up.edu.pe/bitstream/handle/11354/972/CaravedoBaltazar.pdf?sequence=1&isAllowed=y on 12 October 2018.

Möllering, G., & Stache, F. (2007). German-Ukrainian business relationships: Trust development in the face of institutional uncertainty and cultural differences. Cologne: Max-Planck-Institut für Gesellschaftsforschung.

Monteiro, B. (2018). 7 dicas para aumentar sua influencia como lider [video file]. Retrieved from https://www.youtube.com/watch?v=wZnfuWSjkb8 on 25 October 2018.

Montejo, V. (2005). *Maya intellectual renaissance: Identity, representation, and leadership.* Austin: University of Texas Press.

Montelatici, F. (2018). Video interview. 14 November.

Montemerlo, D. (2000). *Il governo delle imprese familiari. Modelli e strumenti per gestire I rapporti fra proprietà e impresa.* Milano: Egea.

Moore, M. H. (1995). *Creating public value: Strategic management in government.* London, England: Harvard University Press.

Moran, R. T., Harris, P. R., & Moran, S. V. (2006). *Managing cultural differences, global leadership strategies for the 21st Century.* Retrieved from http://mimccomwinter2017.pbworks.com/w/file/fetch/114649891/_Robert_T._Moran_Philip_R._Harris_Sarah_V._Moran_Bookos.org_.pdf on 18 Otober 2018.

Moran, R. T., Harris, P.R., & Moran, S. V. (2011). *Doing business with Africans—Northern Africa, East Africa, WestCentral Africa, and Southern Africa (NORTH AFRICA). In:Managing cultural differences: global leadership strategies for cross-cultural business success, eighth edition.* Taylor and Francis. [Books24x7 version]. Retrieved from http://common.books24x7.com.rps.hva.=40158 on 27 September 2018.

Moran, R. T., Harris, P. R., & Moran, S. V. (2011). *Managing cultural differences: global leadership strategies for cross-cultural business success, eighth edition.* [Books24x7 version] Retrieved from http://common.books24x7.com.rps.hva.nl:2048/toc.aspx?bookid=40158 on 10 November 2018.

Moreno, M. & Moreno P. (2012). Formacion de lideres [video file]. Retrieved from https://newmedia.ufm.edu/ video/formacion-de-lideres/ on 12 October 2018.

Motta, G. (2016). *I tempi e I luoghi del cibo.* Edizioni nuova cultura.

Mujtaba, M. G., Afza, T., & Habib, N. (2011). Leadership Tendencies of Pakistanis: Exploring similarities and differences based on age and gender. *Journal of Economics and Behavioural Studies, 2*(5), 199–212.

Mujuru, S. (2012). *Business culture in the Caribbean region.* Retrieved from https://www.theseus.fi/bitstream/handle/10024/45745/Business%20culture.pdf on 7 November 2018.

Musalo, K. (2013). Crimes without punishment: An update on violence against women and impunity in Guatemala. *Hashtings Race and Poverty Law Journal,* 10, 284-290.

Mwangi, M. (2014). *African Leadership: The Youth at a Crossroad.* Retrieved from https://www.iiste.org/Journals/index.php/DCS/article/view/12861/13441 on 11 October 2018.

Nanayakkara, G. (1999). The study of best management practices in Sri Lanka's high performing companies. *Journal of Comparative International Management*, 2(1). Retrieved from https://journals.lib.unb.ca/index.php/jcim/article/view/480/807 on 7 October 2018.

Nathavitharana V. (2017). Can Leadership Be Taught? TEDxColombo [video file]. Retrieved from https://www.youtube.com/watch?v=_2KcTRykSaw on 9 October 2018.

Naver (2018). 리더십, 난중일기에 묻다. Retrieved from https://book.naver.com/bookdb/book_detail.nhn?bid=13221133 on 11 November 2018.

Navi, K. (2018). 7 lessons of leadership. TEDx Islamabad [video file]. Retrieved from https://www.youtube.com/watch?v=MQahU6aGAH4 on 15 October 2018.

Nelson, D. M. (1999). *A finger in the wound: Body politics in quincentennial Guatemala*. Univ of California Press. p.288. Retrieved on 2 October 2018.

Northouse, P. (2012). *Leadership: Theory and Practice*. Oakridge, CA: SAGE Publications.

Nouiri, M., & Mousi, A. N. (2010). *Algeria - Faculty of Economic and Commercial Sciences and Management Sciences Department of Management Sciences*. Retrieved from مذكرة ماجستير مجدي نويري.pdfمذكرة ماجستير مجدي نويري.pdf. on 14 October 2018.

OECD. (2018). *Employment rate of Women of working age*. Retrieved from https://data.oecd.org/emp/employment-rate.htm#indicator-chart on 17 September 2018.

Oghojafor, B. E. A., Idowu, A., & George, O. J. (2012). Application of management theories and philosophies in Nigeria and their associated problems. *International Journal of Business and Social Science*, *3*(21), 72-81.

Ogliastri, E., & Salcedo, G. (2008). La cultura negociadora en el Perú: Un estudio exploratorio. *The bi-annual academic publication of Universidad ESAN*, *13*(25).

Oh-hyun, K. (2018). 초격차 : 넘볼 수 없는 차이를 만드는 격. Retrieved from https://book.naver.com/bookdb/book_detail.nhn?bid=13993934 on 11 November 2018.

Oleson, M. (2004). Exploring the relationship between money attitudes and Maslow's hierarchy of needs. *International Journal Of Consumer Studies*, 28(1), 83-92. doi: 10.1111/j.1470-6431.2004.00338.x.

Oller, V. (2012). *Qué estilos de conducción predominan hoy en las compañías argentinas.* Retrieved from http://www.iprofesional.com/notas/136834-Que-estilos-de-conduccionpredominan-hoy-en-las-companiasargentinas on 14 October 2018.

Oumnia, K. (2013). BUSINESS - Interview: Karim Oumnia, CEO of Glagla Shoes International [video file]. Retrieved from https://www.youtube.com/watch?v=tnuGTMrxRts on 12 October 2018.

Pace, A. & Pace, J. (2005). *Gender Differences in Headteacher Leadership and Management Styles: a Study of a Number of Headteachers in Maltese Secondary Schools.* Retrieved from https://www.um.edu.mt/library/oar/handle/123456789/18932 on 20 October 2018.

Pacesa, N., Zakarevicius, P., & Zukauskas, P. (2011). The profile of Lithuanian manager. *Problems and Perspectives in Management*, 9(1), 56-70.

Pagani, A. M. M. (2018). Interview. 11 November.

Panedas, D. (2014). Experiencias de liderazgo empresarial por Daniel Panedas [video file]. Retrieved from https://www.youtube.com/watchv on 12 October 2018.

Pariona, A. (2018). *What Languages Are Spoken In Argentina?* Retrieved from https://www.worldatlas.com/articles/what-languages-are-spoken-in-argentina.html on 12 October 2018.

Park, J. (2018). Interview. 17 October.

Parris, M.A., Barnes, B., & Vickers, M. H. (2004, October 7-9). *Jamaican entrepreneurship in the 21st century.* Retrieved from https://www.researchgate.net/profile/Lesley_Wilkes/publication/269337763_Managing_in_the_Middle_A_Review_of_the_Middle_Management_Experience_in_the_21st_Century/links/5847849b08ae2d2175703e3b.pdf#page=183 on 4 October 2018.

Passport to Trade 2.0 (2014). *Business Culture in Malta.* Retrieved from: http://businessculture.org/southern-europe/business-culture-in-malta/business-communication-in-malta/ on 4 October 2018.

Paul. (2014). *A tale of two Congos*. Retrieved from http://www.beyondtheheadlines.org/a-tale-of-two-congos/ on 4 October 2018.

PDG. (2018). Telephone interview. 19 October.

Peterson, S., Walumbwa, F., Byron, K., & Myrowitz, J. (2009). CEO positive psychological traits, transformational leadership, and firm performance in high-technology start-up and established firms. *Journal of Management*, 348-368. doi:3510.1177/0149206307312512.

Petrenko, V. (2016, August 29). Training future managers intercultural professional interaction competence in higher education establishment. *World Scientific News*. Retrieved from http://www.worldscientificnews.com/wp-content/uploads/2016/01/WSN-54-2016-165-179.pdf on 13 September 2018.

Pollan, M. (2018). *Gaston Acurio, we can use our cuisine as a weapon of change*. Retrieved from https://www.52-insights.com/interview-gaston-acurio-we-can-use-our-cuisine-as-a-weapon-of-change-peru-food-chef/ on 2 November 2018.

Popelnyuk, A. (2018). FaceTime (iPhone video call) interview. 11 October.

President's Birthday. (2018, August 3). *The Namibian*. Retrieved from https://www.namibian.com.na/public/uploads/documents/5b64083a08edc/Geingob%20@%207 7.pdf on 10 October 2018.

Privitelli, M. (2016). *A study on the relationship between leader empowering behaviour and organisational commitment in Maltese enterprises* (Master's thesis, University of Malta). Retrieved from https://www.um.edu.mt/library/oar/handle/123456789/15808 on 20 October 2018.

PromPeru. (2018). *Perú diverso,milenario y natural*. Retrieved from https://www.peru.travel/es-pe/sobre-peru.aspx on 20 October 2018.

Punnett, B. J., Dick-Forde, E., & Robinson, J. (2005). *Cultural Values and the CSME*. Retrieved from https://journals.sta.uwi.edu/ojs/index.php/cd/article/view/203 on October 2018.

Pushpanathan, A., Ramesh, S., & Nimalathasan, B. (2012). *The Different Leadership Styles and their Impact on Profitability: A Case Study of Women Entrepreneurs in Northern District*. Retrieved from https://scholar.google.com/citations?user=CxeeO3MAAAAJ&hl=en on 5 October 2018.

Raisienė, A. G., Pulokienė, A., & Valickas, A. (2018). Examining Leadership Characteristics at International Multilaterals. *Montenegrin Journal of Economics,* 14(3), 189-198.

Razzaq, F (2018) E-mail interview. 13 November 2018.

Redekop, B. W., Gallagher, D. R., & Satterwhite, R. (Eds.). (2018). *Innovation in Environmental Leadership: Critical Perspectives*. Routledge.

Reggiani, M. (2004). *Leadership. Nuove prospettive e nuovi percorsi di sviluppo*. Franco Angeli.

Republicanew. (2016, August 29). La hora chapina. *República*. Retrieved from https://republica.gt/2016 /08/28/la-hora-chapina/ on 12 October 2018.

Richard, E. (2018). Leadership Argentina [video file]. Retrieved from https://www.youtube.com/watch?v=ibpV-bDUZHE&t=2s on 12 October 2018.

Rickards, T. (2012). *Dilemmas of leadership*. Routledge.

Ripmeester, A., & Witmer, F. (2011). *Looking for work in Portugal. Expertise in Labour Mobility*. Elm.

Riva, N. (2018). Zoom interview. 13 October.

Rodrigues, J. N., & Devezas, T. C. (2007). *Pioneers of globalization: Why the Portuguese surprised the world*. Centro Atlantico.

Rogers, W. (2017). *Edward Seaga helped build a nation.* Retrieved from http://www.jamaicaobserver.com/columns/Edward-Seaga-helped-build-a-nation_86971 on September 2018.

Rolfsen, G. D. (2016). How to start changing an unhealthy work environment. TEDxOslo [video file]. Retrieved from https://www.youtube.com/watch?v=eYLb7WUtYt8&vl=en on 4 November 2018.

Ronen, S., & Shenkar, O. (1985). Clustering countries on attitudinal dimensions: A review and synthesis. *Academy of Management Review*, 435.

Root, G. N. I. (2016). *The differences between horizontal and vertical organizations*. Retrieved from http://pyme.lavoztx.com/las-diferencias-entre-lasorganizaciones-horizontal-y-vertical-5849.html on 3 October 2018.

Rothmann, S., & Welsh, C. (2013). Employee engagement: The role of psychological conditions. *Management Dynamics*, 22(1), 14-25. Retrieved from https://search.proquest.com/docview/1444909433?accountid=130632 on 20 September 2018.

Rowley, C., & Bae, J. (2003). Culture and management in South Korea. In Warner, M. (Ed.), *Culture and management in Asia* (pp. 187-209). London: Routledge.

Ruggieri, R., Pozzi, M., & Ripamonti, S. (2014). Italian family business cultures involved in the generational change. *Europe's Journal of Psychology*, 10(1), 79-103.

Ruiz, C. E., Hamlin, R. G., & Carioni, A. (2016). Behavioural determinants of perceived managerial and leadership effectiveness in Argentina. *Human Resource Development International*, 19(4), 267-288. doi:10.1080/13678868.2016.1147778.

Sabine (2017). *The Fascinating History of the Maltese Language.* Retrieved from https://www.airmalta.com/destinations/malta/blog/detail/history-of-the-maltese-language

Salas, G. (2012). *Negotiating evangelicalism and new age tourism through quechua ontologies in Cuzco, Perú.* Retrieved from http://hdl.handle.net/2027.42/94103 on 15 October 2018.

Salla, M. K. (2018). Mail interview. 14 October.

Sanchez, A. (2018). Telephone interview. 21 September.

Sandoval, A. G. (2014). *La gerencia de empresas by Peter Drucker.* Retrieved from https://www.scribd.com/document/320345000/La-gerencia-de-empresas-por-Peter-Drucker on 11 October 2018.

Santander. (2018). *Algeria: Business Practices.* Retrieved from https://en.portal.santandertrade.com/establish-overseas/algeria/business-practices?&actualiser_id_banque=oui&id_banque=0&memoriser_choix=memoriser on 2 October 2018.

Santos, R. Y. B. (2018). Telephone interview. 18 October.

Sapelli, S. F. (2018). Skype interview. 28 March.

Sawe, B. (2017). *Religious beliefs in Algeria.* Retrieved from https://www.worldatlas.com/articles/religious-beliefs-in-algeria.html on 2 October 2018.

School of Leadership. (2017). Spotlight Session with Raza Pirbhai - CEO KFC Pakistan [video file]. Retrieved from https://www.youtube.com/watch?v=dsBRj5DDKqc on 15 October 2018.

Scroope, C. (2018). *Argentine Culture - Core Concepts.* Retrieved from https://culturalatlas.sbs.com.au/argentine-culture/core-concepts-9f3f5686-9332-429c-be62-192d1adfe333#core-concepts-9f3f5686-9332-429c-be62-192d1adfe333 on 31 October 2018.

SDA Bocconi School of Management. (2014). Mario Monti Leadership Series Full-Time MBA SDA Bocconi [video file]. Retrieved from https://www.youtube.com/watch?v=P4KC9H74ell on 23 September 2018.

SDA Bocconi School of Management. (2014). Vittorio Colao- Leadership series Full-Time MBA SDA Bocconi [video file]. Retrieved from https://www.youtube.com/watch?v=2y7EE-2lo60 on 23 September 2018.

SDA Bocconi School of Management. (2015). Responsible leadership Massimo Magni [video file]. Retrieved from https://www.youtube.com/watch?v=Ryxfu2ZYgic on 23 September 2018.

SDA Bocconi School of Management. (2015). Responsible leadership Ferdinando Pennarola [video file]. Retrieved from https://www.youtube.com/watch?v=g08MNhrz6GQ on 23 September 2018.

SDA Bocconi School of Management. (2017). An Interview with Stefano Sassi, Valentino S.p.A [video file]. Retrieved from https://www.youtube.com/watch?v=f-mH0sWTT_E on 23 September 2018.

SDA Bocconi School of Management. (2017). Leader series EMF con Vittorio Grilli SDA Bocconi [video file]. Retrieved from https://www.youtube.com/watch?v=dOYx2H2WJeE on 23 September 2018.

SDA Bocconi School of Management. (2017). Una leadership diversa a cui non si può rinunciare SDA Bocconi [video file]. Retrieved from https://www.youtube.com/watch?v=P_JKr60Jf5g on 23 September 2018.

SDA Bocconi School of Management. (2018). Leader series EMF con Carlo Messina SDA Bocconi [video file]. Retrieved from https://www.youtube.com/watch?v=NP6EWqWJZlU on 23 September 2018.

Seaga, E. (2010). *Edward Seaga (Volume II: Hard Road to Travel 1980-2008).* Retrieved from https://www.goodreads.com/book/show/15837427-edward-seaga on 12 October 2018.

Selvarajah, C., Meyer, D., & Davuth, D. (2012). The effect of cultural modelling on leadership profiling of the Cambodian manager. *Asia Pacific Business Review,* 18(4), 649-674.

Sena, S. (2018). Audio interview. 19 October.

Senegal: 2018. (2018). *Senegal Country Review*. Retrieved from http://search.ebscohost.com/login.aspx?direct=true&db=buh&AN=129290014&site=ehost-live on 12 October 2018.

Seoulsync. (n.d). Retrieved from http://seoulsync.com/culture/current/important-korean-concepts on 11 Novermber 2018.

Shah, S. A. M., & Amjad, S. (2011). Cultural Diversity in Pakistan: National vs Provincial. *Mediterranean Journal of Social Sciences*, 2(2), 331–344.

Shamba, P. B. & Livian, Y. F. (2014). Le management africain introuvable : Pour une approche de l'hybridité segmentée. Retrieved from https://www.researchgate.net/publication/278777245_Le_management_africain_introuvable on 23 October 2018.

Sheehan, S., & Cooke, B. (1996). *Cambodia: Cultures of the world.* Tarrytown, NY: Marshall Cavendish Benchmark.

Shim, S., Baik, K., & Kim, B. (2014). 한국형리더십의 관계요인과 팀 효과성 간의 관계에 대한 연구. *Korean Academic Society of Business Administration*, 43(5), 1627-1645

Shin, M. (2004). *Convergence and divergence of work values among Chinese, Indonesian, and Korean employees*. Retrieved from http://www.vincentgaspersz.com/wp-content/uploads/2018/07/SJ%20Daniel%20WD%20Reitsperger%20-%20Challenges%20of%20Globalization.pdf#page=108 on 22 September 2018.

Shonhiwa, S. (2008). *The effective cross-cultural manager: a guide for business leaders in Africa.* Cape Town: Zebra Press.

Siborova. O., & Poddubny, A. (2011). *Ukraine as a potential center of nearsourcing*. Retrieved from https://scholar.google.com.ua/scholar?as_q=&as_epq=Ukraine+as+potential+center+of+nearsourcing:managing&hl=uk on 10 October 2018.

Siegers, J. (2015). Pepe Mujica - Lessons from the Flowerbed (full documentary) [video file]. Retrieved from https://www.youtube.com/watch?v=kGHZlqcVx-s on 18 October 2018.

Silseth, M. H. (2018). Interview. 11 October.

Simanauskaite, G. (2016). *Why Having a Job Gives You Wings,* TEDxVytautasMagnusUniversity [Video file]. Retrieved from https://www.youtube.com/watch?v=5MveWw0f-DM/ on 13 October 2018.

Skibitsky, O. (2009). Лідерство та стиль роботи менеджера (Leadership and Managerial style). Київ (Kyiv): Центр учбової літератури.

Skocir, I. (2018). Interview. 12 November.

Smith, L. (2012). *Leadership in today's Jamaica.* Retrieved from http://www.jamaicaobserver.com/columns/Leadership-in-today-s-Jamaica_12977503 on 9 October 2018.

Smith. (2018). *Congo State Oil Company Names New Head Amid Debt-Relief Plans.* Retrieved from https://www.bloomberg.com/news/articles/2018-03-01/congo-state-oil-company-names-new-head-amid-debt-relief-plans on 25 October 2018.

Sodany, S. (20180). The struggling transformations that change a woman: Sath Sodany [Video file]. Retrieved from https://www.youtube.com/watch?v=tVKfibEXTwg on 11 October 2018.

Soemarsono, A. (2017, October). Leadership (Kepemimpinan) [video file]. Retrieved from https://www.youtube.com/watch?v=Sm1Hy-T9R_s on 11 October 2018.

Solares, E. (2018) Email interview. 15 November.

Sologaistoa, R. (2018) *Qué realmente es liderazgo?* Retrieved from https://www.enactusguatemala.org.gt/que-realmente-es-liderazgo on 11 October 2018.

Southiseng, N., Ty, M., Walsh, J., & Anurit, P. (2008). Development of excellent entrepreneurs in small and medium enterprises in Laos and Cambodia. *GMSARN International Journal,* 2, 147-156.

Stankūnas, A. (2018). Skype interview. 9 October.

Statista. (2018). *Dossier Sri Lanka*. Retrieved from https://www-1statista-1com-100019fxw0c05.stcproxy.han.nl/study/47543/sri-lanka/ on 13 September 2018.

Statista. (2018). *Ukraine - main import partners 2017*. Retrieved from https://www.statista.com/statistics/296555/ukraine-main-import-partners/ on 28 September 2018.

Statista. (2018). *Unemployment rate in EU countries.* Retrieved from https://www.statista.com/statistics/268830/unemployment-rate-in-eu-countries/ on 15 October 2018.

Statista. (n.d.). *Italy - Statistics & Facts*. Retrieved from https://www.statista.com/topics/2504/italy/ on 22 September 2018.

Studycountry. (n.d.) *Religious beliefs and spirituality in Jamaica.* Retrieved from http://www.studycountry.com/guide/JM-religion.htm on 4 October 2018.

Sumanasiri, E. A. G. (2016). *An examination of business leadership in Sri Lanka: Cultural modelling of sustainability leadership* (Doctoral dissertation, Swinburne University of Technology). Retrieved from https://researchbank.swinburne.edu.au/file/0105ad78-0bb4-401e-b7d8-abd690a19680/1/Erabaddage%20Sumanasiri%20Thesis.pd on 4 October 2018.

Sumintono, B. (2017). *Development of School Leadership Preparation in Indonesia.* Retrieved from https://www.researchgate.net/publication/320442853_Development_of_School_Leadership_Preparation_in_Indonesia on 1 October 2018.

Sylla, M. S. (2017). *Madou Sylla*. Retrieved from http://madousylla.com/ on 16 October 2018.

Szczepanski, K. (2015). *Indonesia—History and Geography*. Retrieved from https://www.thoughtco.com/indonesia-facts-and-history-195522 on 2 October 2018.

Tavanti, M. (2012). The cultural dimensions of Italian leadership: Power distance, uncertainty avoidance and masculinity from an American perspective. *Leadership*, 8(3), 287-301.

Tecoloco Guatemala. (2012, May 25). *El liderazgo laboral* [blog post]. Retrieved from https://www.tecoloco.com.gt/blog/ el-liderazgo-laboral.aspx on 10 October 2018.

Teklu, A. (2018). Video interview. 24 October.

Telegraph Travel. (2017, 4 April). 18 amazing things you probably didn't know about Senegal. *The Telegraph*. Retrieved from https://www.telegraph.co.uk/travel/destinations/africa/senegal/articles/things-you-probably-didnt-know-about-senegal/ on 12 October 2018.

The Government of Namibia. (2018). *Languages Spoken in Namibia*. Retrieved from https://www.gov.na/languages-spoken on 17 October 2018.

The Observatory of Economic Complexity. (n.d.). *Ukraine (UKR) Exports, Imports, and Trade Partners*. Retrieved from https://atlas.media.mit.edu/en/profile/country/ukr/ on 28 September 2018.

The World Bank. (2018). *GDP per capita*. Retrieved from https://data.worldbank.org/indicator/NY.GDP.PCAP.CD on 9 November 2018.

Thioune, I. M. (2018). Telephone interview. 18 October.

Thompson, C. (2018). *Reflections on leadership and governance in Jamaica: towards a better society*. Arawak Publications.

Thon, V., Ou, S., Eng, N., & Ly, T. (2009). Leadership in Local Politics of Cambodia: A Study of Leaders in Three Communes of Three Provinces. *CDRI Working Paper Series*, 42.

Tichkivskyy, R. (2017). Хто такий лідер та як його виховати? [Video file]. Retrieved from https://www.youtube.com/watch?v=rB4jtKL7_Pk on 10 October 2018.

Times of Malta. (2004). *Talk on stress management by Dr Alfred Darmanin, SJ*. Retrieved from https://www.timesofmalta.com/articles/view/20040118/business/talk-on-stress-management-by-dr-alfred-darmanin-sj.132102 on 12 October 2018.

Tjada, C. (2017, February 17). Money, Power, Family: Inside South Korea's Chaebol. *New York Times*. Retrieved from https://www.nytimes.com/2017/02/17/business/south-korea-chaebol-samsung.html on 8 October 2018.

Toasa, J. (2016). *A new generation of Grassroot leaders bring change to Guatemala*. Inter-American Foundation. Retrieved from: www.iaf.gov/content/story/a-newgeneration-of-grassroot-leaders-brings-change-to-guatemala on 10 October 2018.

Tollgerdt-Andersson, I. (1993). A*ttitudes, values and demands on leadership-A cultural comparison*. Management Education and Development, 24(1), 48-57.

Transparency International (2018). *Corruption risks: how does your country measure up?* Retrieved from https://www.transparency.org/news/feature/corruption_risks_how_does_your_country_measure_u on 11 October 2018.

Trevisani, D. (2018). Skype interview. 15 October.

Trompenaars, F., & Hampden-Turner, C. (2012). *Riding the waves of culture: Understanding diversity in global business*. Nicholas Brealey Publishing.

Trout, J. (2010). *Why Empathy Matters: The Science and Psychology of Better Judgment.* Penguin Books.

Tsegay, T. S. (2013). Some Ethiopian Women Leaders' Perceptions about Their Leadership. *Advancing Women in Leadership, 33*, 75-86.

Tully, J. (2006). *A short history of Cambodia: From empire to survival.* Crows Nest, NSW: Allen & Unwin.

UNESCO Institute of Statistics. (n.d). Retrieved from http://uis.unesco.org/country/LT on 3 October 2018.

United Nations Development Programme. (2018). *Human Development index and its components*. Retrieved from http://hdr.undp.org/en/composite/HDI on 2 October, 2018.

Universia Argentina. (2016). *En Argentina pocas mujeres ocupan cargos gerenciales, según informe.* Retrieved from http://noticias.universia.com.ar/practicas-empleo/noticia/2016/09/29/1144100/argentina-pocas-mujeres-ocupan-cargos-gerenciales-segun-informe.html on 15 October 2018.

USAID. (n.d). *Gender equality and women's empowerment.* Retrieved from https://www.usaid.gov/ethiopia/gender-equality-and-womens-empowerment on 9 October 2018.

Uzzi, B. (2015). Great Leaders Can Think Like Each Member of Their Team. *Harvard Business Review.* Retrieved from https://hbr.org/2015/07/great-leaders-can-think-like-each-member-of-their-team on 18 September 2018.

Van den Bosch, S. (2018). Personal interview. 11 October.

Van der Schaar Investments B.V. Delft the Netherlands. (2012). *How to Act Indonesian*. Retrieved from https://www.indonesia-investments.com/business/working-living/how-to-act-indonesian/item299 on 24 September 2018.

Van der Schaar Investments B.V. Delft the Netherlands. (2012). *Indonesian Business Culture*. Retrieved from https://www.indonesia-investments.com/business/working-living/indonesian-business-culture/item411 on 18 September 2018.

Van Dyk, R. (2018). Personal interview. 11 October.

Van Dyk, R. (n.d). *About*. Retrieved from http://rowanvandyk.com/about/ on 12 October 2018.

Vargas, V. (2018). Telephone interview. 14 October.

VCast Online. (2018). The country manager of iflix Pakistan talks leadership and office culture [video file]. Retrieved from https://www.youtube.com/watch?v=A7isUBLt18U on 15 October 2018.

Velasco, J. (2012). LEADERSHIP: i 5 pilastri per gestire con successo il tuo team [video file]. Retrieved from https://www.youtube.com/watch?v=6GRxsEqGRuE on 23 September 2018.

Viotti, Paul R. & Kauppi, M. V. (2013) *International Relations and World Politics*, 5th Ed. Pearson.

Virginia G. M. (2013). *Investigating leadership characteristics and Attitudes toward creativity according to agency context for agriculture extension agents in Uruguay* - PDF [Book]. Retrieved from https://docplayer.net/58356572-Investigating-leadership-characteristics-and-attitudes-toward-creativity-according-to-agency-context-for-agriculture-extension-agents-in-uruguay.html on 13 September 2018.

Visit Norway (2018). *Innovation Norway*. Retrieved from https://www.visitnorway.no/ on 9 October 2018.

Visitoslo. (2018). *Norli Bookshop*. Retrieved from https://www.visitoslo.com/en/product/?TLp=15403 on 12 October 2018

Visser, W., & Tolhurst, N. (2010). *The world guide to CSR: A country-by-country analysis of corporate sustainability and responsibility*. Routledge. [Books24x7 version] Available from http://common.books24x7.com.rps.hva.nl:2048/toc.aspx?bookid=37878

Von Doepp, P. (2005). *Party cohesion and fractionalization in new African democracies: Lessons from struggles over third-term amendments*. Retrieved from http://search.ebscohost.com/login.aspx?direct=true&db=buh&AN=19651324&site=eh ost-live on 13 September 2018.

Wade, B. D. (2016). *La chronique du Coach Kader*. Retrieved from http://reussirbusiness.com/tag/leadership on 17 November 2018.

Wall, K., Cunha, V., Atalaia, S., Rodrigues, L., Correia, R., Vladimira Correia, S., & Rosa, R. (2017). *WHITE PAPER – Men and Gender Equality in Portugal*. Lisboa: Institute of Social Sciences of the University of Lisbon.

Wanasika, I., Howell, J. P., Littrell, R., & Dorfman, P. (2011). Managerial leadership and culture in sub-saharan africa. *Journal of World Business*, 46(2), 234. Retrieved from https://search.proquest.com/docview/856201620?accountid=130632 on 20 September 2018.

Warburton, K. (2013*). Indonesian Business Management Style*. Retrieved from https://www.worldbusinessculture.com/country-profiles/indonesia/culture/business-management-style/ on 27 September 2018.

Warner-Søderholm, G. (2010). *Kommunikasjon og kultur: Regionale orskjeller i forretningskultur i Norge*. Retrieved from https://www.magma.no/kommunikasjon-og-kultur-regionale-forskjeller-i-forretningskultur-i-norge on 2 November 2018.

Warner-Søderholm, G., & Søderholm, A. (2018). *Ansattes preferaser for Lederkommunikasjon.* Retrieved from https://brage.bibsys.no/xmlui/bitstream/handle/11250/2501359/Ansattes%20preferanser%20for%20lederkommunikasjon%202018.pdf?sequence=4&isAllowed=y on 28 September 2018.

Well Grounded. (2017). Leadership development in the Congo Basin / Développement de leadership dans le Bassin du Congo [video file]. Retrieved from https://www.youtube.com/watch?v=1cK22wP9S2o on 18 October 2018

Well Grounded. (2018). Well, Grounded - Leadership Development Programme 2017-2018 - long version [video file]. Retrieved from https://www.youtube.com/watch?v=KsuNhfIl2Oo on 18 October 2018

White, P., Arcienaga, A., & Gonzales, C. (2010). *Argentina's Innovative Capacity – Which Direction?* Retrieved from http://www.corporateinnovationonline.com/wordpress/wp-content/uploads/2010/06/Argentina-Arriving.pdf on 13 October 2018.

Wickramanayake, N. (2018). Skype interview. 1 November.

Widianto, S. (2018) Skype interview. 8 November.

Widianto, S., & Harsanto, B. (2017). The Impact of Transformational leadership and organizational culture on firm performance in Indonesia SMEs. *The Palgrave Handbook of Leadership in Transforming Asia*, 333-340. doi:10.1057/978-1-137-57940-9_27.

Willis, D., Lucas, C. & Breitbarth, A. (2013). *The History of Negation in the Languages of Europe and the Mediterranean.* Oxford: Oxford University Press.

Windtrebusinessdactor. (26 April 2011). Claudio Belotti - Come è cambiata la Leadership? [video file]. Retrieved from https://www.youtube.com/watch?v=GyVwz9068WI on 23 September 2018.

Wong-MingJi, D., Kessler, E. H., Khilji, S. E., & Gopalakrishnan, S. (2014*)*. Cross-cultural comparison of cultural mythologies and leadership patterns. *South Asian Journal of Global Business Research*, 79-101. Retrieved from Proquest: https://search-proquest-com.rps.hva.nl:2443/docview/1508550613?accountid=130632 on 1 October 2018.

World Bank Group. (n.d). Retrieved from https://data.worldbank.org/indicator/SP.POP.TOTL?locations=LT-LV-EE&view=chart on 8 November 2018.

World Economic Forum. (2018). *Global Gender Gap Report 2017 Italy.* Retrieved from http://reports.weforum.org/global-gender-gap-report-2017/dataexplorer/#economy=ITA on 17 September 2018.

World Population Review. (2018). Retrieved from http://worldpopulationreview.com/countries/ between 2 October and 13 November 2018.

Yemer, H. (2009). *Applicability of Transformational Leadership Models in the Ethiopian Context*, Walden University. Retrieved from https://search.proquest.com/docview/305075584accountid=130632 on 23 October 2018.

Yeonhee K. (2013). Business not as usual: The key to success for Korean global leaders, Ted@BCG [video file]. Retrieved from: https://www.ted.com/talks/yeonhee_kim_business_not_as_usual_the_key_to_success_for_korean_global_leaders#t-50010 on 2 November 2018.

Yonsei University. (n.d.) Understanding Korean Politics, 5.1 The Korean Economic MIracle Empirical Check [video file]. Retrieved from https://www.coursera.org/lecture/understanding-korean-politics/5-1-the-korean-economic-miracle-empirical-check-kuWXi on 13 October 2018.

Zattoni, A., & Ravasi, D. (2000). Grandi imprese e grandi gruppi in Italia. *Economia & Management*, (2), 55-72. Retrieved from http://emplus.egeaonline.it/it/61/archivio-rivista/rivista/3337611/articolo/3337641 on 26 September 2018.

Zepp, R. (2011). Perceptions of leadership in three professions in Cambodia. *International Journal of Business and Social Science,* 2(3). Retrieved from http://ijbssnet.com/journals/Vol._2_No._3_[Special_Issue_-_January_2011]/28.pdf on 27 September 2018.

Zúquete, J. P. (2011). The flight of the eagle: The charismatic leadership of Sá carneiro in Portugal's transition to democracy. *Leadership Quarterly*, 22(2), 295.

Selected previous CCBS editions

World without words
The cross-cultural context of gestures in international business
2012, HvA CCBS minor
ISBN 978-90-79646-11-1

World-wide workforce
An intercultural benchmark of global recruiting practices
2015, HvA CCBS minor
ISBN 978-90-79646-25-8

Where cultures meet
A cross-cultural comparison of business meeting styles
2013, HvA minor CCBS
ISBN 978-90-79646-17-3